Toward
an Effective Critique
of American Education

The Lippincott Foundations of Education Series

Under the Editorship of
John Hardin Best and *James E. Wheeler*
Rutgers University

Toward

an Effective Critique

of American Education

James E. McClellan
TEMPLE UNIVERSITY

J. B. Lippincott Company
Philadelphia / New York

Preface

This book grew out of many things. It began with a course I used to give for graduate students at Teachers College, Columbia University. This course was called "Education and Social Policy," or something like that, and it tried to show how policy proposals for education were linked up with other sorts of public policies. The students didn't have the proper background for such a course. Who does? A proper background would have included a sound knowledge of educational thought and practice, of economics, political science, sociology, and, most important, political philosophy. But with graduate students in education who are going into positions of great responsibility, a teacher can't wait until everyone is properly prepared. You just go ahead with what you have. That's what we did, and that's how this book got started.

Here at Temple University where I continued to give the same course to the same sort of students, I came to see the whole matter a bit differently: It isn't so much a matter of opposing *this* grand social-and-educational design against that one; it's more a matter of careful criticism of a specific literature—the contemporary policy proposals that people are reading, talking about, and acting on where decisions are being made. It wasn't hard to identify such a body of literature, but it was very difficult to find sustained, relevant criticism of it. Case in point: The works I treat here were all reviewed in more-or-less educational journals, but all those reviews read as if the book reviewed were *sui generis,* completely separated from any continuing body of critical thought. The problem became that of devising relevant *canons* of criticism right within the *activity* of criticism itself. That problem took more time than I could find in the conduct of regular academic work; therefore, I was fortunate to receive a most generous grant from the John Simon Guggenheim Memorial Foundation which enabled me to devote a whole year to this study.

Two other kinds of experiences made a great deal of difference in the direction of this work. Some friends of mine brought me into Washington as educational consultant to the President's Committee on Juvenile Delinquency and later to the Office of Economic Opportunity. That experience proved to me that the old categorization of "issues in education" reflects the internal problems of a particular institution, the public school system, and not the issues of education *per se.* The legal, fiscal, pedagogical, and philosophical problems all shift decidedly when you move education out of the school system and into new institutional arrangements. From this it follows that you can't set up in advance the categories in which to relate and compare the policy proposals treated. You can't, that is, unless you are willing to accept the structure of a particular institution as *defining* what education is.

Which brings me to the second kind of experience that shifted the direction of this book. Taking advantage of other friends in the academic world, I traveled around a good deal, trying out these ideas in various sorts of meetings, conferences, symposia, colloquia, etc. I found that many ideas which I had heard whispered around here at Temple University were also being whispered by other colleagues throughout the country. I've summarized those ideas under the heading "The Public School Movement." We simply no longer treat educational policy as a matter of establishing convenient house rules for a single institution. Those of us who have gone to, taught in, and become emotionally involved with public schools, the uniquely American version of public schools, find it hard to accept that that institution is merely one among a multitude of educational possibilities. A Catholic church, by definition, is not merely one denomination among many, nor is a public school merely one among a society's many educational options. For "public school" has come to *mean* "the institution providing all the basic education for all the people." We have seen a most amazing social and political movement aimed at completing and perfecting that institution. Quite naturally, we have seen policy proposals for education judged by their effect on the public school, thus defined.

But when one begins to take seriously that "public school" and "education" are not synonyms, you also have to ask for other sorts of *reasons* for policy proposals. What sorts of reasons are relevant? What kinds of argument are persuasive and why? Are there decisive reasons for accepting policy proposals? Or are decisions on policy subject to something other than reason? I found my colleagues throughout the nation asking these questions with a radical intent. It's a bit frightening to realize that the good solid institutional sanction is no longer sufficient to justify anything—anything proposed for future policy, anything accepted as present policy. It's also liberating, and I tried to get that feeling into this book.

From all this you can see that it would be impossible to list all the subjects of my indebtedness. But simple honesty demands that I make a public bow to my colleagues in the Department of Foundations of Education at Temple University, especially to my long-time friend and collaborator, B. Paul Komisar. He is almost always the person referred to when the phrase "a colleague of mine" appears (as it so often does) in the text. I should mention in the same breath Professor Thomas F. Green of Syracuse University with whom I have argued these essays, literally, from one end of the country to the other. Paul Nash, Robert Guttchen, Rubin Gotesky, Joanne Reynolds, Harold Taylor, Elizabeth Flower, and many, many others will recognize where my arguments have changed in response to their criticisms.

My thanks go also to Stanley Salett, now Assistant Commissioner of Education for the State of New Jersey and to Louis D. Eigen, now Vice President of Grolier, Inc., who brought me down to Washington and introduced me to the realities of policy planning. A very special gratitude is owed to the students from various universities who have helped refine these ideas as they made their slow progress from lecture notes to printed page.

Finally, I am genuinely grateful to the five major writers on educational policy whose works I've treated here. My gratitude is not personal but professional. This body of literature—the works of James Bryant Conant, Theodore Brameld, Jacques Barzun, B. F.

Skinner, and Paul Goodman—is part of our best thought on education. By no means is it the most distinguished body of literature in the history of mankind, but it is still our most valuable resource as we face the really tough job of devising new educational policies for the new institutional environment now emerging. These men didn't *have* to write on educational policy; it is for us a clear and unearned benefit that they *did* apply their minds and emotions to education—that most fascinating and frustrating arena of human action.

James E. McClellan

Temple University

Table of Contents

Toward

an Effective Critique

of American Education

1

The System, The Establishment, and The Search for a New Politics

I. THE PUBLIC SCHOOL MOVEMENT

It is foolish to proclaim the day and hour that the Public School Movement died, equally foolish to assign its precise moment of birth. No one can doubt, however, that there was such a movement—a vast, inchoate surge of feeling among the people and of ideology among the intellectuals—from which emerged a distinctively American way of educating the young.

The American way of educating, like the American way in general, has been a resounding success. The primary and secondary schools of the nation enroll practically all the youngsters of school age who have any chance of profiting from instruction. There is sufficient standardization in teaching arrangements throughout the nation that a child may enter school in one locality and graduate in another, having made many moves in between, all with minimum administrative difficulty. Wherever a child or youth attends school in this country, the chances are extremely good that he will find:

1. A formally well-educated corps of teachers, averaging more than a baccalaureate in higher schooling, holding jobs that are secure and reasonably well paid.

2. A sturdy, sanitary, and reasonably spacious building as his place of instruction.

3. An efficient, orderly and generally humane staff of professionally trained administrators and supervisors.

4. Some, if not always immediate, access to medical, dental, counseling, and other social services.

5. A local lay public having a high level of interest in schools and participating through open, democratic processes in their operation and control.

6. (Since the passage of The Elementary and Secondary Education Act of 1965) a complex but fairly well balanced system of financial support to meet the ever-rising costs of schooling.

7. Enough instructional materials (primers, textbooks, laboratory and shop equipment) to promote efficient classroom teaching and to provide some opportunity for individual use after class or at home.

8. A program of studies which, commensurately with his age, can be varied to accommodate his particular abilities, interests, and probable vocation.

9. A continuing and conscious effort to represent, in the life of his school, the nation's ideals of tolerance, respect, and fair play for *all* human beings.

Each of these points summarizes an achievement of unquestioned historical significance. The expression "Public School Movement" is just an abbreviated way of referring to the political impetus which, over a long period of time and through enormous expenditures of energy, money, and frustration, has made those achievements possible. However easy it may be in retrospect to "explain" the American system of education by the manpower needs of industry or by the dissolution in this country of Old World patterns of family and kinship, the fact remains that *building* the American public school from its precarious origins to its present pre-eminence did not occur automatically but only because of a major political effort by several generations of brilliant, resilient leaders and literally millions of dedicated teachers, parents, and friends of youth.

Perhaps the most impressive evidence for the success of the American way of education is the impact it has had on the educational policies of other nations. It is patent throughout the world that nations seeking material prosperity and political freedom regard a system of free, compulsory, and comprehensive public schools as a necessity for achieving those ends. Help from the United States in support of education in emerging nations is a model of how the rich can truly help the poor—not by giving to them but by working with them. A proper item of export from the United States to the "Third World" is not the impossibly expensive American high school but the indefatigable Public School Movement which, in time, made that high school possible.[1]

These splendid achievements tempt one to say that the Public School Movement in America passed away because it had achieved its purposes and therefore lost its *raison d'être.* Yet this is to propound a paradox, for never before in the nation's history—itself a record of continuous interest in education—have we been so preoccupied with questions of educational policy. Perhaps it is not that the degree of our concern is greater today than at other times in our history but that our concern is so deeply bifurcated. On the one hand, we are striving to perfect the public school system (which includes most non-public schools), while on the other we are beginning to question most of the basic assumptions which underlie the whole Public School Movement. In such circumstances, it is not unexpected that our educational discourse often seems pathologically dissociated from the realities of the world.

Nowhere is this dissociation more easily noted than in the present strain toward educational equality for Negroes, especially the poor Negro. On one level, it seems quite clear what has to be done to elevate the Negro to full equality of educational opportunity but very, very difficult to do it. In the South, segregation must be ended and fully (not tokenly) integrated schools provided for all children of both races. In the North, the radical disparity between schools of the slums and schools of the rich suburbs must be eliminated once and for all. *Beauty of school environment, richness of cultural resources, and competent concern in teachers are all more necessary in slum than in suburb, and all are glaringly, blatantly absent just where they are most needed.* Continuous massive political efforts are required in the South, while an economic and planning program of greater scale than the whole of the present "War on Poverty" is necessary in northern cities, in order to overcome the severe educational deprivation of a large proportion of our Negro youth. The concern presently devoted to this aspect of educational policy is paltry when compared with the magnitude of the problem.

On another level, we are not *exactly* sure what needs to be done. Are our "best" suburban schools really such excellent institutions that we can *define* equality of educational opportunity as duplicating for Negro children the same facilities now enjoyed by a minority of whites? Without even raising at this point the complex question of cultural pluralism, and without making the routinely odious remarks about misplaced "middle-class values" in Negro schools, we still have some serious reservations. Is the moderately expensive modern school building—architecturally indistinguishable from a moderately expensive modern warehouse—the only model for a beautiful environment to nourish the aesthetic sensibilities of Negro youth? (Or *any* youth?) Is there only one path of culture to bring a young person to full membership in his civilization—i.e., the path that leads from "Run, Spot, Run" to "Problems of Democracy"? And have we really found a way to develop both competence and concern in all the two million teachers we must employ just to run our system of public schools?

Here is the bifurcation, the dissociation. The educational goods we have acquired belong by moral right to *all* the children of *all* the people. But we have lost our erstwhile secure confidence that we know (or, by adding an additional one per cent to our budget for research, can soon find out) how to achieve *all* educational goods; to put it another way, we are no longer entirely sure that the goods we know how to achieve are really so important that they justify everything we do, including some pretty obvious evils, in the name of education. The "we" here means not only self-conscious intellectuals; "we" includes practical politicians, schoolmasters, and parents as well, that is, people responsible for deciding *how much* and *what kind* of education children should receive. All doubt that "more" and "the same" are always the appropriate answers.

The Public School Movement might have adapted to its concern the old Populist motto about democracy: There's nothing wrong with American education that more American public schools won't cure. Today, we have achieved enough distance to detect the assumption on which this faith rested:

1. To the extent that all children are inducted (by legal compulsion if necessary) into a free, publicly supported and publicly controlled, comprehensive school system, to that extent we have achieved full equality of educational opportunity. Most of the time and by most of the Public School Movement it was held as a corollary that equality of educational opportunity guaranteed all the other equalities ordained by the Creator and enunciated in the Declaration of Independence.

2. Only a citizenry educated in that kind of school will possess the high level of individual judgment and common loyalty required to perform the duties inherent in a democratic state. This assumption justified taking the rich man's money to educate the poor man's child; in case assumption (1) did not suffice, assumption (2) would always justify taking the poor man's child and educating him in a middle-class school.

3. Such a school will not only preserve, it will selectively refine and purify our popular culture. This formulation borrows from John Dewey; the point was made particularly to counter the charge that mass education meant cultural debasement.[2] Thus, the Public School Movement could encompass efforts toward cultural as well as political or social reform and could rely on the fundamental, albeit often exasperated, loyalty of the socially and culturally *concerned* intellectuals.

4. The public school (cf. 1 above) is by nature an open institution, always responsive to sympathetic criticism and appeals for positive reform. Local control through popularly elected officials will guarantee that the school be responsive to rational persuasion. (By the time it became a point of ideological controversy among various factions in the Progressive Education Association, whether a radically unorthodox independent school represented an alternative *to* or an experimental model *for* the public school, it was all over for both progressive education and the Public School Movement; for they were not really two different things.) [3]

5. Another way of proceeding from (2) was to assume that

the same school which prepares a citizenry (very often of non-citizen forbears) to execute the duties of a democratic state will also prepare both the workers and managers in the American economy. The Public School Movement could encompass men who had very different ideas about what kind of economy was American—whether "mature" and controllably stable or expanding and inherently cyclical—and equally different ideas about how it ought to be run—from complete laissez-faire to democratic collectivism. However, from all points of view, it could be agreed that more literate, responsible, and ambitious workers and managers would help the economy.

6. Operating from the same thesis of free competition in an open market, most Protestant denominations were willing to compete for educated minds; Jews could assume that better educated Jews would still be Jews, whatever their wishes might have been. The Public School Movement could thus count on the support of educationally concerned and active Protestants and Jews. (Catholics built their own schools where they could afford to; their schools increasingly came to be marginally differentiated from public schools. On none of the assumptions (1) through (5) did the Catholics offer a genuine alternative to the Public School Movement. To disagree on (6) only left the Catholic educator fighting legalistically for the right and the money to run his own version of the public school. His tragedy was partial victory.)

Since there are more people today than there were in 1915, probably more people today believe assumptions (1) through (6) than did so fifty years ago. But these assumptions no longer really pertain. It is not that they have been found to be false when measured against the realities of the world; rather, these realities have so changed that these assumptions no longer (as truly they once did) pertain to something very important.

In a society where most of the people are poor and constantly threatened with real want, "equality of opportunity" means only one thing: a fair shake at getting rich. In a society where everyone could easily be guaranteed freedom from want, what does "equality of opportunity" mean? How important is it?

In a society where the ballot box was not merely the symbol but the reality of access to power, democracy did seem to depend on a marching together of literacy and suffrage. In a society profoundly divided between a rich minority and a poor majority, education to promote social integration seemed necessary for social survival. It is hard for us to recapture either of these concerns. When we think of the importance of voting it is not of the well-informed newspaper reader who puts aside all demagoguery and votes, as a social atom, on the pure merits of the case; it is of the masses of disfranchised poor who can use the ballot to alleviate their exploitation, and we need effective demagogues and demagogic techniques to make it work. When did it become apparent that American society was not going to pull apart at its economic, ethnic, or racial seams? The Depression proved it to some; Truman's victory over both Dewey and Wallace should have convinced the last pessimist. Society may be dividing disastrously between age groups and between sexes, but we have no educational agencies for healing these two breaches.

When the distinction between academic and avant-garde culture is disappearing and when "proletarianization of culture" (to borrow Toynbee's expression) is proceeding apace in *all* the creative arts, how significant is it that we have a mass education designed to purify and refine popular culture? Who is to purify the purifiers? Refine the refiners?

The school's responsiveness to change has proved a very interesting phenomenon, one that requires a reversal in an old French proverb. For it has been discovered that schools change very slowly, but that the more deliberately and skillfully the school is organized for change, the more adaptable and responsive it becomes. Thus the more it is the same thing, i.e. a bureaucratic system, the more it changes. But this is not what the believers of assumption (4) had in mind.[4]

The accelerating rate of technological change has had two sometimes contradictory results for the school's role in preparing workers and managers. On one hand, for full participation in the advancing technical cultural, there is no point at which education is complete. Learning, unlearning, and re-learning are continuous; and school-like training programs are a necessity. On the other hand, it is not at all clear what proportion of our young are actually going to be involved in the economy as technical workers or managers. That is to say, assumption (5) used to be *about* something very important: how to prepare the masses in the skills and attitudes necessary to keep the economy going. But today, who are the masses? What does "prepare" mean? What skills? Do we want a docile labor force? Who is "we"?

If "religion" is taken to mean a set of institutions called churches with rituals and creeds that possess only a historical interest and importance, then schools need not teach religion. If "religion" is taken to mean the pursuit of ultimate meaning and reality, then a school is a rather shallow place if it ignores religion. At one time it seemed as reasonable to look upon the school as an institution which prepared an individual, as a social atom, to choose his religion as he chose his candidate for office, his job, and his daily purchases. But what has been presupposed about religion when it is treated that way? Who today would make that kind of presupposition?

In sum, the Public School Movement has left us an institution which serves as a model to the world. It serves a large proportion of its clientele very well in a large proportion of its endeavors. Where it presently serves less than adequately, e.g., to the Negro poor, it would be *relatively* simple, considering the effort and money which went into its creation originally, to perfect and complete the school's mission in society. However, it does not happen that way because the Public School Movement rested on certain assumptions which today we regard as irrelevant when not blatantly false.

An individual under such conditions might go mad, but institutions are sturdier. We keep it going, even as we try to rebuild it from keel up, even as we try to think anew in what direction it ought to go. The fact is that we order and direct an institution by establishing *policies*, a word which sounds quite odd when applied to an individual. One could say, if he chose, that the school is in a state of crisis. Perhaps one should say that the politics of education needs to be reconstituted, or, perhaps better, re-instituted. To make clear what that means, let us turn our attention to the very complex word "politics" and to words closely related to it.

II. WHAT IS POLITICS?

In accordance with the license issued to every philosopher, I propose to approach the definition of terms through Greek origins. The word "politics" is a derivative from πόλις, a term combining the extension of the English word "city" with the intension of that word plus the terms "state" and "society" as well. But the

Greek word πόλις is not without antecedents of its own. Classicists recognize a close connection between πόλις and πολύς, meaning much or many, now a common prefix in scientific and other polysyllabic discourse. Albeit without proper scholarly sanction, I should like to add another antecedent to πόλις namely πολος, meaning axis or axle, the fixed point around which other things revolve, an interesting Greek word which continues its life in the modern sciences of geometry, astronomy, and magnetism. Both the notion of multiplicity and the notion of polarity are necessary to a proper understanding of the idea of politics and the other terms derived therefrom.

As I am using the term, a problem or issue belongs in the realm of politics only if there is more than one real or genuine interest involved. This in itself establishes the philosophical (metaphysical) position from which I speak. If one believes in the Reality of an Absolute Good, through which all lesser goods receive such goodness as they possess, then one would not be at all concerned with politics, in the sense of the term used here. For this sense of "politics" assumes that multiplicity, diversity, and ultimately conflict among real goods are, in principle as well as in practice, an ineluctable condition of all existence, and particularly human existence. (It is not a mere coincidence that another Greek word closely related to πόλις is πόλεμος, meaning "war.")

A political order, then, may be defined as one way of creating concert in action from conflict in interest. It is not the only way. Pure force and fraud can also succeed in making men act in unity, often against their individual interests. Extermination never is effective ultimately, for conflict of interest is a structural feature of social life; hence, killing or driving off the persons who happen to occupy certain positions in that structure will not eliminate conflict, though it will seriously weaken the society—as attested by many examples in the history of war-like Western nations.

A political order differs from pure force and fraud by virtue of the second metaphor buried in the idea or the πόλις: the metaphor of polarity, or fixity at the center of revolution. A political order conciliates conflict according to a system or rules, and that system—linked with the society's basic myths, history, and philosophy—maintains a constancy even as particular compromises and reconciliations of interest fluctuate in response to changing external conditions. As a society becomes more differentiated in function and ramified in structure, its governing rules must become explicit and systematic; that is, the rules must distinguish between the basic principles governing the making of decisions on one hand and the particular decisions made according to those principles on the other. Again, the Greeks knew this distinction clearly: Lycurgus and Solon were revered lawgivers not because they formulated particular decisions but because they established systems which would continue indefinitely to generate particular decisions as required. In contrast, King Solomon, for all his wisdom, never grasped this fundamental requirement of a political order.

Note that a political structure does not preclude the presence of force and fraud in determining a united course of action from diverse interests. But in a political structure neither force nor fraud operates freely; both are constrained by rules. The oracle at Delphi might well be a fake; but the appeal to Apollo was a rule-directed way of resolving conflict. History's most remarkable instance of the use of force within a political structure, the Nazis' policy of genocide, operated according to an elaborate, albeit inconstant and inconsistent, system of rules for determining who was a Jew and of what degree of "guilt." Inside the extermination camps, we are told, behavior often reverted to the primitive or pre-political, rules having been replaced by sadistic whims in the guidance of conduct. This reminds us of another basic principle of politics known and honored in Greek thought: No political order is ever guaranteed to survive; cultural evolution, unlike genetic evolution, is reversible. Primitive ways of resolving conflict always lie close beneath the surface of any political order, as is seen so clearly in the savage behavior we euphemistically call "international politics."

The term "policy" may now be considered as a derivative from "politics." A policy for education would be a set of statements formulated and accepted according to the following principles:

1. The genuinely conflicting interests in the society as a whole must be acknowledged. A statement asserting that Siwash College will serve the educational needs of every young man and woman without favor or discrimination could have no operative value as policy. For there are inherent conflicts between the educational needs of the clever and the dull, the industrious and the lazy, the mature and the immature, the vocationally committed and the

vocationally undecided. A statement which is supposed to direct the conduct of an institution must at least acknowledge these conflicts.

2. The statements must be the product of some rule-directed activity, e.g., a decision of a court or administrative agency, a duly-processed piece of legislation, the proceedings of a duly-constituted school board, the dicta of a duly-elected president, or a majority vote in a duly-formed faculty assembly. When, as occasionally happens, such policy statements conflict, the rules must specify an order of precedence, if we are to determine what is actually the *policy* in the case.

In the logic of the term "policy," it is impossible for one institution or organized system of institutions to hold two contradictory policies, e.g., for a college to admit all high school graduates on a first-come-first-served basis and to admit only the academically qualified. There may be contradictory feelings, pressures, tendencies, desires, and beliefs; but these contradictions must be resolved, according to *some* set of rules, before a *policy* can be said to obtain.

3. These two conditions are necessary for the appearance of policy, but they are not sufficient. One other factor is logically necessary; two other factors are in practice indispensable. In order to complete the logical meaning of "policy" we must add another idea suggested by πόλις, namely "police." For a set of statements does not constitute a policy unless its directive force on conduct is enforceable. This condition requires the capability of imposing penalties for non-compliance. A linguistic analysis of the concept "policy" would show certain interesting features in this element of enforcement. For example, it is a sufficient explanation for an organization's punishing a member that the member violated the organization's policy. But compliance with policy is not, in itself, a justification for an organization's extending special rewards to a member. Even at a testimonial dinner honoring a retiring school principal, one would want to say something more than that the principal had followed the policies of the school board for thirty-two years. One would want to say at least that he had faithfully executed the policies for this extended period. It is the faithfulness, not the policy-execution itself, which merits the reward. What would we say if a superintendent regularly announced that his official actions were directly contrary to the school board's stated

policies, e.g., on faculty tenure, racial integration, and building maintenance? Either the superintendent is in error or the institution's stated policies are not its actual policies.

4. Thus the concept "police" is the crucial one for discovering what actually *are* the policies of any institution. What purport to be policy statements, that is, the statements found in college catalogs and speeches of school board presidents, often have nothing to do with policies. *"Cherchez le gendarme"* if you want to find out actual policies, for Apollo does not announce policies nor enforce them with his father's thunderbolts. In practice, a *social* system with its own rules, functionaries, and folkways is needed. In short, a polity is required; by "polity," I mean a social organization capable of carrying on politics, generating and enforcing policy.

5. There is yet one further conceptual point which must be added to the complex idea of policy; again, we may find a hint in the Greek. The term πολίος has an interesting history of its own, appearing first as a simple color-term meaning white, later gray, from which it came to signify old or venerable; and with that significance it got caught up in the expanding connotations of "πόλις." This suggests something very important about a polity. In a certain sense, the ultimate rules of argument are timeless; the laws of logic constitute eternally fixed poles about which discourse on any topic may revolve. A properly drawn deduction, a relevant use of evidence, an appeal to a universalized concept of justice are valid moves in educational policy discourse because they are valid moves in any discourse, anywhere, at any time. But a polity is always local and temporal. Its parts have age—some parts more, some less. Its concerns are immediate, of the moment. But its ways of handling those concerns are mediated by rules which are not altogether universal but partly conventional, somewhat arbitrary, yet functional in making politics *polite*. This last derivative from πόλις (like its Latin equivalent "civil") is as necessary to understanding the true nature of a polity as is the tougher "police." A polite respect for the ways of our fathers is neither blind conservatism nor mocking hypocrisy. A polite respect for the arguments of one's opponent is neither subservience nor condescension. A *polity*, then, is a social organization aiming at rational argument and resolute decisions; hence the existence of an effective polity depends on disseminating the rules of politeness as much as the laws of logic.

Let us now introduce the central question which defines what this book is all about: How can we build an adequate polity for American education? That question presupposes that we do not now have an adequate polity. It may not be obvious that we do not, for we do have an amazing plethora of policy-making bodies for American schools. Every state has one or more. Every college has its own, likewise every school district. Washington has dozens—official, unofficial, and quasi-official. Every academic discipline and every professional association will debate policies as regularly as the calendar turns. Conflicts of interest are apparent throughout the educational world, and all the apparatus of politics can be seen in their periodic resolution. Enforcement is not lacking; it is common to speak of "policing" decisions arrived at through the politics of education.

Does all this add up to an adequate polity for American education? I believe not. Whenever one encounters serious thought and genuine interchange in educational policy arguments—from Congressional committee hearings to the monthly meeting of the Classroom Teachers Association in X-ville—those arguments are directed toward finding a specific course of action which will maintain or enhance the functioning of that particular institution. When one hears educational policy discussions *outside* the context of immediate and narrowly circumscribed decisions—from the pronouncements of the Educational Policies Commission to the annual policy statement of the president of X-ville's school board—one hears hot air. It is among the duties of a citizen in a democracy to tolerate his quota of ceremonial nonsense; that perpetrated under the label "educational policy" is bearably benign, albeit boring.

The serious deficiency is where talk is serious, as if we could make just and rational decisions on what kind of education we ought to have in this country, when, in fact, all these decisions are bound by the requirement to maintain and enhance our existing *institutions* of education. But the Public School Movement *is* dead, and we can no longer assume a reasonable correspondence between what is good for the schools (as presently instituted) and what is good for education. But that forces us to the question: Just how *are* schools now instituted?

The third section of this chapter is an attempt to answer that question conceptually, i.e., an attempt to develop the terms and definitions necessary for an intelligent description of American schools. At best it would have the inevitable inaccuracies of partial description, and it may be further marred by simple errors of fact. But I believe that any move toward an intelligible politics of education will have to begin with this or some very similar *way* of describing our present institutions. This way is the other side of the same coin which proclaims, "There is *no* System of education in America; there is rather an infinite multiplicity of systems." When one is searching for the precise, detailed description of what is actually going in in X-ville High School, then the variety, the lack of system, is the correct starting point. Only from that perspective can one see the subtle nuances that make X-ville High so importantly different from Y-ville. On the other hand, when one asks what kind of civilization we want to become, what kind of education we must have to become so, and what institutional policies are necessary to bring these things about, one must start from the other gate: There is a System of American education, and it is the function of intellect to make it explicit.

III. "SYSTEM" AND "ESTABLISHMENT"

In his *Education of American Teachers*, James Bryant Conant speaks forthrightly of the conflict between "Educationists" and "Academics." As we shall see in some detail in the next chapter, Conant's remarks contain some misleading and tendentious statements but overall probably fewer than one might find in any other treatment of this admittedly difficult subject. But in his *Shaping Educational Policy*, published less than two years later, Conant has dropped *that* distinction and speaks rather of "the Establishment," an undefined group whom he occasionally contrasts with "subject matter professors." Let us agree that Conant may use whatever terms he finds convenient, but it is to misuse a very important concept to label the Educationists, "the Establishment." One can well understand *why* Conant switched titles: it reduces animosity to use the quasi-comical term "Establishment." Especially when the conflict arising from *Education of American Teachers* threatened to break into open warfare, it tended to soften the atmosphere when school superintendents and deans of colleges of education could speak and think of themselves rather wryly as the "Establishment."

But it *is* confusing. The term "Establishment," as certain British writers use it and as it has been adapted by American sociologists, refers *not* to a particular political or economic interest group but to a somewhat amorphous collectivity that tends to concentrate at the top levels of all interest groups, or, rather, the top levels of all interest groups that carry significant weight in politics.[5] Thus, among the leadership of the major political parties, the civil and foreign services, major industrial corporations, the army, the church, and even the Trade Union Councils of Great Britain, one finds a surprising proportion of "public" school men, Oxbridge graduates, and "old county families." It is obviously difficult to determine exactly what proportion of such people would *not* be surprising, since one would have to factor out such variables as intellectual ability, aspiration, and parental "push." Hence, the notion of "Establishment" is not a precise, statistical concept. It is a way of expressing a *feeling* about British society in general: although the system does allow for competition among conflicting interests, it also protects a favored group, one which will win regardless of who wins the election, the strike, the newspaper war, or whatever.

I want to argue that there *is* an Educational Establishment in this country, that it includes but is not restricted to the collectivity Conant earlier had labeled accurately if inelegantly as Educationists, and that much of our literature on educational policy disastrously identifies the nation's need for education with the adornment of the Establishment. In other contexts, I shall suggest some reasons for thinking it likewise an error to treat educational policy as if the Establishment did not exist. But now I have to clarify how these terms are being used.

From nursery school through graduate and professional school in this country, there is one ladder of educational success. An American who has failed to achieve a post-baccalaureate degree is *ipso facto* a drop-out and a failure, though various degrees of near-success are recognized, and more or less commensurate rewards given for near-achievers.

The existence of an educational ladder of this sort is nothing new. Very likely the Library of Alexandria stood in a similar relation to primary schools in the Hellenistic world that the graduate school (Columbia, Harvard, Berkeley, etc.) stands in to primary schools in this country. But two twentieth-century developments have profoundly altered our educational system, making it very different from its Hellenistic forebear.

First, an ideological movement, one which found its political expression in the Public School Movement, made it politically imperative that all youngsters be *forced* to enter upon that single system of education. Second, a complicated set of historical changes, among them a sweeping technological revolution, tied the school and economy together to an absolutely unprecedented degree.

The ideology in question we shall call Educational Democracy. Its roots extend only into the eighteenth century, whereas the idea of political democracy or religious democracy can be traced much further in the dendrites of history. But it was only in the twentieth century that the full institutionalization of Educational Democracy occurred. In institutional terms, Educational Democracy may be expressed this way: if a primary school which prepares youngsters to enter a higher school is the best schooling for any child; and it seems to be, for it is chosen consistently by the rich and cultured who could have *any* kind of schooling for their children, then all children have a right to it. Since parents cannot be depended upon to secure this right for their children, the state must provide and compel the children to attend such schools.

The actual arrangements which emerged brought with them certain consequences that had not, likely could not have, been forseen by those who made this ideology central to the political evolution of America. One possibly unexpected consequence is that schools organized on this basis must retain youngsters for the total length of time it is believed necessary, for whatever reasons, that youngsters remain in any school. Put another way, you cannot run compulsory schools exclusively for failures, that is, youngsters who have proved unsuccessful in the traditional academic schools. The poor showing of the English secondary modern school is a very late confirmation of what should have been obvious to any American schoolmaster of the year 1900.[6]

Another consequence is that in no pluralistic society will the state secure a monopoly on schools (that is a tautology: one criterion, but not a sufficient one, for saying that a society is pluralistic is the absence of a state monopoly on schooling), but as the dominant producer the state schools will set the form and tone for everything done deliberately, systematically, in *all* schools. This follows logically as the converse of the first statement of Educational Democracy: if it is the duty of the state to provide and compel attendance at the best *kind* of school our culture knows, then (assuming the state is doing its duty) what the state provides *is* the best kind of school and all others will emulate it in those features which are significant. It follows institutionally from the fact that all schools must articulate with the next highest step in the ladder. The Roman Catholic parochial schools articulate fairly well with undergraduate colleges, but they have not fitted so neatly into the *next* higher level of graduate schools, which are dominated by the science faculties. But parochial schools must articulate or perish, as leading Roman Catholic educators are quite aware. In short, between state and non-state schools only marginal differences can obtain.

Other consequences from institutionalizing Educational Democracy include a vast increase in the number of educational functionaries of all sorts, the growth of special cultural forms—music, literature, pageantry, and argot—to express these institutions and relate them to the larger society, and the establishment of complex forms of political and budgetary control over school practices. How easy it is with hindsight to see that both national championship football and National Merit Scholarships follow from the decision by the Committee of Ten (1893) that public high schools should provide as high quality academic training as the educational logistics would permit. Colleges *will* be filled with school boys interested in fun and games, and high schools *will* surely produce an allotted proportion of high-quality scholarship. And thus is laid the institutional basis for the educational Establishment.

The second, i.e., economic, development which transformed the nature and function of our educational system is more difficult to name. It includes aspects of what has been called the Second Industrial Revolution, the Technological Revolution, the Managerial Revolution, the Revolution of Rising Productivity, the Paper Revolution, and many other things. What it signifies here is simply this: an individual's participation in the economic life of the nation is increasingly conditioned by his participation in the school system. From the junior high school drop-out who becomes practically unemployable to the Ph.D. in physics who moves into the R. and D. laboratories of an industrial corporation, every individual's access to a productive role in the economy reflects, *more or less but increasingly more,* his success in the system of formal schools.[7] The same is true of his life as a consumer, not only because income varies fairly closely with educational success but even more because tastes do.

It is a very difficult problem in social research to show *exactly* how closely connected are economic and educational success, especially when attention is shifted from relatively meaningless overall figures ("a high school diploma is worth $114,260.25") to the details of specific industries, specific income, and educational levels. It is even more difficult to show how this connection has changed over time, for the data from earlier generations are simply not available. Needless to say, on a topic so emotionally loaded and so unsusceptible to precise analysis, a great deal of nonsense has been and will be written. What follows may be a contribution to the literature of nonsense, but I take it as a matter of common, everyday observation that at least the following points are true:

1. Job qualifications for entry into nearly all occupations include an increasingly high and specified level of formal schooling.

2. Admission to specialized training programs includes an increasingly high level of formal schooling. This is true not only of old-line professional schools, almost all of which now require a baccalaureate for admission, but also of training courses for such occupations as insurance salesman and undertaker which only a few years ago were open to almost anyone. Licensing for practice is tied so closely to the training program that the educational requirement for the latter will almost completely exclude those who do not meet it. In one state, the requirement of successful completion of the tenth grade for entrance into a beautician's training course was challenged in court, but the requirement held. Within a few years the requirement of a high school diploma probably will be standard.

3. The state of affairs described in 1 and 2 cannot be explained solely or even primarily by the knowledge and skills acquired through formal schooling and deemed necessary for successful practice or training in the several occupations. A bachelor's degree may be quite a proper requirement for entry into law school, but its propriety is not a function of the specific knowledge and skills possessed by holders of that degree, simply because there *is* no specific knowledge or skill common to the baccalaureate, or to the successful completion of the tenth grade of high school, or to the

Ph.D. in physics. In recognition of this, wherever specific knowledge or skill is necessary for an occupation or training course, entry is determined by standard examination as well as by formal educational requirements.

4. As the requirement of formal schooling for entry into training programs is increased, these programs themselves become more and more indistinguishable from formal schooling. This merging of form between school and all training courses—law course to barber course—provides a "pragmatic" justification for the increased requirements: it *becomes* true that only those who have successfully completed a specified level in the "regular" school system can successfully complete the training course. It often becomes a source of justifiable pride that an ostensibly "practical" training course has higher academic standards and achievement than a corresponding course in the "regular" school program.

Because all these points of articulation are in constant flux, any attempt to chart precisely the educational system of the United States is bound to fail. But the upshot is clear: Democracy ordains that any school attended by any child be open equally to all; employment practices in an increasing number of occupations dictate that a certain level in school be attained before one can enter or even train for that occupation. Let us now use upper-cased "System" to refer to the complex of institutions which result. It would take many volumes to discuss all the consequences of this System for our society. Its effects permeate every aspect of our economic, political, and cultural life; but for understanding the literature of educational policy, a few effects must be made explicit.

1. Economically, the regular System is an automatic beneficiary of any educational upgrading that occurs anywhere in the total economy. It would not have to operate that way. One could well imagine a scheme in which a youngster could leave the System at *any* point to enter a specialized training course which, at its conclusion, would demonstrate very high-level, intensive standards. But that imagined course would, in effect, *have* to succeed with everyone who entered it, for a reject would have no other place to go. The only way to increase the educational standards anywhere in the economy and, at the same time, maintain mobility in and out of the ever-expanding number of job classifications is to *delay* exit from the System. Thus, the increasing number of non-System

schools, with their increasing resemblance in form and function to the System, are in no sense competitive but strictly complementary. This gives us the first clue to a functional definition of the (Educational) System: It is that part of the total educational enterprise of the society which automatically receives more students, *or* better students, *or* longer control over students, *or* some combination of the above, whenever a decision is made to upgrade educational requirements anywhere in the nation's economy.

It is the political impact of Educational Democracy which guarantees that there shall be a System. The ever-closer tie between education and economics guarantees that the System will continue to grow in power and influence over more and more aspects of life.

2. Still speaking economically, the System exists, functions, and grows because it fits admirably into the organizational mold of the rest of American society. In principle, there is a point beyond which expansion of the System is uneconomic, i.e., the point at which time taken away from the production and consumption of non-educational goods would *not* be surpassed by the consequently increased productivity and consumptivity (scans like "7" in International Morse) when the worker returns to the job. But except in one or two instances, we have not yet reached that point. One possible exception is medical education. Our prolongation of the training period for the M.D. has no doubt increased the skill and the economic "hunger" of the young doctor, but it is possible that his total contribution as producer of medical service and consumer of Buick automobiles might be increased if his pre-service training period were shortened—especially since his lifetime in-service training will continue to expand almost indefinitely. Another exception is the astronaut, whose training is preposterously long when measured against the length of time he produces the service of flying spacecraft. But these are exceptions; the rule is as follows:

For the foreseeable future, the continued growth of the System *can be justified* by its contribution to the nation's productivity and consumptivity of non-educational goods. Given the growth of more or less similar educational systems in all industrialized nations, one is led to believe that the System is indispensable to any society which is tied to an indefinitely expanding "growth" economy, of which more will be said later.

The Establishment, then, may be defined as the leadership of the

System. What was said earlier about the System can be person-
alized and applied to the Establishment: There is an ineluctable
drive toward raising the schooling requirements for almost all the
goods of life, including employment which still functions as a general prerequisite for access to other goods. This drive will, again
ineluctably, enhance the power, wealth, and prestige of the Establishment, *as a whole.*

But scarcely any particular instance of this drive will benefit all
segments of the Establishment equally. On the contrary, the relative advantage of various segments can be quite contradictory. The
Establishment, then, is not a unified political and economic group.
It is, rather, a congeries of shifting, unstable alliances of subgroups,
all united in fact if not yet in feeling by their sharing, however
unequally, in the growth of the System.

Let me illustrate with a not-quite-hypothetical case. Suppose a
large corporation, the AIX Corporation, has a number of specialized training programs, including a very well-known and respected
management-development program which over the last three
decades has become the only avenue to middle and higher level
management positions in the AIX Corporation. This corporation
has long preached the virtues of general education as a background
to management; but since its management-training programs had
assumed a rather specialized knowledge of economics and the principles of accounting, marketing, and business administration, admission to the training program had favored the graduate of the College of Business over the graduate from the College of Arts and
Sciences. Finally the AIX Corporation finds itself able to, and
therefore does, require both a bachelor of arts degree and a master's
degree from a graduate school of business for entry into its
management-development course. Now the System obviously benefits from that decision, but not equally in all segments. Assuming
honest and informed academic counseling, the very bright and
eager high school graduate who formerly was advised to pursue his
intended career in business by enrolling in the College of Business
will now be pointed toward one of the academic departments of
the College of Liberal Arts. Standards are strengthened in the latter, threatened in the former. The AIX Corporation is regarded as
a leader in management-development work; adoption of its new
policy by many large corporations may well be expected to follow,

with consequences for the System extending down into the early years of secondary school. The College of Business may respond by tightening its standards, intensifying its program, and producing a B.B.A. who compares favorably with the more expensive product holding the A.B. plus M.B.A. Or, more likely, it may shift its emphasis to a graduate course in business to provide candidates for the management ranks of the AIX Corporation and others. Any such response is costly and unsettling. If it can do so without being too obvious, the College of Business (assuming that it now serves mostly an undergraduate clientele) will oppose the AIX Corporation's decision to "raise standards" for its management-development course, while other members of the Establishment will applaud that decision.

Examples are numerous: The decision of the College of Dentistry to admit only college graduates will have effects on a small, private junior college specializing in "pre-dental" courses which are quite different from its effects on the College of Arts and Sciences at the state university. The decision of General Motors to restrict initial employment to high school graduates not only affects the Flint (Michigan) Public Schools in very definite ways; it also has different consequences for the University of Michigan, Michigan State, and the state colleges which provide teachers. The response of different members of the Establishment in these different institutions will surely be varied. But as a whole, the Establishment's response to G.M.'s understandable, albeit deplorable, personnel policies will be significantly different from that of the Urban League or the Congress of Racial Equality.

Many more examples of this sort could be given—e.g., the increasing importance of local educational resources in determining the location of new industries, the merging of the educational Establishment with the leadership circles of government and industry, etc. Indeed, these topics will recur as we look later at the connection between the System and the political economy it serves.

I have mentioned two *causes* for the present System: Educational Democracy and school-based employment. (I do not call these "basic causes" for I am sure that both the ideology and the economics of the System could ultimately be explained by more fundamental structural features of American society.) To this point, the *consequences* of the System have been discussed as if the causes were always working together. For the most part they do; otherwise the System would not have the strength it does. But in at least one crucial area, these two causes operate quite contradictorily. Increasing sophistication in the production of goods and services increases differentiation in employment; not only does it increase specialization among occupations, but it also increases stratification within any given industry or occupational classification. The reasons for this are partly in the nature of technology itself, partly in the nature of social organization, particularly the rationally structured corporation which, whether under public or private control, seems inevitably to become the dominant form of social organization in the modern world.[8]

But the System is ideologically opposed to all distinctions among persons, especially to invidious stratification. Each individual is entitled to the best education possible, regardless of future career or niche in a highly stratified system of employment. Now the ideology is often softened a bit to make it read "Each individual is entitled to the education which is the best *for him*," whence derives the doctrine of individual differences frequently encountered among Educationists. According to this doctrine, each child is unique, possessing needs, aspirations, and potentialities which distinguish him from every other child in the universe, and the school must respect that uniqueness in tailoring an educational program for *him*. There is yet another corollary of Educational Democracy which to some extent counteracts the doctrine of individual differences: a common school experience uniting all citizens is indispensable to the successful operation of the peculiar political institutions known as American democracy.

Reconciling these various corollaries of Educational Democracy is easy as long as we stay strictly at the level of ideology. But the System, the final product of the Public School Movement, is not a set of ideas but a set of institutions. And reconciling various ideological strains with economic and technological necessities in the everyday life of schools has been a continuing and arduous task. In some ways the most complex and subtle part of this task must be performed in the primary schools, for here the basic patterns of authority, work, equality, and differentiation must be established. But because the task is so subtle and complex, there is little to say about it in an overview such as this. For our purpose, it is enough that the primary school gets the System started.

Secondary Schooling: More visibly affected by ideology and economics is the American comprehensive high school. When "comprehensive" is taken in its two complementary pedagogical senses —taking all of an age group from a given geographic region *and* providing a full range of curricula—the ideological base is clearly visible. Note also that comprehensive high schools have some rather obvious economic advantages. In principle they should be relatively cheap, for they do make efficient use of increasingly expensive equipment and personnel. But that is really a minor consideration. Education is going to be an increasingly expensive enterprise, however miserly the public becomes in granting it support. There are strong pressures to make high school attendance compulsory to age eighteen; there is a constant upward pressure in teacher salaries and increasing costs for overhead—administration, supervision, debt service, new buildings, etc. There is a really powerful effort underway to force schools to invest in the terribly expensive "hardware" derived from computer technology.[9] With all these pressures operating, it is not at all clear just what institutional form is, or will be, the least expensive way to organize secondary education.

No, the significant economic fact is that the uniformity-diversity pattern of the comprehensive high school has its mirror image in the nation's economy. The finely differentiated roles in economic production are foreshadowed in the minutely "tracked" and "streamed" curricular programs of the secondary school. Rarely have two graduates from a large comprehensive high school shared all their classes. In principle, this fine differentiation reflects careful guidance—courses and sections being assigned to each student on the basis of his individual aptitude, interest, and vocational plans. In practice, it is not important that administrative problems of scheduling more usually determine who goes where and when. The *fact* of infinite differentiation, not justice or rationality, is what the school and the productive economy share.

But the uniformity of status has its obvious correspondence in the economy also when men and women are regarded as consumers not producers. A highly sophisticated productive system produces a mass market. Boys and girls have to learn their roles as mass consumers as well as the skills and knowledge necessary to become differentiated producers. The socio-psychological devices by which the school accomplishes this largely unintended training have been described by a number of astute observers. As an ever-larger proportion of the population reaches the point of satiety in rationally desirable goods, "consumer education" ceases to teach the virtues of thrift and the techniques of comparison shopping, in order to get on with the more important business of turning out avid mass consumers. The officially unrecognized "teen-age" culture of the comprehensive secondary school has made great strides in motivating the purchase of useless objects; it remains only to give more time and energy in this direction.

Teacher-Training: Both socially and architecturally, the *structure* of the comprehensive secondary school accords admirably with the structure of the economy. But if this structure is going to function, there must be as highly individuated corps of teachers as of students. An effective, up-to-date, comprehensive secondary school cannot be conducted with teachers that come exclusively from Forked Lightning State College, formerly F.L. State Teachers College, *née* F.L. Normal School c.1896. Neither can the school be run without *some* graduates from Forked Lightning; they will possess certain necessary skills and attitudes not possessed by the less numerous Ivy League teachers.

In itself, the need for a highly diversified, indeed stratified, teaching staff in primary and secondary schools is no problem. American higher education is as complexly and subtly stratified as the Grand Canyon, and equally well surveyed and mapped, as I will point out later. The administration of any school should be able to find *somewhere* exactly the conformation of qualities needed for a particular job of teaching, counseling, coaching, supervising, assisting, or whatever. The System functions as a structured system because it is possible to find persons who can perform the necessary functions.

But this need becomes a problem because the administration cannot look just *anywhere* in the ranks of higher education for personnel. A complicated series of laws and decrees have been established in each state, setting the qualifications for entry into school employment and regulating minutely the conditions for retention and advancement in that occupation. Differences among the several states' laws were and are marked, often capricious and whimsical. So the harassed administrator, needing all sorts of employees, some with highly specialized skills and knowledge, finds his labor market rather severely restricted. That is a problem, one we must pause briefly to explore.

It is our task in this section to explain how the System works. It is not yet time to evaluate it, in part or in whole. But for the sake of understanding it is necessary to distinguish between the *motives* and *forces* leading to certification, by which I mean the whole apparatus and the *apparatchki* regulating entry, retention, and advancement in school employment. It will also be necessary to distinguish both from the *effects* of certification.[10]

By "forces" here I mean the circumstances that get people worked up enough to enable certification to emerge in its present form. Ancient common law recognized the right of the sovereign to decide who might be a teacher, especially of young children. The sovereign's right in this regard was limited, at least in English law, by the rights of corporate bodies to regulate their internal affairs. In general, in this country at least, the state as sovereign has generally required that teachers be persons of reasonably good character who will not conduct their classes or themselves in a scandalous fashion. But legislation is one thing, and quite old; effective regulation is something else, and relatively recent.

During the relatively unregulated period which saw a vast expansion of the elementary schools and then of the secondary schools of this country (a process that began in the last quarter of the nineteenth century and should have been completed before 1930 except for rather untoward conditions generally), there were scandals aplenty. Venality and corruption were common when local lay boards could choose teachers and principals *ad lib*. Even more prevalent was simple ignorance (on the part of local boards) of what intellectual and personal qualifications were needed in the emerging System. But, even with the best of intention and insight, the local board would have been severely limited in the qualifications it could set and maintain: the processes for supplying the System with qualified teachers had not been worked out.

There were indeed scandalous conditions, first noted and attended to in the cities, later picked up and corrected by legislation on a statewide basis. Thus certification by the state went hand in hand with the provision of adequate teacher-training facilities. In time, the "political" appointment of ignorant and sadistic adults as teachers of children ceased to be a constant *cause celébre*. The general law here is perhaps a tautology: in a healthy democratic society, whenever there are scandalous conditions (as judged by that society's current morality), appropriate political action will be taken to correct those conditions. This accounts for the political *force* of the certification movement.

The *motives* of those engaged in establishing certification were in general the same found in other reform movements of the time. The term "irregularity," as it might appear in a newspaper report, "Irregularity Discovered in Public Works Department," has come to be a euphemism for unproved crime; but the reform movement was often out to eliminate irregularity in its extended sense, meaning *anything* not according to rule. Thus "irregular" and "unregulated" come to be synonymous in the reformer's vocabulary. In its early stages, then, certification was *not* a matter of the System's using the police power of the state to enforce the System's rules. On the contrary, the System emerged with the rules: *re*form was primarily a matter of establishing *a* form. It is not only in respect to school affairs that reformers were first of all regulators.[11]

One of the *consequences* of certification, not properly speaking a motive, was the emergence of the System itself. Another, which was not experienced acutely until after World War II, is that raising standards of certification by increasing the *number* of college *courses* that must be taken by any person wishing to enter, remain, or advance in a given occupation is a relatively slow but effective way of raising salaries in the System as a whole. The more *specific* the course requirements for a particular position in the System, the more certain and rapid the effect in raising salaries for that position and all others above it in the same "line."

As a result, the forces, motives, and consequences of certification combine to make courses in Education a central feature of the state's control over the corps of teachers. In the early days of the Massachusetts Bay Colony, a testimonial of good character by a minister was required of anyone who would be a schoolmaster. The same principle has to be followed by any state authority which takes cognizance of its schools and the welfare of the pupils in them: the state must require its *especially* trusted citizens to attest to the qualifications of those who would be teachers. But who are its especially trusted citizens? In default of an established church, we establish a secular institution—the Department of Education—which takes on the role of examining character. And we attach Education to the academic world, with extraordinary results which we will examine later.

For both ideological and temperamental reasons, Educationists are concerned with the character of their students in a way which can be rather easily distinguished from other academic types. Once when I was a very junior and eremitic instructor at a large university, I overheard an interchange between another teacher and a clerk in the registrar's office. These were pre-IBM days when faculty members were required to bring semester grades directly to the registrar. The clerk had noted that my colleague, who like nearly everyone else on campus was completely unknown to me, had left a blank beside a student's name. "But, sir," she said, "you must put in something—a W if the student was passing the course at the time he withdrew or an F if he was failing."

"Then mark it F. I have no idea who he was or what he was doing."

When he said that, I knew at least that the professor was not a member of the Department of Education. If the Educationist had not known the student, he would not have admitted it. If he had no reason to believe the student was failing, he would have assumed that he was passing. The professor of Education may never know any student with the depth or intimacy that sometimes is found in the relation between student and professor of other disciplines, but he will try to know every student well enough to spot the potential scandals in advance and to weed them out. The standards for acceptance are not high, perhaps, but then when a seventeenth-century minister affirmed that a parishioner was "of good character," he too made a rather minimum judgment. In either case, it was probably enough to eliminate those teachers who, under decent conditions, would do positive harm to their charges.

How nicely courses in Education satisfied the motives of the school reformers! They were forming a new sort of educational institution, broader in scope and function than any known before. Both teaching and "pupiling" (to use B. O. Smith's terms for the institutionalized act of receiving instruction according to rules) [12] were new habits to a large part of the school population as that institution spread among classes and groups previously free from its influence. One could no longer just assume that any young woman who presented herself as a prospective teacher possessed by second nature the discipline, order, and regularity one expects of the New England schoolmarm. There simply were not enough of the latter to go around. So a great many young men and women had to be trained in those virtues, and quickly. A quasi-academic program emphasizing the technique of pedagogy was an obvious necessity. The basis for the Educationists' membership in the Establishment lay precisely in their ability to satisfy that need.

A great deal has been written about the "abdication of responsibility" on the part of colleges and universities because those institutions did not take on the entire task of teacher-training in the period of greatest expansion of the elementary and secondary schools. It could not have happened that way. In response to a movement common to all of Western civilization, American colleges were coming to demand graduate training as a requirement for teaching, and graduates of graduate schools were very scarce. Furthermore teacher training in that time was not, properly speaking, an academic enterprise. It would have been out-of-place, if not repugnantly otiose, in a genuinely academic environment. Even so, American colleges and universities did make a major effort in teacher education, often straining their resources and academic heritage to do so.[13]

Pedagogy, however grandiose its claims, was and is an eminently practical kind of training. Its major content, indeed, in the era of the normal school, was the subject matter of the lower schools, taught in the ordered, regular fashion in which it was to *be* taught to the younger pupils. The idea of a course in teaching method was to make teaching methodical. Even courses in "principles" of education show the same tendency; in America, teachers must become themselves bearers of the discipline, order, and dedication which in centralized school systems are imposed by bureaucratic authority from a national ministry. In a later generation, Educationists would be attacked for wishing to destroy ordered and methodical teaching in order to replace it with something formless and disordered called Progressivism. But even until today and even in such hotbeds of radicalism as the experiments in team teaching sponsored by the Harvard Graduate School of Education, courses in education are designed to effect order out of chaos, to *achieve* a method and a form which may be institutionalized.

As for the effect of legislating courses and degrees as requirements for school employment, this was the one area in which the combined corps of teachers of *all* subjects and *all* grades as well as *all* administrative and special service staff had, however poorly understood, a united, common economic interest. From this common base, interests diverge to a greater or lesser extent. It is easy to see how this works: the more courses in Education required for *any* teaching position, the more restricted the labor market for teachers. Since all other professional employment in the school requires, first, certification, and, second, experience as a teacher, the more restricted the labor market for teachers, the more restricted the market for all higher, better-paying, less drudging positions. Beyond that, interests are not quite so common. School principals like to see the requirements for that position jacked up, but teachers who want to become principals do not. High school teachers have somewhat different interests from those of elementary teachers. But when the teaching profession acts as a united political entity, its weight is significant. Everyone in the System benefits from raising or maintaining the requirement of courses in Education, though not all equally, of course.

This discussion of the motives, the forces, and the effects of certification, was in the nature of a brief comment on teacher-training as a constituent institution in the System. I want to add two comments on the story told above. First, if I have correctly understood the history of the rise of Education, that history will provide the grounds for supporting neither the Educationist nor the Academic segment of the Establishment in their internecine struggle. Anyone who attempts to draw a moral from that story will simply draw a blank. Consider the last point, i.e., that certification requirements restrict the labor market and thus in the long run raise wages for all professional employees in schools. Is this good or bad? Is there an adequate measure of how high teachers' salaries ought to be? Astute observers agree that teachers are becoming increasingly concerned over non-economic goals such as respect, dignity, and a chance to do the best teaching they can. In pursuit of these goals, teachers insist on a distinction between their interests and those of supervisory personnel, which means that the old common front for raising standards of certification is broken; which means, in turn, that teachers are turning to direct collective bargaining as a supplement to the job-restrictive techniques of certification in order to protect their special interests, which then come into conflict with those of "higher" professional employees of the school.[14] Is *this* good or bad?

From the point of view of the growth of the System, certification would seem to be an absolutely necessary aspect of the Public School Movement. Legal coercion had to be employed to force articulation among the various segments of the System—the common (elementary) schools, the secondary schools, the colleges, the teacher-training institutions, and (last in appearance but essential in function) the graduate schools—each of which had traditions and forms of control clearly distinguishing it from all the others. In turn, the System was essential to the growth of the kind of economy and national policy which have been inherent in America since we entered World War I, even though it took some disastrous events to make us recognize what that scheme was.

Has the System been a blessing or an evil to the millions of Americans who have been teachers and pupils in it? Anyone who would even attempt to answer that question seriously is mad. There is simply no standpoint from which to pronounce a moral judgment on the history of certification and the consequent growth of Education.

My second comment is to disclaim what may seem to be implied by the first. I do not believe that the events of our educational history were inevitable. Rather, careful scholarship will reveal them to be the outcome of consciously adopted policies of reasonable and responsible individuals, whose efforts we summarize (perhaps misleadingly) in the expression "Public School Movement." It was inevitable, *in rerum natura*, that the consequences of their policies were frequently different from those intended. It was also inevitable, in the basic dialectic of social life, that institutions thus created acquired a will-to-survive which persists after their original purposes have changed. But the System was not inevitable, nor was the growth of Education. Someday our historical knowledge may be detached enough that we can truly understand just how it happened.

The Liberal Arts College: Perhaps the most difficult task of historical understanding is to grasp how the liberal arts college, that archaic offshoot of a strange series of historical accidents, should have become the *key, central* institution in the whole System. Perhaps this last claim is not obvious; it will become obvious if we contrast the position of the liberal arts college with that of another institution serving an age group overlapping that of the college— adult education. The city of Philadelphia, just as an example, has an honorable tradition of adult education. If one wants to learn a skill or trade one can find a number of schools—public and commercial—willing to provide the teaching. If one happens to be a follower of some religious or political prophet, e.g., Elijah Mohammed or Henry George, he can find a school in Philadelphia to give instruction in the details of the prophet's teaching. Subject only to general health, safety, and embezzlement codes, these schools are free of political control. It is a part of the general educational policy of this nation, the Commonwealth of Pennsylvania, and the City of Philadelphia that such institutions be allowed to teach whatever they like to whomever they like.

This is a precious freedom; its price, indeed, is isolation from the nation's system of schools. A certificate of successful mastery of a course at the Henry George School will entitle one to enter a more advanced course at the same school, and little else. A certificate in welding from a garage mechanics' school may have value in getting its holder a job anywhere in the country but only because that certificate specifies completion of the Underwriters Laboratory examination in welding, an examination established by a quasi-public polity, national in scope.

In contrast to such "free" institutions, the American college today is not isolated but intimately bound up with all sorts of institutions, educational and otherwise. The fact is that the undergraduate, liberal arts college is *the* gateway to economic and social advancement. This statement expresses a fact which is no surprise to the multitudes of parents and children seeking college admissions. But its recency and present naturalness go strangely together. Only one or at most two generations ago, all the traditional professions offered several paths of entry, and an undergraduate degree was scarcely ever a requirement for any of them. Outside the traditional professions, a college education was popularly regarded, rightly or wrongly, as a positive bar to economic success: the "college boy" was stereotyped as much inferior to the man of practical experience in business, in industry, even (from our point of view, astonishingly) in a literary career. Hemingway rejected college and achieved success; F. Scott Fitzgerald went to Princeton and, in the eyes of his own time, to failure. And that was only one generation ago.

Conant's *The Education of American Teachers* was subjected to a good deal of buffeting by the Educationists because it proposed a certain relaxation of course requirements for teaching certificates. What went unremarked, because unremarkable in our time, was the unquestioned assumption that all school teachers should go to college, preferably a liberal arts college. Only three decades ago a four-year period of teacher-training was a goal which many regarded as utopian, one which required justification by an elaborate theory of the social (i.e., more than merely teaching) role of the educational profession.[15] Now that the goal has become fact, no one even notices it, much less tries to justify it.

If this institution does, indeed, control access to leadership and even employment in every phase of our economic and political life, it also has other functions which argue for its centrality in the System. Plato recognized long ago that the way in which a society regulates its nuptials is *the* most significant factor in determining the happiness of the πόλις; and in the United States today, the undergraduate college serves as our primary agency for deciding who shall meet and marry whom, at least among sons and daughters of the middle class.

Plato's authority may be invoked again if we point to the political role of the college as the bearer and arbiter of the higher culture which the Greeks would have called simply "poetry." Censorship of poetry is a political decision. The movement to reduce censorship to the vanishing point is only extending to the larger society policies which were earlier established for college life.

There is no need to add more evidence: any institution which controls access to the economic, familial, and cultural institutions of the society may reasonably be called "key" or "central." Indeed, the most paradoxical point about the liberal arts college is that we should have to *argue* for its centrality in the System. It is a strange blindness, particularly prevalent among college professors in America, that the term "higher," when used in the expression "higher education," means somehow elevated above sordid economic and political functions. Such blindness is not found elsewhere in the world; it was not found always in America. The establishment of Harvard in 1636 was as self-consciously political as any other act of that most self-consciously political body, the General Court of Massachusetts Bay Commonwealth. The same political quality carried over to the decision to make an external Board of Overseers the highest policy-determining agency of Harvard College.[16] Very much the same could be said for the establishment and governance of other colleges in America during the colonial period.

The last quarter of the eighteenth century in America saw the appearance of a political generation scarcely equaled in the history of Western civilization. It is not surprising that these men who were so much at home in the world of politics should have turned their attention to educational policies. From Jefferson's *Notes on Virginia* to the essays submitted to the American Philosophical Society in 1810, the generation of Revolutionists and Founding Fathers had thought of educational policy as inherently a central concern of politics, both theoretically and practically. In this spirit and with a paean to the power for progress locked within the liberal arts, leaders in the newly united states, from New Orleans to Michigan, established state colleges as one phase of a general effort toward civic virtue and cultural enlightenment.[17]

But shortly thereafter the connection between responsible politics and college policy was effectively broken, not to be re-established until our own times. Several reasons may be offered in explanation of this rupture: John Marshall's decision of 1819 in the Dartmouth College Case had not utterly separated educational and governmental concerns; but, in affirming the sanctity of contract, this decision had made it more difficult for partisan legislatures to meddle in the internal affairs of chartered institutions. Furthermore the country underwent something of a revulsion against the humanistic and nationalistic political ideals of the French Revolution, ideals which had inspired the founding of the early state universities, witness particularly the charter of the University of Michigan in 1817.[18]

But the strongest factor separating liberal arts education from responsible politics was of an entirely different order. Those who had fought the Revolution and founded the Constitution regarded America's citizenry as her greatest resource, to be husbanded, nurtured, and perfected if America was to survive as that lonely little nation on a far continent. But after the full effects of the Louisiana Purchase began to be felt, a great change occurred. Not her citizens but her inexhaustibly rich land was America's great treasure; not Man but God was to be praised and honored. The Great Awakening, as a religious phenomenon, fit this change of mood most admirably. And, as Donald Tewksbury has convincingly demonstrated, colleges were founded, grew, and prospered not because of responsible political decisions but because of good luck and enthusiasm, mostly denominational in tone. Enthusiasm could easily wring a charter and occasionally a few dollars from a state legislature. Enthusiasm could entice a few youngsters from the farms to the cold comfort of a firetrap frame building. Enthusiasm could persuade a student of Timothy Dwight to teach for poor bread and board at some distant and struggling college. As the eighteenth century knew so well, religious enthusiasm and responsible politics cannot co-exist. As the college became the prime goal and example of religious enthusiasm, it lost its place in the deliberations of a responsible polity.[19]

The history of education was different on the continent and in England. The impetus given by Napoleon's schools to French military and cultural imperialism was carefully noted in every European capital. The effect was gradually to transform institutions of higher education—new technical schools and ancient universities alike—into extensions of the emerging systems of schools. There were subtle and revealing differences between the way nationalism worked itself into English and continental systems, and equally interesting differences among the latter. But by 1914, from Madrid to St. Petersburg the basic pattern was similar: higher education was *de jure* an arm of the national state. Academic freedom, *Lehrenfreiheit und Lernenfreiheit,* existed where and to the extent that national policy dictated. In education as well as in foreign affairs, reason in support of policies always ended with *raison d'état.*

The United States, which had followed closely the European schemes for ubiquitous primary schools and was to lead the world in the development of publicly supported and controlled secondary schools, paid relatively little attention to its congeries of institutions of "higher" education. It did institute a system of agricultural education unique in history; we have yet to find economic and political solutions to the problems created by the success of this educational venture. We created institutions to train the enormous numbers of teachers required by our burgeoning public schools; however primitive some of these institutions appear in retrospect, the very strength from which we view them today shows that they were at least adequate to the tasks they undertook. We developed graduate schools which slowly became the peers of their European counterparts. In all these developments, public policy directly intervened: federal policy in the case of agricultural education, state policy in supporting, selectively, graduate, professional, and technical schools and local policy predominantly for normal schools. There a curious thing happened. Although never of central concern in public policy discussions, *undergraduate liberal arts education eventually worked itself into a position of institutional centrality in all these and indeed practically all other educational programs.*

A full historical treatment of this paradox would require certain qualifications, but I believe that full elaboration would make it appear even more paradoxical. There is no doubt that early reformers of graduate, professional, and technical education saw their task as one of by-passing the classical language curriculum which dominated the liberal arts college. But without conscious planning, it has turned out that an ever lengthening program of liberal arts studies has become the *via regia,* often the *via sola,* to *all* other sorts of training. This unofficial but rigorously enforced policy is actually of more practical import in our national life than that emanating from those public and quasi-public bodies which define our "official" educational policies.

In the process, of course, the liberal arts college has changed greatly, as indeed what American institution has not? Somewhere, however, there must be a moral in the success story of the liberal arts college. Quite apart from any overall planning and without any conscious or central direction, this formerly peripheral institution has moved into the very heart of our entire social system. A careful sociological study of the structural and functional connections between the liberal arts college and the other dominant institutions of the society would explain how the college maintains its central position. But the moral, if there really is one, would be different. The very freedom from central planning has enabled the colleges, all two thousand of them and each in somewhat its own way, to change and grow in response to the world about. We can speak of the success of the liberal arts college as *one* institution only because it is *not* one administratively. Try to explain *that* to an educator visiting from the Soviet Union!

The Graduate School: At the top stands the graduate school. The data about graduate education in the United States have been collected with some care and need not be repeated here.[20] There are two points, however, that may be emphasized:

In the graduate school, the final step away from the local community has been taken. The professional loyalty of a professor in the graduate school is not to the local campus or institute which houses his work; it is and ought to be to the international community of scholars—dead, living, and yet unborn—who pursue Truth through his discipline. Put more prosaically, the people with whom he can communicate most significantly in his specialty are less likely to be his campus colleagues than his fellow specialists scattered throughout the world, in contact through periodicals and periodic conferences.

Teaching in the graduate school is regarded by many as the most preferred spot in the System: salaries are generally higher, teaching loads are lighter, facilities for research are much superior to those found in a purely undergraduate college, and opportunities for travel, service, and power are greater than elsewhere in the System. In principle, however much the demand for college teachers may have stretched its holes, there is a highly selective screening process for membership in the graduate school. Thus a fundamental contradiction appears in the structure of the System: Ideologically it is committed to egalitarianism and pluralism; but its most valued positions are occupied by a small number of men and women who have achieved their status through rigorous competition in the strictly academic game. These men and women—naturally jealous of their perquisites and jealous in promoting the game in which *they* have succeeded—set a model for action in the System quite contrary to the official ideology.

Politically also the graduate school finds itself in a contradiction. On one side, it is part of the truly revolutionary movements in our society. Research, by definition, is directed toward *new* discoveries. This is the central truth in the otherwise absurd idea that "science" has captured higher education. The point is that whether one is constructing a bevatron or re-constructing Beowulf, the benefits are in new knowledge; and new knowledge, feeding into the technology of our physical world *or* into the de-mythologizing of our psychical world, is inherently a revolutionary force.

But the attitude of the graduate professor is not usually so revolutionary. He is more likely to have the scholar's ideal of contemplation than the activist's ideal of revolution. Indeed, with an activist ideal, the graduate professor is likely to be less than effective in his pursuit of Truth.

Furthermore, and this may not be exactly a different point, the professor in the graduate school has no good material reason for wanting revolution, particularly social revolution. He has secured a relatively favored position in society and is not inclined to see that society as basically flawed. It would, indeed, be a rather sick man who would denounce a System just because that System had amply rewarded him.

From the graduate school down to the primary grades, this same contradiction filters, diluted, of course, by many other ideas and purposes. Yet when the claim is made that "the school" is inherently torn between promoting change and resisting it, the graduate school furnishes the paradigm case.

GLOSSARY

In this section, I have coined some technical terms to indicate my sense of what are the most *prominent* features of the educational landscape of the moment, not necessarily its most valuable and persevering traits.

The System: There is not, and in all probability ought not be, a free market for educational goods in this country. One can go out and buy education at any level and for about any price one wishes to pay, but the producers of even the most expensive education *of some kinds* operate within a protected market. They are subsidized by the state in all sorts of ways, ranging from direct, total financing out of tax revenues to a minimum set of tax concessions and other franchises accorded non-profit institutions. One way, then, of defining the System would be to say that it includes all and only those institutions of primary, secondary, and higher education which share in this protected and subsidized market.

But this purely economic definition would miss the feature which gives the systemic character to the System: legally each of the elements (primary, secondary, higher) is defined and regulated in terms of the others. Thus, a primary school differs legally from a communal baby-sitting operation because it must staff itself with graduates of colleges and universities, which can admit only graduates from secondary schools, which must also be staffed with graduates of colleges and universities and must accept youngsters who have completed primary schools and so on. So this *legally* systemic character could also be used as a basis for defining the System.

However, that would ignore certain informal, quasi-legal attributes that are as influential as the purely legal or economic features of the System. For example, a college is legally defined in various ways in various states, and its autonomy in granting degrees is severely limited in some states, while in others a charter confers almost unlimited license. Unless a certain proportion of the faculty of a college hold advanced degrees from the graduate faculties of recognized universities, the graduates of that college will suffer many disabilities which the state chartering it cannot control. Its graduates will not be admitted to graduate and professional schools, they will not be allowed to teach in the primary and secondary schools of neighboring states, and they will not be afforded all the employment advantages accorded graduates of colleges "accredited" by quasi-legal groups.

I intend that the definition of "System" not be merely economic, or legal, or other, but functional, in the sense that it points out what happens because of the interrelations of these educational institutions. Through the operation of various political and economic forces which are not very well understood, there is a continuous, possibly accelerating, expansion of the protected market of education. There are more strict and better enforced compulsory school attendance laws; there are higher requirements for formal schooling for various jobs and job-training programs. The System is that part of the nation's total educational enterprise which automatically expands when there is an extension in any protected sector of the education market. For example, suppose that the Board of Underwriters prepares a new and more difficult examination for electricians. This creates an expansion in education, but not in the protected sector specifically, for much of the training necessary to pass the new examination will be given by commercial training schools, union schools, or industrial training shops. But let us suppose that the Board of Underwriters decrees that a high school diploma will be regarded as a *prerequisite* for taking the examination to become a licensed electrician. This means that a certain number of boys who would have left school at the minimum legal age in order to get the training and experience required for the electricians' license will now stay in school until graduation. Provision must be made for continuing their technical and general education. Teachers must be secured from colleges, and teachers for *those* teachers must be secured from graduate schools. Provision must be made for counseling the would-be electricians, teachers, and professors. The teaching at all levels must be supervised and administered by trained personnel who must be taught by even more highly trained personnel. The System, then, in one way of looking at it, concatenates those educational institutions legally and logistically so that all have to expand when any one aspect of the protected segment of the educational market expands.

The System is somewhat like the penumbra of a shadow: there is a sharp line around it only *after* you draw it. Thus, any increase in the number of youths who stay in secondary schools until graduation will also increase the amount of medical service, nursing service, dietary service, and legal service required by the secondary schools. Are we to say that medical schools, etc., are, because of that fact, parts of the *System?* Then what about architectural schools and schools for the building trades? I should prefer to *try* to draw a line between *educational* services and other services given under the auspices of the school. Such a line, in the final analysis, is arbitrary. For example, the work of a public health nurse in a junior high school might be classified as "educational" while she is teaching a class in "health education" and "other" when she conveys the same information (and probably with greater effectiveness) to an individual child in the nurse's office. This is arbitrary. On the other hand, it is not arbitrary to recognize that when a local school district decides that only registered nurses will be allowed to teach the required courses in health education, a very minor but real structural connection between the nursing school and the public school has been established, and the nursing school has become, to that extent, a more integral part of the System.

It might happen that a state should require all social studies teachers to take a course in constitutional law, taught by a person possessing a law degree and a license to practice. Such a requirement would make the law schools of that state (to a minor degree) part of the System. The increasing amount of litigation in which local school boards find themselves engaged does increase the market for lawyers but does not, in itself, make law schools part of the System, as the term is used here.

Another way of drawing the line is to distinguish between the effect of a *general* rise in the economy and a specific growth in the school system on, say, a school of law or medicine. From the fact that a given industry is growing by a certain amount one cannot tell whether that rise will have a greater or lesser effect on the demand for doctors or lawyers than an equal amount spent on schools. But the System is that part which automatically expands whenever *any* industry decides to increase the amount of schooling required for some particular job.

Establishment

The Establishment includes *all* the leadership class in the System. In some parts of the System it is very easy to distinguish workers from leaders, in other parts very difficult. Mobility into the Establishment is very high, for, as is the case with many other industries, the rate of increase in supervisory personnel is greater than the increase in production-line employees. In the case of schools, the productivity of the front-line employee has not increased proportionally; indeed it probably has declined.[21]

The hard-boiled language of economics effectively communicates certain facts about public school education, but it does not serve to demarcate the Establishment. No institutional nor monetary criterion will catch the political reality of the Establishment. One can say that having primarily administrative or supervisory duties is a criterion, but then it all depends on what kind of administrative duties, some of which are very narrow and clerical in nature. One might say that an income of $15,000 per year separates the Establishment from the rest, but that would make the vice-principals of many high schools members and many college professors non-members, even though the first may be concerned with only schedules and student discipline while the second may be a leader in something that really matters.

Nor is there a social class or "mutual understanding" basis for distinguishing the Establishment. Members do not know one another personally; there is no common set of identifying marks in dress, speech, or values by which they can recognize one another. There is very little mutual respect between deans of graduate schools and elementary school principals.

Yet both must act in ways which overall are strictly determined by the mutual dependency of these institutions. *That* is what makes them members of the Establishment. Such a definition, admittedly very rough, enables us to distinguish the member of the Establishment from a classroom teacher or routine, clerical administrator. The duties of the latter two can be described strictly in relation to the particular level of the System in which they operate. But the responsibility becomes located *somewhere* to make sure that any particular educational level or service or subject matter articulates adequately with all the rest. This task of articulation is handled in many, many different ways in the System, for there is no overall bureaucratic structure in which it can be "rationalized" or codified. But it does get done, sometimes by a continuous series of smooth adjustments, sometimes by great wrenches of effort. The difficulty is that although many and varied institutions and activities within institutions go to make up the System, the value of no particular institution within it can be defined exclusively by its contribution to the functioning of the whole. Thus one can say truly of the public high school that it serves to continue the education begun in primary schools and to prepare a certain proportion of the youngsters for further education in college. But if one should assert or imply that its functions as a pipeline in the System is the *only* value the high school serves, one would clearly be wrong. For the high school serves certain distinctive values that pertain to it alone. And the same is true for all other levels in the System.

It is the function of the Establishment, then, continuously to adjust and reconcile activities necessary to the pursuit of *distinctive* values (of a level or of a subject matter, etc.) with activities necessary to the continuation of the System. Sometimes this adjustment is relatively simple: there is a difference between teaching a high school general science course as a terminal course (i.e., for youngsters who will have no further formal instruction in science) and as a preparatory course for further work in high school and college science. This difference is one of emphasis and degree, rather easily compromised and adjusted in the same classroom. Sometimes the conflict is more severe. The distinctive goal of a high school guidance program is to help each youngster to understand himself or herself as a person unique and precious, having a history and a future in a world possessing many genuine values but not entirely responsive to uniqueness and individuality. But the value of the high school guidance program for the System is to con as many youngsters as possible to maximize their efforts in academic study, at whatever cost in other aspects of personality so long as that cost does not act reflexively to cut down academic achievement. The need for academic talent at the next level is apparently insatiable; thus, as far as the System is concerned any diminution of academic effort and any rejection of further academic study by an academically talented youth is sheer loss, "wastage," as the English would say.

Taken by itself, of course (and that is the way writers on educational policy usually take it), this con game is an ethical monstrosity, a clear violation of the fundamental moral premise that human beings must be treated as ends, not means. But, of course, if the distinctive value of the high school guidance program is taken *just by itself*, it is socially irresponsible. One can extend personal sympathy to that small minority of high school counselors (and even smaller minority among those who teach them their jobs) who recognize the moral conflict inherent in their role. For their consolation it may be noted that counselors are clearly members of the Establishment on my definition.

Educationists and Academics

We can say that every "professional" worker in the System is either an Educationist or an Academic. But I should prefer to use those terms to distinguish two *sometimes* conflicting interest groups in the Establishment. As mentioned earlier, the easiest way to spot this conflict is to ask whether a person's institutional status will be enhanced by raising the requirement for that and lower statuses by increasing the number of credits in Education courses or in some other field of study. (Everyone in the System benefits every time any requirement is raised for entering the System, and all those at or above any particular status benefit when the requirement for that or a lower status is raised. But not all benefit equally, the difference being a function of the specifics of the increased requirement.) Yet in any particular political engagement, lines may be drawn in quite different ways, for rational arguments and moral sentiments are not without quite significant effect. The arguments may run from the pitifully jejeune ("Anybody who really knows his subject can teach it." Confronting the equally inane response, "We don't teach subjects, we teach children.") to the very sophisticated, e.g., Myron Lieberman's attack on the myth of "liberal" education in teacher-training.[22] But the differences in attitudes and values are not easily resolved by rational argument. The traditions and origins are different: the Educationist is rooted in the primary and secondary schools. Teachers there constitute a single profession only in the sense that there are common criteria which all must meet, and those criteria include specific courses in Education taken at the undergraduate college level. Therein lies the mass of the Educationists, though their members and supporters are everywhere in the System.

The basic locus of power of the Academics is the departmental structure of the graduate school. Here college teachers are not only trained but formed into distinctive professorial types. The same pattern has extended itself into the undergraduate college, whence come departmentally sensitive high school teachers and department chairmen. Some of the more Academically oriented high schools now recognize science, English, or history "majors" in the high school program. At least one state, California, has already made an Academic department major a requirement for certification at the elementary school level. A non-graded, departmentalized primary school is undoubtedly the next extension of the graduate school structure within the System.

The intention here is to pass judgment on neither the Educationists nor the Academics. It is rather this: despite the fact that their interests sometimes conflict, they coincide on the vast majority of issues that arise. Neither may have much respect for the other, but neither could run the System alone. Sophisticated leaders of both sides realize it.

Nor can Academics and Educationists simply divide the System between them. There is no returning to a dual system, one culminating in higher education for a small minority, the other in fixed jobs for the majority. The connection between the System and the rest of the society is too symbiotic to make division sensible; and in running the System, the Academics and Educationists stand in an inseparable relation of mutual dependency. Illustrations are innumerable. In discussing Conant's work, I will argue the impossibility of conducting an advanced placement program *for* the Academics without calling on the technical skills and "personnel point of view" *of* the Educationists. Reciprocally, the Educationists could not even begin to talk seriously about the "scientific" status of their instruments and techniques without organizing themselves as a minor, subsidiary *department* in the Academic hierarchy. If the teaching of any subject in the primary schools loses its connection with the spirit and content of the parent discipline in the Academic world, the teaching will go stale immediately, for there is no traditional, "folk" base on which techniques and content of teaching can be built. On the other hand, the enormous and ever-increasing intellectual distance between Academic research frontiers and primary school instruction means that the Educationists' professed role as bridge between graduate school faculty and public school faculty is indispensable, even when practice cannot measure up to profession. As a colleague of mine remarked in another connection, the marriage between the Educationists and Academics "may resemble Ethan Frome's, but it is no less compelling for that."

This, then, is the System—with its Establishment, its Educationists, its Academics—as American as Mom and napalm. Whatever may be happening to education in this country, it is a central and inescapable truth that the System is thriving.

IV. THE SYSTEM AND THE FEDERAL GOVERNMENT

The fact, however, that the System thrives is no guarantee that it ought to. Such questions as Who shall be admitted to the ranks of the managerial elite? Who shall be allowed to meet and marry whom? How shall the higher culture of our civilization be regulated and supported? are properly political questions, in the proper sense of the term "political" employed here. Does this mean that the federal government ought to be responsible for making educational decisions? There are valid points to be made on each side; as the old World War II saying had it: "Anyone who isn't confused doesn't know the whole story."

It is easy enough to argue in favor of a more active and responsible role for the federal government in the formulation of educational policies. Conflict of interest achieves institutional dignity as well as legitimacy in the deliberations of the Congress. Legislative rules are fair and equitable; laws made by Congress tend to have continuity without rigidity. The Supreme Court has proved itself an able defender of the rights of individuals in most, unfortunately not all, affairs in which conflict may arise between the interests of an individual and those of the government itself. The executive branch has learned to utilize the creative technical talent of the intellectual community of the nation, a factor which will be increasingly important as issues and problems of educational policy become increasingly technical.

Finally, we must remember that the government of the United States is a democratic polity embracing *all* the people of *all* races, creeds, and economic conditions. Since schools have become of such structural significance in the lives of the nation's people and institutions, basic policies affecting education should be made within the polity embracing the widest constituency; and that polity, without question, is the federal government.

It should not be cause for wonder that the federal government measures up fairly well by the criteria we would naturally apply to any polity. For our criteria are ultimately derived from our political experience; and the most striking fact about the political experience of Western civilization since the American and French Revolutions is the enormous sum of passion, intellect, and life itself which has been expended in forcing political institutions to accord with those criteria which we vaguely label "democratic." History's indictment would be cruel indeed if all the mind and will which have gone into reform of the political life of so favored a nation as the United States had been quite in vain. I believe that only a person whose criteria for a polity derives from a source other than historical experience itself could claim literally that *all* is vanity.

Having said all that, I now wish to argue that the political issues facing education in America today ought *not* to be debated in Congress, nor argued before the Supreme Court, nor "processed" by Presidential memoranda. My reasons are quite simple: one of the most basic criteria which we would apply to any political system is that the polity itself must be neutral with respect to the interests contending on any particular point. This criterion is difficult to satisfy in practice. The state has to be separated into various "powers"; a condition of more or less civilized warfare between different branches has to be maintained. But the principle is relatively simple: when, for example, the Congress is legislating, then the interest of other branches of government and non-governmental interests must be regarded without prejudice. This principle has been notoriously violated in the case of the Congress and the Defense Department; but even in violation, its simplicity is apparent.

However, on the *fundamental* conflicts of interest facing education today, the whole of the federal government must stand as one side. The issues are entirely prejudged in the basic structure of the government itself.

For the essentially contested question is this: Just what *is* education in the United States of America today? This question sounds like a request for a definition, and surely one can construct a formula to answer it. One can say, for example, that education is that discipline of thought, will, and emotion which enables a child to become a free and whole person in a free and whole society. But such a formula, useful *as* a formula, becomes operative in policy debate only when it's filled in. Just what disciplines of thought, will, and action *will* enable a person (What person?) to become free (What is to be free?) and whole (Wholly what?) in a free and whole society? (What's *that*?) Etc. Such questions admit of no final and definitive answers, but they do (at least they *should*) exert a pervasive influence even on such mundane disputes as the relative value of the 6-3-3 or the 4-4-4 system of school organization. For such matters as school organization *are* relative, relative to the really profound questions of what sort of civilization we are and are to become by educating our children one way instead of another. In the sense of the "political" employed here these really profound questions are themselves political.

And on those questions the federal government is already committed. I don't mean this administration or that, this particular Commissioner of Education or that one—I mean the federal government as a structural and historical entity. For the federal government is an integral part of a growth economy, and a growth economy puts certain inexorable demands on all other aspects of a society, including that society's conception of education. There is one fundamental requirement of any growth economy: To achieve a maximum rate of economic growth consistent with (particularly financial) stability. This requirement can be met most efficiently in a society (like the United States) which is devoted to two further principles: (i) constant technological change for increased productivity, and (ii) the use of physical violence against any threat to the nation's economic superiority. These requirements and principles are inherently connected; their point of connection is the federal government of this nation.

The federal government is already committed; I do not mean this or that administration or political party but the organized social system we call the government. For the three principles of economic behavior—constant and controlled technological change, economic growth to the degree compatible with financial stability, and the use of physical violence to protect and defend the economic superiority of this nation and its allies *vis à vis* the rest of the world —are inherently connected; and our governmental system is inextricably intwined with all three.

Any segment of our economy which is not progressing toward full industrialization, does not show a profit (either pecuniary or social), or does not exhibit growth will necessarily either cease to function or be subsidized by the federal government to the point that it can keep up with a growth economy. In fact, the major political activity of the federal government lies in deciding which segments of the economy are to be subsidized—how and how much— in accordance with the above principles. Policies for education made within the rules of the federal government will necessarily be decisions on how and how much to subsidize schools and colleges so that they can make their full contribution to a growth economy.

This is not to say that there are no political problems of education *within* the economic assumptions of the federal government. The conflicting interests of research and teaching for a limited supply of top-line scientists provide one clear case of a political issue, and the federal government will have to reach some kind of decision on the matter. The guiding concern will necessarily be what proportion of talent for teaching and what for research will maximize in a medium run (for example, twenty-five years) the contribution which the scientific community can make to the nation's economic growth. That is an interesting problem, especially from a technical or logistical standpoint, and we can expect increasingly sophisticated arguments to be advanced and policies adopted to solve it.

The relative importance of the humanities, the social sciences, and the natural sciences—pure and applied—constitutes another political issue quite reasonably handled within the assumptions of a growth economy. After all, as James Bryant Conant once put it, any proffered curricular offering must prove its value either as contributing to a man's efficiency as a worker or to his loyalty as a citizen. Surely there is an optimum balance of these complementary purposes. So long as the conflict remains merely any internal struggle for students' time, it resembles more the *bellum omnia contra omnes* than a political process. The debate among various academic departments could (not necessarily would) achieve greater dignity and relevance if it moved from College Hall to Capitol Hill.

There is yet another and perhaps more important political issue which can and ought to be argued within the basic assumptions of economic growth. What priority should be given to the development of relatively poor human material as opposed to our most favored human resources? It is very like the problem that the Soviets faced in agriculture: given a condition of absolute shortage should they maximize the exploitation of their good Ukrainian land or open new farms in Siberia or do both with what relative priority? The British faced this problem in manpower development. They responded with an admirable series of Parliamentary Reports and a dismaying lack of political courage when it came time to act on them.[23]

The federal government in this country has already begun to subsidize compensatory education and to favor those colleges which will attempt the immediately less profitable job of developing underdeveloped human talent, which is, in all probability, an excellent move for long-range economic growth—especially since most of the subsidy of private philanthropy rewards those colleges which attract those already well-favored academically.

In short, with due reservations and full recognition of its shortcomings, one can well recognize that the policy-making bodies of the federal government do constitute the polity most capable of establishing well-formed policies for education within the general assumptions of our present social system, assumptions which derive from economic considerations. It is possible and, within proper limits, legitimate to conceive of education as an economic commodity, the policies governing its production and distribution subject to the same requirements as those for any other aspect of the growth economy.

But what are the "proper limits"? Where and how does it become possible to debate the basic assumptions of the growth economy? What are the philosophical and social conditions necessary for a responsible polity *not* structurally dependent on the assumptions of a growth economy?

Let us look once again at the basic idea of a polity. Is the term to be regarded as merely a Hellenized version of the word "citizenry," defined as the sum of all the persons legally citizens of a certain nation-state? In that case we have no need for the term "polity"; whatever we want to say about the class of citizens we can say using the term "citizenry." Let us restrict the term "polity" to rules, customs, conventions, and skills which make possible *rational* debate on a political question. By this definition the federal government of the United States in all its branches is a polity as we have noted, in many ways an admirable polity. But the *particular* rules, customs, conventions (in several senses), and skills that make rational debate possible within the federal government do not allow certain political questions to arise, where "political" questions means those involving genuine and legitimate conflicts of interest within a relatively stable ongoing social system. Quite specifically, within the polity that is the federal government one cannot raise seriously the questions: What is education? Who has the right to the best education our society can provide? What fundamental knowledge and skills constitute our culture? Within the rules of debate in government these questions have one and only one legitimate answer: Those deserving education are those maximally related to the system of economic growth. According to the norm of universal citizenship, everyone has such a right to education. The "War on Poverty," for example, is devoted entirely in conception to securing this right for those who were formerly denied full participation in the system of economic growth. That there is another legitimate conception of having rights and being a citizen is simply unallowable in the politics of the federal government.

Likewise we have learned from the disasters and threats of disasters of this century what knowledge and skills we must possess if we are (i) to maximize the production and consumption of goods within the nation and (ii) to maintain adequate power to kill "enemies" who might threaten the system of production and consumption. But is this corpus of knowledge and skills the only legitimate conception of the arts constitutive of our culture? That question cannot be raised seriously in the context of government, and *that* is the most serious question of all. (See * p. 56.)

Where would we find, then, an adequate polity? In answer I should like to turn back to the connotations of πολις. A group of dissidents could not draw up a statement of the rules to constitute a new polity for debating the nature of education. A polity is a polity by virtue of sharing a "language," in the rather specialized sense in which Michael Oakeshott employs the term:

> The language of desire and aversion, of preference and choice, of approval and disapproval, of praise and blame, of persuasion, injunction, accusation and threat. It is the language in which we make promises, ask for support, recommend beliefs and actions, devise and commend administrative expendients, and organize the beliefs and opinions of others in such a manner that policy may be effectively and economically executed. . . .[24]

Only as one comes to use language in that sense—to follow its rules, to participate in its customs and conventions, and to master its skills—does one come to membership in a polity.

The language in which we can "organize the beliefs and opinions of others" on the question What is education? cannot be found in the trade union negotiations of teachers and administrators, nor in the economic planning of various levels of state and federal government. This language will be found, to use the other half of Oakeshott's distinction, in the "literature," the "texts," which constitute the paradigm cases of the living polity. In that literature the particular institutions of the System are not the central concern, but rather man, his nature and destiny, knowledge, will, and action —in short the ancient concepts that define a philosophical concern with education.

What has happened is tragi-comic. The great historical texts embodying a philosophical concern with education have been generally ignored by serious historical scholars, i.e., those who seek to understand how ideas and arguments guide men's conduct. Instead, these historical tests—from Quintilian's *Institutes of Oratory* to John Dewey's *Democracy and Education*—seldom find their way into the academic world at all and then usually as bowdlerized, pre-digested pap for undergraduate teacher-trainees,—young men and women who in general find it impossible to organize their own beliefs and opinions with any degree of clarity, much less influence those of others. Those who occupy the seats of power, particularly in the central institutions of the System, are doubly removed from these texts, both because they seem appropriate to the young and weak and because they are associated with "professional educationists," an expression obviously synonymous with "anathema." Thus, there are those who could profit from a study of this language in the sense of acquiring easy familiarity with certain standard arguments, mastering the uses and misuses of the central concepts, and sensing the moral progress which its literature traces; but those who could seldom do. Those who do study this literature have no further use for its language, which they rightly reject as "impractical."

None of this mattered so long as the Public School Movement together with its basic assumptions provided the actual political impetus for educational progress. It did not matter whether or not there was precision and clarity in thought about education; it did matter terribly that school buildings were erected, teachers trained and hired, curricula organized, and books provided. Only now that the Public School Movement no longer defines the goal and process of education in this country does it become existentially important to refine a language of educational policy.

It isn't necessary to advocate a "return to the classics" in the study of educational policy, for that turn comes rather naturally when men seriously confront the issues that divide them and argue for policies on which they can unite. The key to the whole point is that one word "argue." We are not lacking in a literature of educational policy. Much of it is trival and boring, but some writings are inspired by brilliant insight and profound passion. Notably lacking, however, is a critical metaliterature of educational policy. Writers write and readers read, but *arguments* seldom appear. Progress in thought is not evident. Worse, the System and its defunct ideology is not informed nor illumined by that writing and reading.

The emergence of a language of the sort Oakeshott envisions requires a critical literature *about* the contemporary writings on educational policy. The present work is an essay toward that critical stance. I have selected five contemporary writers more for their inherent interest than as representative of anything else. I have not hesitated to treat them with as many different styles of criticism.

Notes

THE SYSTEM, THE ESTABLISHMENT, AND THE SEARCH FOR A NEW POLITICS

1   Since writing this paragraph, I have had the opportunity to watch United States educational aid missions at work in some of the poorer nations of Latin America, and I am no longer sure that the description is accurate. There seems to be, too often, an attempt to build a System before there are schools in these countries. My description, however, still represents the ideal, if not always the actuality.

2   John Dewey: *Democracy and Education* (New York, 1916) pp. 23-26.

3   This is as convenient place as any to pay tribute to L. A. Cremin's *Transformation of the School* (New York, 1961), a work which informs much of this chapter. See also Harold Rugg: *Foundations for American Education* (New York, 1947) Chapter XVII.

4   Paul R. Mort: "Studies in Educational Innovation from the Institute of Administrative Research, An Overview," in Matthew B. Miles (ed.): *Education and Innovation* (New York, 1964) pp. 317-328.

5   E.g., E. Digby Baltzell: *The Protestant Establishment* (New York, 1964).

6   Edward A. Krug: *The Shaping of the American High School* (New York, 1964) Chapter 8.

7   Leonard A. Lecht: "The Changing Occupational Structure with Implications for Education" Center for Research and Leadership

Development in Vocational and Technical Education, Ohio State University (Columbus, 1966) mimeographed.

8 Cf. Solon T. Kimball and James E. McClellan: *Education and the New America* (New York, 1962), *passim*.

9 James F. Ridgeway: "Computer-Tutor," *New Republic*, June 4, 1966, pp. 19-22.

10 Lucien B. Kinney: *Certification in Education* (Englewood Cliffs, 1964) Mr. Kinney makes a sharper distinction than I do between requirements of *specific* competence for teaching and the general requirements for any post of public trust (cf. Kinney, p. 36). Later one sees why he takes that view; for he considers certification very narrowly as a civil service procedure. His arguments are persuasive, especially pp. 137-143.

11 The reference is to the English Regulators of 1687, leaders in electoral reform, rather than to the Carolina vigilante groups.

12 B. O. Smith: "A Concept of Teaching" in Smith and Robert Ennis (eds.): *Language and Concepts in Education* (Chicago, 1961) pp. 88-90.

13 Merle L. Borrowman: *The Liberal and Technical in Teacher Education* (New York, 1956) pp. 78-92. Borrowman shows how wide were the disagreements on procedures and how near the unity among academic spokesmen (in the period 1865-1895) that "the colleges had a responsibility to provide professional training as well as liberal education for teachers." (p. 91).

14 Fred M. Hechinger: "Money and Power Are the Keynotes of a New Year" *New York Times*, September 10, 1967, p. E9.

15 Cf. William Heard Kilpatrick: "Professional Education from the Social Point of View" in *The Educational Frontier* (New York, 1933). Kilpatrick affirms that the depression made it possible to raise standards for entry into the teaching profession. It would be an interesting but very difficult study in economic history to determine whether there was, indeed, an increase in the proportion of college graduates in public school teaching from 1929 to 1939 and whether that increase (if any) could be accounted for by the absence of other opportunities. This might shed light on why America did not suffer from an "unemployed intelligentsia," that phenomenon which many saw as an important cause for the rise of Fascism in Europe during the same period. See W. M. Kotschnig: *Unemployment in the Learned Professions, An International Study of Occupational and Educational Planning* (London, 1932). Just a little later than Kilpatrick, Goodwin Watson wrote "Preparation of Teachers" for *The Teacher and Society*, First Yearbook

of the John Dewey Society (New York, 1937). Watson was careful *not* to assume that the preparation of teachers should be accomplished in a regular four year liberal arts college; in fact, he argued that the kind of experiences most needed by prospective teachers could not be found in a regular academic environment. But even so, Watson finally fell in line by holding out the ideal that all teachers be prepared in a special-type *college*, an institution whose major competence (even on Watson's analysis) seems to be in selecting and sorting rather than educating. (*Op. cit.* p. 319-322.)

16 Samuel Eliot Morison: *Harvard College in the Seventeenth Century*, 2 vols. (Cambridge, 1936).

17 Frederick Rudolph: *The American College and University, A History* (New York, 1962) Chapter 2.

18 "The Catholepistemiad or University of Michigania" reprinted in Edgar W. Knight and Clifton L. Hall (eds.): *Readings in American Educational History* (New York, 1951) pp. 214-215.

19 Donald G. Tewksbury: *The Founding of American Colleges and Universities Before the Civil War: With Particular Reference to the Religious Influences Bearing Upon the College Movement* (New York, 1932).

20 Rudolph, *op. cit.* Chapter 16.

21 Charles S. Benson: *The Economics of Public Education* (Boston, 1961) Chapter 11.

22 Myron Lieberman: *The Future of Public Education* (Chicago, 1960), Chapter VII.

23 *E.g., Higher Education* ("The Robbins Report") 1963, *Half Our Future* ("The Newsome Report") 1963. These documents are still available from Her Majesty's Stationery Office, London.

24 Michael Oakeshott: "The Study of 'Politics' in a University," reprinted in his *Rationalism and Politics* (London, 1962) pp. 321-322.

Since writing this chapter I have had the opportunity to read much of John Kenneth Galbraith's *The New Industrial State* (Boston, 1967). Two points which I had taken to be my own original observations are stated by Galbraith with greater precision and authority than I could lend them: (i) that in educational policy argument, the federal government speaks as the voice of the "industrial system," and (ii) that that voice is not the appropriate one to articulate goals and interests other than economic. (Galbraith, Chapter XXXIII) I do not find in Galbraith any *clear* idea of how "university presidents" and other spokesmen are to create a responsible polity outside the federal government. He says that "there must be some political force for accomplishing what the industrial system ignores and, indeed, holds to be unimportant." (p. 345) He promises to "come to this in later chapters," and he does reiterate and expand the proposition, assigning primary political obligation to the academic, scientific, and "general intellectual" communities. But on *where* and *how* this political obligation is to be met, Galbraith seems to return to the conventional advice to elect better federal Congressmen. Odd.

2

James Bryant Conant:
A Man-Made System
and Vice-Versa

If a foreign visitor to these benighted shores were required to take his views about the policies governing American education from one, and only one man, he should have to consider all the men treated in this book and many others besides. Yet there could be only one sensible choice at the end of that consideration. If any one man spoke for and to American educational policy (granted that in a most important sense no one man does or can)—that man would be James Bryant Conant.

But if one studies carefully what Mr. Conant is now saying, one is struck by the absence of clear, logical argument, by enormous lacunae in the factual information offered in support of his policy proposals, and by the contradictions between the high, universal values he espouses and the narrow, parochial values which his policies actually serve. Now just my saying that there are these lamentable shortcomings in Mr. Conant's statements of educational policy does not establish the case—it must be shown.

Section I of this chapter, entitled The Elder Statesman of American Education (pages 61-88), sets out to show it by, first, a close,

59

textual analysis of a typical passage from a typical Conant book, *Shaping Educational Policy*, and, second, by an extension of the same technique to his recent and more important work, *The Education of American Teachers*. The reader is hereby warned that he may find this section rather rough going. Arguments are analyzed to greater detail than you may think necessary; you may be willing to grant me my case against Conant's latest writings before I have finished stating it. But please follow me carefully through all of Section I, for the politically more important arguments of Sections II and III depend on understanding precisely how and why Conant's recent proposals fail to persuade the reason. Indeed, the precise deficiencies in Conant's recent proposals set the questions to which this chapter as a whole is addressed: Given the weaknesses of his arguments, why is Conant our most influential spokesman on educational policy?

The answer to this question lies partly in Conant's intimate, personal involvement with the major historical events of this nation since 1933. Section II, entitled The Nation's Servant (pages 88-104), discusses this involvement through a study of how and why the phenomenon of Conant appeared on the American educational scene. Consequently, we discover that Conant's qualities of character give his words a power that goes beyond mere rational persuasion; he possesses influence *despite* the weakness of his arguments.

But in Section III of this chapter, entitled The Arguments (pages 104-115), we come back to the very form of argument itself; and there we find that the direction of Conant's bias, as revealed in the first section, is closely analogous to the bias in *our* ordinary, sensible, unreflective, un-serious conception of the *form* policy argument ought to take. From that point of view, Conant has influence *because* the fallacies in his reasoning are so close to the fallacies in our own.

In the end, of course, we shall still be baffled by the phenomenon of James Bryant Conant. But that should not be surprising. After all, how do we look upon the history of this nation in the twentieth century? Are we not baffled, amazed, shocked, and (from time to fortunate time) wryly amused at our own recent history? Of all the thinkers treated in this book, only Conant is intimately a part of that history. The tragedy in this story is that neither Conant nor his arguments ever transcended those limits.

I. THE ELDER STATESMAN OF AMERICAN EDUCATION

Shaping Educational Policy

This book is like a musical composition without a melodic line; it is like a film with interesting images but no plot. As a colleague of mine described it, *Shaping Educational Policy* is the pure phenomenology of educational politics—an accurate portrayal of the shifting appearance of the surface of things, with no attempt to separate underlying reality from mere appearance.

If one follows educational politics as a day-to-day activity at the state capital, the absence of resolution, in both the moral and dramatic senses of the term, is the dominant characteristic. Issues appear and disappear without being resolved; groups oppose one another with a great show of hostility but without the sturdy resolve to reach a decision. This same quality of irresolution serves as the form (or lack of it) for *Shaping Educational Policy*.

I wish to show this absence of resolution, first, by a rather detailed criticism of a half-dozen pages of this book, a section central to Conant's policy proposals, and, second, by extending the same form of argument to other sections of the book. Later I will try to show how similar analysis can be extended to Conant's other works.

Let us begin in microcosm. On page 26 of SEP, (*Shaping Educational Policy* hereafter abbreviated as SEP; see list of Conant's books at end of this chapter), Conant provides a "list of ten problems now facing our public schools." They are:

1. The reform of instructional methods and materials including the new developments in foreign language instruction in the lower grades and the new courses in physics, chemistry, mathematics, and biology.
2. The advanced placement program.
3. The improvement of instruction in English composition.
4. The introduction of new techniques including T.V. and programmed instruction.

5. The recruiting of more intellectually able young people into the teaching profession.

6. The education of students of limited ability in the high school.

7. Vocational education.

8. Teaching reading to the children of disadvantaged families.

9. The slum schools.

10. Segregated schools.

Having asked us to consider "how many [of these problems] fall outside the interest and competence of the establishment," Conant goes on to say: "The first five items involve changes which were not initiated by the establishment and some of which have been resisted by the Old Guard. The first two require active leadership by subject-matter professors, not professors of education. The last item is political; the establishment has never dared tackle it."

What are we to conclude? The quaintness of "the Old Guard" and the question of just who are "subject matter professors" left apart, it seems clear that Conant wants us to believe that the first five and last "problems" . . . "fall outside the interest and competence of the establishment." (The last term, remember, is a technical one, extremely important for understanding Conant's conception of educational politics; by it, he means the collectivity including teachers organized in affiliates of the National Education Association, public school administrators, professors of education, and former members of one or more of the above groups presently employed in educational work in a state government or in Washington. In short, "Establishment" means approximately the same as "Educationists" in the "System," as these terms are defined in the first chapter.) It is indeed difficult to analyze the interest and competence of such a complex phenomenon as "the establishment," and no one has more experience to bring to the task than Conant. But he does not do it. He merely asserts (p. 27) that, with respect to the first and second items, "None of these developments were taken up with enthusiasm by those who had been determining policy; but what is more important, *these and similar reforms can not now be discussed or planned without the participation of subject matter professors.*"

Here we have a truly amazing statement joined by a semicolon to what is patently either a truism or falsehood, the latter given the distinction of italic type. It is amazing to say of the reforms in the teaching of the natural sciences, mathematics, and foreign languages that none were taken up with enthusiasm by those who had been determining educational policy, particularly school boards and superintendents. Were they removed *en masse* and replaced by new ones? How was power mustered to do so? Were there *no* connections between the enthusiasm which greeted the first tentative efforts of the Physical Sciences Study Committee or Max Beberman's work at the University of Illinois on one hand and the rapid development of similar reforms in other fields? (Conant himself calls it a "chain reaction.") Were all these reforms actually perfected in the face of hostility or apathy and then pushed through despite resisting administrators and school boards? Perhaps Conant, who arrived back in this country during the first year of the Sputnik era, actually knows a story that proves false our usual interpretation of how teaching reforms were greeted; but here he does not tell the story but makes instead that literally unbelievable statement.[1]

As for the italicized sentence quoted just following, perhaps my experience is so improbable statistically that it can be ignored, but I have heard parents, teachers, children, radio commentators, and television comedians, among others, discuss these reforms without the participation of subject-matter professors. I have known school boards and high school departments to plan the reform of their programs without the participation of professors. But my experience may be totally illusory, and Conant may be right in saying that it cannot happen.

Or perhaps he means that it ought not happen? What could be the referent of "it"? Public discussion and planning? That would represent a rather presumptuous censorship by Conant, would it not? We must be perfectly clear on this matter. Conant has no right to tell parents, children, and television comedians that they *ought not* discuss anything whatsoever in the absence of subject-matter professors. If there are some topics which people ought not discuss, then subject-matter professors ought not discuss them. There can be no moral or legal *privilege* to discuss any topic; in a free society, everyone has a *right* to discuss whatever anyone is permitted to discuss.

Therefore, Conant cannot be taken seriously when he says that

"*reforms can not now be discussed or planned without the participation of subject matter professors.*" May I suggest what he must
have meant in writing that sentence? It is rather a trite prudential
counsel to the following effect: If one is preparing new curriculum
materials in various academic disciplines, attempting to represent
the most advanced thought that can be taught successfully at the
secondary school level, and if one is training secondary school
teachers to use those materials, one will find it necessary to draw
upon those who know, at least in general terms, the nature of the
most advanced thought in each discipline. At our present level of
technology, this requires persons who are designated "subject matter professors." A very sophisticated computer-based information
and retrieval system can at least be imagined, however, such that
those men and women who are capable of participating in the most
advanced thought of an academic discipline would be free from the
necessity of participating in the preparation of secondary school
materials and teachers. Thus there is no logical necessity in Conant's statement; "*can not now be discussed or planned*" means no
more than that we have not any technique for doing this job other
than employing the persons who have the necessary knowledge and
skill to do it. This last can reasonably be regarded as true but
scarcely newsworthy.

Conant then turns to the second item in his list, but by now we
are not quite sure what it is a list *of*. First called a "problem," then
a "reform," then a "development," this item has now become "this
significant phase of the educational revolution." And as such,
Conant says, it "leads me to consider the way the establishment has
developed organizations to enforce its decisions." (p. 27) (Whenever "establishment" appears in SEP, read "Educationists.") For
eleven more pages, he does consider organizations of Educationists
with never another mention, except *en passant*, of advanced placement. What he has to say about such organizations produces some
further amazement, as I will indicate later, but let us for a moment
consider advanced placement *as a problem*. There is nothing problematical in the *idea* that young men and women of high school age
and superior mentality might profit more from an introductory
college course than from the usual high school courses. There is
nothing problematical in the *idea* that entering freshmen who have
taken college-level courses while in high school should not have to

repeat those courses but be allowed to enter more advanced courses in the college sequence.

But in regard to advanced placement, there are a number of problems, i.e., decisions which involve choices among genuinely conflicting values, and there are some difficult tasks that must be performed in carrying out any decision. As an example of the latter, consider that a successful program of advanced placement requires that a certain number of youths be recruited, selected, and entered upon a special sequence of advanced courses rather early in their secondary school careers. Does *this* task fall, in Conant's words, "outside the interest and competence of the Establishment"? One would think that the talents of academic advisers and guidance counselors are particularly relevant right here; and, indeed, one can easily hypothesize a causal connection between the meteoric rise of the advisement-counseling branch of the Educationists and its role in making possible the advanced placement sequences in high schools.

So recruitment, selection, and retention of advanced placement students must call upon "the interest and competence of the establishment." But there is also a problem for policy here: we cannot *precisely* identify at age thirteen or fourteen those youngsters who will be able to succeed in college-level courses at age seventeen or eighteen and enter higher into their college sequences the year following. But unless youngsters are started on advanced placement sequences in their last years of junior high school, they will not be able to take college-level work as seniors or, in some cases, juniors. There are three basic strategies that can be adopted with respect to this problem. (a) One can reduce to some acceptable minimum the chance that anyone who could profit from advanced placement will be denied the opportunity for it. This strategy requires vigorous recruitment and rather lax criteria for selection. Or (b) one can reduce to some acceptable minimum the chance that anyone who *cannot* profit from advanced placement will be forced into unnecessarily difficult and time-consuming academic study. This strategy requires minimal recruiting and very high standards for acceptance into advanced standing sequences. Finally (c) one can seek a compromise between these first two strategies which, pushed to their limits, might yield, alternately, nearly everyone or nearly no one in advanced placement courses. Since everyone will choose (c), the *problem* becomes one of balancing the limits so that the operation becomes acceptable to persons and groups who would *tend*, in opposite directions, to favor strategy (a) or strategy (b). Conant never *argues* explicitly in favor of a particular compromise position. He seems, rather, to assume that, because he recognizes the unacceptability of the extremes, any mean he adopts is Golden. But, of course, that won't do. The genuine issues of policy arguments are seldom between mean and extreme, they are far more often between *this* compromise position and *that*. The fact that Conant does not follow through with a detailed analysis of just *where* lies a reasonable compromise between strategies (a) and (b) is typical of his reasoning on tough, dialectical issues.

There are other tasks and problems in carrying out advanced placement. At the college level, tests of the student's actual achievement in various disciplines have to be constructed and administered. But the construction of such tests takes time, and their use implies a commitment to a student, extending backwards into his first years of secondary school and forward to his last years of college. The academic department which depends on advanced placement tests in assigning a student to classes is saying in effect that it will hold its own curriculum sufficiently stable that the work done by the student through his advanced placement sequence in high school will profit him enough to justify the extra work done there. If success on an advanced placement test means that an entering freshman would take Mathematics 101 instead of Mathematics 100 his first semester but rejoin his less industrious or less able classmates for Mathematics 102 the second semester, he might well question whether advanced placement was worth the effort.

But tests will tell only whether the student has learned the subject matter which had been designed, built into textbooks and teacher training, and eventually taught as part of his high school curriculum, the total process taking a rather long time. Does the college department wish to forgo the flexibility it has when it assumes the entering freshman to be completely innocent of all subject matter, in return for the advantage of having a much more knowledgeable freshman? Most college departments in mathematics and the natural sciences will answer yes and enter into "active leadership" in deciding what knowledge the entering freshman should possess and in preparing materials to insure that he gets it. Most departments in the social sciences and humanities will answer no, while languages, foreign and domestic, seem on the verge of switching from no to yes. On these questions, Educationists in general are relatively uninterested and incompetent, both terms now used in their technical, legal sense; but when advanced placement courses begin to demand really significant increments of student time and energy, of teaching talent in the school faculty, and of administrative effort in dealing with public relations problems arising from parents whose aspirations for their children have been thwarted or uncomfortably extended, then the legal interest and competence of the Educationists is not to be denied.

In the foregoing discussion of advanced placement, I have assumed general agreement on the following proposition: a high school student should be asked to do more than the relatively undemanding but meaningless busy work of ordinary academic courses only if that additional work will be beneficial. There are many kinds of benefits: either increasing the chances of being accepted at the college of one's choice, *or* increasing the range of course choices available when one enters college, *or* learning something of genuine value in itself. Many people would not accept that proposition, arguing either that since knowledge is an unlimited good, schools are justified in forcing all the academic subject matter they can into students or that since whatever adolescents do when they are not studying would be useless at the infrequent best, harmful to themselves and society in the more usual cases, schools are justified in forcing all youngsters to master all the academic subject matter possible. I have never seen Conant argue the second case and I should be surprised if he even *feels* that way. On the first case, he distinguishes in varying ways between those youngsters who can learn academic material rather painlessly and those whose talents lie elsewhere. With reference to the academically talented, he *would* argue, I believe, that for their own good and the good of their country and the preservation of democratic freedoms in a world threatened by various forms of totalitarianism, they should be challenged to perform to the limit of capacity. That appears to me a shameful doctrine; but to one who holds it, the matter of advanced placement is a much less complicated issue than it is for those who hold contrary views. But once the complexity of the issue is recognized, it is no longer possible to say that the *problems* of advanced placement, in principle, are outside the purview, the "interest and competence," of anyone who *chooses* to consider the questions involved. Advanced placement is a *problem* for *public* policy.

However, Conant does not present any argument showing why or how Educationists have no interest or competence concerning advanced placement. He merely asserts it, and that assertion "leads [him] to consider" educational organizations and state politics. This is the stream-of-consciousness literary technique applied to educational discourse. It is a clear example of the "phenomenology" of educational politics, where seldom if ever do those who must decide issues really think them through; instead minds wander where they are led, until the time for action arrives and what is done is what is being thought of *then*.

Exactly this same sort of mind-wandering is seen in the ten pages Conant devotes to "organizations serving the interests" of Educationists. It may be instructive to follow a few statements for illustration:

1. The regional accrediting agencies, of which the North Central Association of Schools and Colleges is by far the most powerful, serve "in practice" only to discredit the very few schools and colleges which are "scandalously inferior."

2. Regional accrediting agencies did serve to bring a modicum of order into schools and colleges, but the widespread use of national tests in college admissions procedures has reduced the effective "power" of the association over the individual school or college.

3. The North Central Association accepts the "concept of the comprehensive high school" and shows no interest in recent efforts to increase the number of able students taking advanced academic courses.

4. "*In short*, the regional accrediting associations are not in a position to plan a modern high school curriculum for the academically talented nor to come to grips with the problems of the acceleration of the more able students. . . ."

5. "I venture the opinion, *therefore*, that the era of nationwide school policy planning by unofficial agencies reflecting only the opinions of the establishment is drawing to a close." (Pp. 25-29, emphasis added.)

Let us follow this progression. Statement (1) would seem to answer the question: What standard of educational quality, if any, is guaranteed by regional accreditation? Statement (2) would answer the dual question: What is the good of a regional accrediting agency? What power to accomplish this good will the agency possess in the future? For statement (3) the appropriate question concerns the ideology of the regional accrediting agencies. For those unacquainted with the work of regional accrediting agencies, these questions are of some interest; for example, statement (1) would be relevant information to a parent considering a private school advertised as "Fully Accredited by the North Central Association."

But none of these questions is the one which Conant was led to consider. Without a pause, however, he *summarizes* the three statements ("in short") as (4). But it happens that (4) is not in any sense a summary of what went before. It may or may not be true. I happen to believe that it is, and its truth will be shown by argument quite different from that presented in (1), (2), and (3). Only (3) has any conceivable relevance to (4), and its relevance depends upon the truth of some statement to the effect that the present ideology of the North Central Association is so deeply embedded in the political structure of the Association that any attempt to use that agency for curriculum planning would be either futile or prohibitively difficult. This latter proposition would be very hard to establish; indeed, it is easy to show the opposite by noting a general tendency of Educationists' ideology to change quite rapidly following shifts of political power in the nation. Indeed the same organizational structure is used at different times by Educationists to serve very different ideological purposes, e.g., the late and unlamented Educational Policies Commission.

(Statement (4) *is* true because it is implied by a general principle of educational politics, a principle suggested but never fully understood by Conant, namely that curriculum planning is a process requiring the reconciliation of genuinely conflicting interests; therefore, it ought to be carried on in a politically responsible context. But any regional accrediting agency is responsible only to a narrow range of interest. From which argument, (4) and many other important propositions follow.)

Thus (4) is a true statement, though not for the reasons nor in the sense Conant stated it, but (5) is merely a jumble. The assumptions are extraordinary: that there ever was such an era; that the regional associations are "unofficial agencies reflecting only the opinions of the establishment"; that they are the only such agencies or else that remarks through (4) apply equally to all other such agencies; and, most unaccountably, that (5) can be regarded as a conclusion ("therefore") from anything which preceded it.

Conant is not obligated to present a full treatment of the complex issues involved in advanced placement procedures or to undertake a thorough analysis of the power structure of various educational organizations, for he is not obligated to write a book on educational politics at all. Even after he has said that he wishes to use the "problem" of advanced placement as a demonstration that Educationists have no interest or competence in matters of educational policy, he has no obligation to delve any more deeply into the details of the questions than he has done in the present book. The matter at issue is whether these difficult policy questions, such as the degree of interest and competence of various groups competing for roles in curriculum planning, are to be argued in a straightforward, logical fashion or treated with the rambling mind-wandering exhibited in the work under consideration here. It is not that logical reasoning would require a longer work. With the explicit and judicious use of simplifying assumptions, Conant could probably have constructed a logical argument in no more *space* than he actually used.[2] However, it would have required more active *thought*.

I have treated only a half dozen pages of that work. Yet a similar analysis applied to any section of the book would produce similar results. Expanding the focus, thus inescapably losing some definition, we can see that the book as a whole has the some formlessness as does the section which has been examined in some detail. Conant's conclusions are really matters of meta-policy, i.e., policy *about* the formulation of school policies. In addition to his remarks on higher education, he advocates two basic propositions at meta-policy. These are:

(I.) The policy-making machinery in each state should be strengthened by the creation of a prestigious, long-term, non-political, appointive, lay board of education, which sets policy for a chief state school officer who, in turn, administers a strong state department of education, the latter representing the Establishment, not merely Educationists.

(II.) The development of nationwide educational policies should be the responsibility of an interstate commission, created by compact among the states themselves and approved, in accordance with Article I, Section 8 of the Constitution, by Congress.

Interspersed with the advocacy of these propositions are many entertaining, gossipy little stories about the operation of various state departments of education. The absence of any theoretical framework makes these stories, like much of the work of political scientists, rather pointless albeit diverting. But the stories are *merely* interspersed with the advocacy. It is not only that both these proposals are timid and weak; neither is actually supported by substantive argument, however loosely we construe the criteria for logical support.

What purports to be an argument for (I) comes down to the fact that New York State has a department and Board of Regents of the sort Conant proposes. One can surely expect the next statement to be that a causal connection holds between the organization of that department and a superior quality of education in New York State. But what we are told is that the "Board of Regents published a 100-page pamphlet" on educational change, the Commissioner of Education (New York's chief state school officer) published a Catalog of Educational Changes containing accounts of "hundreds of new programs" and, even more important, "the names and addresses of those to whom one may write for further information. No one could ask for a better response from a state system. . . ."

Conant is simply wrong in fact. Several people who are quite competent to judge such matters *have* asked for a better response.[3] But even if one held on purely ideological grounds, as Conant *sometimes* seems to do, that it violates fundamental principles of political morality for state educational officials to do more than serve as agents for the distribution of information, particularly information about Ford-Foundation-sponsored projects,[4] it still would not follow that all states ought to establish the form of organization found in the New York Board of Regents. To do the limited job Conant wants done, three people are required: one to go about the state asking superintendents what is being done to promote change in their schools, a clerk to compile and distribute information gathered by the first, and a third to petition the legislature for money to support the first two.

In short, Conant has presented no case for his explicit claim that a particular form of organization—including a prestigious lay board, appointed chief school officer, etc.—is necessary to carry out the limited function of distributing information.

This is not to say that support for Conant's claims *could* not be secured. But it should be pointed out here that in respect to his first claim (that distributing information from state education offices suffices to make a significant difference in education in schools) securing supporting evidence would appear very difficult. Many studies over a long period of time have attempted to discover just what *does* make a school or system of schools responsive to change, hence susceptible to improvement. Anyone familiar with the many different solutions that have been proposed to the problem of increasing the flexibility or adaptability of schools and the extreme difficulty of demonstrating the actual effectiveness of any one such solution or combination of them finds it incredible that there should be *any one* response to "the educational revolution" than which "no one could ask for a better." There may be evidence to make us credit this claim, but Conant will have to conduct new research if he is to secure it.[5]

On the second part of his proposition (I.) *viz* that a particular form of organization is the proper one for a state department of education, Conant may be quite right but not on the lines he chose to argue. If he were serious in believing that information distribution were the only proper function of a state department, it simply would not matter how the department were organized. But if, as would seem more reasonable and consistent with his other views, he actually proposes that the state department of education provide a wide range of services and supervision to local school systems, then the organization *is* important. And if most of the students of educational administration are correct in their evaluations, the form of organization proposed by Conant is probably more desirable than some other forms, specifically better than in Indiana and Illinois, where a chief state school officer is elected on a partisan ticket, with a departmental staff serving under a spoils system. On this claim Conant is probably right, but there is nothing in *Shaping Educational Policy* that would give him grounds for saying that he is.

The rationale for the second proposal made by Conant, (II.) above, depends on the prior acceptance of the assumptions in (I.) That is, only when Conant has provided good reason for accepting state departments of education as the basic element in policy-formation *within* the several states (leaving aside his strange notion that policy-formation can be reduced to information distribution) does it make sense to argue that a compact *among* state departments is the best way to organize for nationwide policy-formation.

Conant's own discourse is, on the surface, rambling and inconsistent, but a careful reconstruction of his case will produce a more rational argument and reveal the *form* essential to the whole book. Here are what appear to be the four fundamental moral and political premises supporting his case. Later it will be necessary to examine exactly *how* they support it.

(i) Because educational policy-making is a public responsibility, it ought not be allowed to devolve untended upon any unofficial agency, even such well-intentioned agencies as represent the Establishment.

(ii) The Constitution of the United States properly reserves to the governments of the several states the right to establish, support, and direct public schools. Local school districts are creatures of the state government and can be made subject to any degree of central control that the state constitution permits and the state legislature desires.

(iii) The only alternate public agency is the federal government itself, but it would be politically impossible as well as administratively monstrous to create a U.S. Office of Education possessing the power and personnel necessary for national educational planning.

Given these premises, one could easily see that any proposed organization for educational planning which was *not* an organ of state government would be eliminated from further consideration. But the three premises given so far do not provide criteria for choosing among the various options within the state level. For that we add a fourth, which, with alliterative license, we may call the premise of prudential polarity in educational planning. At one pole:

(iv-a) If educational planning is to be effective, it must eventuate in policies that are reasonably stable over a reasonably long period of time. And at the other pole:

(iv-b) If educational planning is to be effective, it must be flexible and responsive to advancing knowledge in various disciplines and to changes in purposes to reflect political pressure at local, state, national, or international level.

It is not difficult to show the various boundaries within which to interpret the term "reasonably" in (iv-a). There are certain natural periodicities in education; there are also certain conventional periodicities in schooling which have the force of second nature, to be violated only after careful assessment of consequences. It is natural to think of education as being the major activity in the first quarter of a human life. It is second nature to think of schooling as divided into primary and secondary phases, as taking place inside buildings designed and constructed for that purpose, as conducted by persons employed more or less full-time for that job, etc. It is the rhythm within this latter category of conventional expectations which sets the meaning of "reasonably." A sequence of courses in secondary school mathematics which carries a gifted youngster into advanced college work is five or six years in length. It takes about twice that length of time to prepare the course materials for that sequence. About two and one-half years of special training (in colleges) are required to prepare a student in the *specific* skills and information necessary to be an elementary school teacher. Well constructed school classrooms cost about $20 per square foot, certain auxiliary services included; with reasonable maintenance, they last a maximum of forty years. A high-level educational administrator has a maximum "service" life of about twenty-five years, out of a much longer professional life which includes classroom teaching, graduate study, apprentice-type training, and non-school employment.

This list of conventional "periods" could be extended indefinitely. But, as it stands, it is sufficient to draw Conant's first conclusion from (iv-b): the biennial-meeting state legislature, while it very satisfactorily meets requirements (i) and (ii) above, is *not* the appropriate organ of state government to effect educational planning. Even if a legislative body could, very uneconomically, provide itself with a technical staff possessing the competence to design or evaluate mathematics programs, teacher training courses, school building plans, qualifications for school administrators, etc., all these would have to be done again whenever a new legislature was elected. This violates the requirement of reasonable stability. On the other side, to establish a state education department consisting exclusively of public school administrators would violate the first part of (iv-b); while allowing that department to become exclusively the province of professionals, including "subject-matter professors," would violate the second part of (iv-b), and possibly (i) as well.

Let us *for the moment* accept these criteria which have been constructed from Conant's rather rambling discourse. What positively can one conclude about state organization for planning and administering education? Does it follow from the second part of (iv-b) that a continuing political influence is best provided by a lay board of non-professionals (either elected or appointed on a rotating basis) or might some more imaginative arrangement be devised? For example, assuming that a state has a competent professional department of education and a working plan for the future, continuous political responsiveness might be extended in time and expanded in function. Since education is the largest avenue for the expenditure of funds in most states, the education committees in the state legislature should be able to muster the ablest and most experienced state legislators.

Or a special lay advisory committee might be attached to the governor's office, serving as a channel for ideas from non-establishment professionals as well as other parties having an interest in education. Or the governor's office might sponsor a biennial or quadriennial conference like the White House Conference on Education, beginning with local committees setting their own agenda and sending their conclusions and delegates to the next higher level, culminating in, for example, a week-long conference at the state capital.

None of the above suggestions seem in the least valuable, for reasons which I will present just below. The point, however, is that any one or any combination of them satisfies Conant's criteria as well as do Conant's own proposals. The logic of arguing from criteria to particular cases is that *the criteria provide a basis for rejecting unworthy proposals, but they do not imply any specific proposal.* For this particular kind of argument, the criteria-to-case *form* is highly appropriate, as Conant must have sensed. The form is that employed by the Supreme Court in many of its recent rulings, e.g., that concerning reapportionment of state legislatures. The Court translated a series of previous decisions and constitutional provisions into what is essentially the *criterion* of one-man-must-equal-one-vote, and then left it to state courts and state legislatures to find equitable processes of change and to formulate new arrangements which accord with the criterion.

It is highly useful for Conant to formulate criteria for the organization of policy-making bodies in education. It is quite legitimate for him to report that, of those bodies he has seen, the New York State system for schools and the California system for higher education satisfy the criteria best. But it is clearly fallacious to claim that they satisfy them uniquely.[6] And even to claim that the California or New York systems satisfy the criteria better than, for example, South Dakota's system requires that Conant make judgments on highly contingent, shifting matters of fact—quite different from the historico-moral judgment that goes into the formulation of the criteria themselves. Conant's special competence, that which his experience and wisdom qualify him for extraordinarily, lies in the area of general policy, not specific matters of fact.

Let us recapitulate briefly before deciding the significance of the point. So long as he does not have to give any *reasons* for his statements, Conant can say anything which seems to him more or less plausible; his readers can then accept what he says on his authority, or they can reject it for the same reason or for none. Progress in thought cannot occur under these circumstances: free association is reputed to be of some value in mental therapy, but is useless in the formulation and support of educational proposals. To put Conant's ideas on state departments of education in a *form* that permits critical evaluation, I reconstructed his argument, formulating criteria that are, as closely as I can make out, the actual controlling beliefs in his own writings. Let it be noted that, for anyone who is committed to the American tradition of local, public control of schools and also seriously concerned about effective educational planning for the conditions of modern life so very different from those under which our school tradition emerged, Conant's premises are almost impossible to deny. The power of the man as the conscience of American education springs more from his ability to follow the underground stream of our moral beliefs than from what he articulates on the surface.

But what follows from accepting these criteria is *not* any particular institutional arrangement for a state department of education. In fact, given the wide variation in political structure and tradition among the states and regions of this country, the moral one would expect to be drawn from Conant's argument, when that argument is made explicit, is that wide variation in institutional form should be encouraged, new and imaginative solutions to the problem of balancing professional competence and political sensitivity should be sought.

Notice that this appeal for "imaginative new solutions" is not in this instance the trite sort of thing one could say about any sort of problem. On the contrary, in this connection it is something very specific. Conant's first three premises imply that educational planning should be a function of state governments. Now consider (iv-b) once more. Is it sensible to hold that *one* form of political control will work equally well in all states? In one-party states and in two-party states? In two-party states where election districts for the state legislature are almost all "safe seats" for one party and in states where there is effective party competition for nearly all seats at nearly every election? In states that have effective income or sales taxes as a major source of state revenues for education and in states where nearly all school money must be raised by local *ad valorem* taxes? In states with strong civil service systems and in states that have large areas of patronage? These variations are known and emphasized by Conant in SEP. Then why does he think them irrelevant when it comes to the matter of an institutional form for balancing professional and political control of education? The answer lies in Conant's identification with the System, which he recognizes as threatened by the mob. If one adds to each of the criteria "and do so in such fashion that the System is not threatened," then Conant's strong, non-Educationist department, prestigious non-professional board, etc., would seem to be surely the most plausible if not the only solution. It will be the work of Section II to show how his mind works on this matter.

But before turning to why Conant identifies with the System, I wish to enter a personal demurrer to his belief in the possibility of resuscitating significant policy-making in education at the state level. In some part, the difficulty is financial. Everyone knows that states vary enormously not only in wealth and income to be taxed for education but also in their willingness and ability to provide for schools. By "ability" I mean such things as state constitutional limitations on indebtedness, maximum taxing power allowed to local districts, basis of state support to local districts, and so forth. It would take many years to achieve a degree of uniformity in those matters sufficient to *guarantee* equal financial support behind every school child and college student, regardless of state of origin. But our national System, as discussed above, will move us necessarily toward that guarantee. The individual state's policy-making importance will be thereby severely threatened if not immediately destroyed.

But the problem of equalizing financial support among the states is a technical one, and, were there will enough to do so, it could be solved. There is, however, a more compelling reason for considering the state capital no longer appropriate as the locus of educational policy-making for the nation. Washington provides a stage setting for political argument that simply cannot be matched in Albany or Harrisburg, to say nothing of Pierre or Concord. Hearings before Congressional committees command the most powerful and the most talented spokesmen for the conflicting points of view toward education found in the nation. These hearings—the documents presented and the confrontations that occur—attract the attention of the mass media; and, more important perhaps, they elicit the *critical* reaction of journalists, commentators, and editors who systematically ignore "educational" news from the state capital.

Even if state legislators were fully as competent individuals as members of Congress, and even if the planning staff of the state department of education were fully as well qualified as their counterparts in the U.S. Office of Education, deliberations in the state capital still could not command the overall talent, time, and dramatic tension which attend corresponding deliberations in Washington. The only way to arrest this trend would be to prohibit Congress, the President, and the Supreme Court of the United States from discussing educational policy *at all*. That is even less feasible politically and constitutionally than is the gradual movement of educational planning to Washington.

The gradual shift of the political control of education to Washington seems both inevitable and desirable. Conant discusses the problem of racial segregation as one which especially indicates the need for strong leadership at the state level (SEP, pp. 38-47). He writes: "The first matter to be attended to is the formulation of a *state* policy. . . . The state, by legislative resolution or by the action of a powerful and respected *state board, should declare that the public schools as far as possible should be comprehensive schools* . . . (i.e. [racially] mixed schools . . . I conclude therefore that the *power of the state to establish school districts is a fundamental fact . . . and state policy must be examined and clearly stated"* (SEP, pp. 43-44).

Legally, the power of the state to establish school districts may be fundamental, but it is not unlimited; e.g., it is subject to the various decisions of the Supreme Court declaring segregation of schools by races unconstitutional. Morally, the impetus toward equality in education did *not* arise from the states. In fact, it is almost exclusively at the state level of government in most of the South that the bitter and effective counteraction to Negro equality was taken.[7] Politically, it would be relatively simple in some states to pass a legislative resolution declaring a policy of comprehensive high schools, but I fail to see how such a policy "could be relatively easily enforced by state authorities" (SEP, p. 44). Enforcement would require that the legislation establish a clear-cut formula for what constitutes a "comprehensive" school, and it would have to authorize "state authorities" to withhold state financial aid to the local school district or to restrict the taxing and borrowing powers of the district which fails to comply with the formula. *That* kind of legislation would not be easily secured in any state, Northern or Southern, which really has a problem in integrating its schools.

As we follow the consequences of Conant's adherence to premises (ii) and (iii) (p. 73), we are impressed by the logical consistency of his thought and at the same time amazed that a man of his experience and good sense should hold such opinions. There must be more here than meets the eye. The only explanation that holds up when examined in the light of all his writings on education is this: Conant's insistence on the state level as the primary political control of educational planning stems from a deep conviction that the Establishment must be allowed the maximum freedom from outside political intervention. Whatever may have been the case in 1787 when the Constitution was drawn up, today the state government has no organic, natural relation to education —unlike the local community on one side and the federal government on the other. Thus, the state government in principle and in practice is the weakest public organ for satisfying premise (i) above. And undoubtedly Conant, consciously or unconsciously, wanted to locate the public concern with education there.

One can say either that Conant wants to see the public *interest* in education clarified or the public *control* of education weakened. The two amount to the same thing. This gives us a clue to Conant's apparently anti-Educationist bias, which is really not that at all. Conant knows, perhaps better than anyone else, that the System cannot run without the Educationists. Their technical expertise and their acceptance of ambiguity are alike indispensable to the System, but they do occupy a political position out of proportion to their services. The Educationists have learned to play their role as liaison with public authorities very adroitly. They use their connection with the public as a lever in academic politics and their academic status as a shield in public politics. So long as the public interest in education is left unclear, and one can easily see that it *is* unclear, the Educationists can give it whatever clarity and consistency they believe helpful. Through the Educationists, the voice of the public becomes clear and powerful in the deliberations of the Establishment.

In sum, Educationists have developed considerable skill in molding public opinion when they can and in bowing gracefully before it when necessary. Thus they have acquired power within the Establishment to which they are otherwise unentitled. Conant, being a gentleman, would never put it so, but I think his aim is not to destroy Educationists but to break up the blackmail power they exercise within the Establishment. And that means severing the connection with effective public control. Only thus can we understand what Conant's proposals for the intra-state political determination of educational policies amount to: (a) turning educational planning over to the Establishment, (b) under the general supervision of non-Establishment laymen who will see that the System adequately serves the economy, (c) subject only to gross budgetary control by a state legislature, i.e., by the weakest of all general representative bodies in the political system of the nation. Conant wants the state government merely to provide a *forum* wherein the Establishment can reconcile its internal conflicts of interest and ideas before presenting plans for the System to the scrutiny of those who must provide the money.

It is necessary to be completely fair about Conant's proposals, for the objections to follow reflect a radical disagreement with his strongest case, not his weakest. Conant himself has really only one argument for his position:

"One hardly needs to argue that state legislatures have no business making political footballs out of substantive educational issues. Yet if the professionals in the field are to have a decisive voice in establishing the broad guidelines of educational policy, then ways must be found to cope with the divisive forces operating [sic] American . . . education *before* they submit their fate to the ultimate control exercised by those who provide and regulate support" (SEP, p. 59).

This statement was directed particularly toward higher education, but in the context of Conant's wholehearted espousal of the New York State Board of Regents as the model for state planning of school-level education, what he says here can be taken to apply, *mutatis mutandis,* to education as a whole within any state. And let the weight of his point be felt: *can* one find a case in which a state legislature has gone against professional opinion and made an educational decision which *anyone* would seriously regard as liberal and responsible? The fact is, of course, that professional opinion comes to be the *definition* of "liberal and responsible." The horror stories of the consequences arising from legislative meddling in education, i.e., acting contrary to professional advice, are as old as the history of education itself and as new as each week's issue of *Time.* If, as Conant seems sincerely to believe, the option is between (a) a weak and divided voice in the Establishment leading to legislative control of education on a pork-barrel basis and (b) a clear directive from the Establishment to the legislature stating the needs and programs of the System, then one would be foolish indeed to prefer (a). But the point of radical thinking, always, is to find the third option hidden behind what sensible men see as an exhaustive disjunction.

There is a second argument in favor of Conant's proposal which he does not mention. To provide a publicly supported and responsible forum in which the Establishment can work out its plans for the System is not only to admit conflict of interest but also conflict of idea. The Establishment contains many stuffed shirts and vested interests. It also contains a large proportion of the nation's intellectuals; i.e., men and women who devote their lives to discovering, testing, and acting on ideas. Considering one of the criteria mentioned earlier for any educational planning—that the planning must provide for flexibility and experimentation in education to match the rate of change in other aspects of life—it is clear that the Establishment is more likely to provide imagination and foresight than any other segment of the nation. Its superiority over most state legislatures in these qualities would seem commanding.

This praise of the Establishment must be qualified. There is no more disgusting display of narrow self-interest than the daily politics of Academia, unless it is the daily operation of a large school system where outright dictation denies even the shadow of democratic politics. Academic specialization has all but replaced the broadly educated, humane scholar who might argue and judge wisely on a wide range of human concerns. There is no reason to prefer the faculty of a "typical" school or college to the legislature of a "typical" state with respect to general wisdom and sensitivity to public good, qualities which would seem the prime requirements for a legislative body. But Conant is not proposing that the Establishment legislate, though he comes fearfully close to that conclusion. Rather, he proposes that the Establishment *plan*. To plan well requires, among other things, the imaginative projection of ideas; and the academic training more or less common to all the Establishment does provide a discipline in separating idea and interest.[8] That discipline would seem indispensable if the System is to be kept adjusted to the rest of the society, especially to the growth economy which provides its principal *raison d'etre*.

The System's need for nationwide policies provides a third reason for accepting Conant's proposals, which would allow the Establishment to plan education under public auspices within each state. Even without the somewhat cumbersome inter-state compact which Conant advocated and is apparently going to succeed in establishing, the Establishment has proved that it could run a nationwide System of education, run it rather equitably, keep the curriculum as uniform and up-to-date as is technically possible, and respond as adequately to changing economic demands as any other conceivable system of educational control. The Establishment already functions as a control system in education very much as Adam Smith's "unseen hand" was supposed to function as a control system in laissez faire economy. In both cases one can well argue that political interference is at best useless, more usually a menace.

In order to achieve the full benefits of a nationwide (as opposed to a "national," i.e., federally-controlled) system, it will be necessary to eliminate some of the more glaring financial inequities among states and regions and to extend and expand the principle of Merit Scholarships many times its present scope. The federal government's taxing power will have to be used to accomplish both these ends, but on Conant's premises it must be possible to provide federal money without invoking federal policy-making in education. One need not accept all Conant's premises to be convinced that he is correct on the conditional claim that *if* adequate and equitably distributed funds were made available to the Establishment through the state governments, the Establishment could and would provide the connecting nerves and sinews to guarantee that the System functions on a nationwide scale.

Here, then, are several good reasons for accepting Conant's general position that the Establishment be given a very loose if not altogether free rein in planning and running the System. One can accept that position without endorsing all his specific notions about how public authorities and Establishment relate to each other in each state. These are good reasons, but are they good enough? His is a strong case, but must we accept it? Before answering, we must see in some detail how it would work.

The Education of American Teachers

This is the test case. Here focus the conflicts of interests within the Establishment, here intersect the demands of the System and the demands of the economy. So far as the college and university segments of the System are concerned, here is where the greatest number of students are affected; and numbers mean a number of different things. So far as the schools are concerned, the most fundamental personnel policies are determined by state authorities who set training and certification standards for teachers, matters over which the local school has little control. Concerning state politics it is sufficient to note that intense pressures for extending and opposing pressures for abolishing certification requirements are regularly felt at each session of the legislature. As far as the parent-public is concerned, "the school" is mostly "my child's teacher." When any teacher proves less than completely competent, the increasingly well educated parent-public will immediately and rightly condemn the policies guiding teacher-training and certification.

In sum, teacher training is *the* crucially sensitive issue of educational policy. It is not surprising, then, that in most respects, *Shaping Educational Policy* is merely an extension of the position Conant had adopted earlier in his *Education of American Teachers* (1963). The latter contains two very different kinds of policy proposals for the training of teachers. The first kind is (like most of SEP) really meta-policy, i.e., policy for the making of policy. Here Conant advocates that teacher-training be recognized as a function of the university as a whole and that the university president certify graduates as adequately prepared to teach in schools. This advocacy raises quite interesting questions which will be considered below.

But on his second kind of proposal in *Education of American Teachers*, (hereafter abbreviated as EAT), namely specific course requirements for various teaching positions, it is sufficient to point out that Conant himself recognizes that the most important policy questions have already been decided when one attempts to formulate a teacher training program in semester-hour requirements. Conant's honesty and translucence of mind are nowhere more easily observed than in his discussion of the training of elementary teachers. On page 154 of EAT he announces that he will give us his "conclusions and recommendations" on this matter, and he promises to provide us "with supporting arguments." Very soon we encounter a typical question, whether a specific course in the diagnostic and remedial techniques for teaching reading should be required of all prospective primary school teachers. Conant answers yes and provides a paradigmatic "supporting argument": "I have actually visited such courses during my travels around the country, and I was impressed by the importance of providing this valuable experience for future teachers." (EAT, p. 157)

(To a logician that statement may not appear a very convincing argument, but to certain administrators Conant's way of supporting his views is apparently quite persuasive. I offer the following evidence: In the early spring of 1963, I (among *many* others) received invitations from two rather prestigious universities, one on each coast of this continent, to enter my name as candidate for the post of director of teacher-training. In both cases and in almost identical words, the prospective job was described as "implementing the Conant report on teacher education"—this only two weeks after the official date of publication of the book! The part of the Conant report referred to, of course, was the second, that concerning specific programs of courses for different teaching specialties. One does not, in two weeks time, reorganize a university so that, *as a whole*, it takes responsibility for educating teachers. Needless to say, I declined.)

Leaving aside minor matters of course content, here is the important issue: should we officially, explicitly invest in each university or college the responsibility for deciding which of its graduates shall be allowed to teach in schools? To do so is not only to put policy in the hands of the Establishment, it is also to put the decision into that polity—the myriad of academic forums—where for very good reasons the non-academic public is effectively excluded. Surely it is legitimate to inquire *why* we should treat the basic policies governing teacher-training as if they were academic questions. Conant gives us two reasons, one of which is vitiated by his own activity, while the second is seen to follow from the most questionable assumption of the whole enterprise.

The first reason for turning teacher-training over to the individual college or university is that only so will each institution have the freedom to make most effective uses of its own resources— professors, laboratories, traditions, students, etc. This would be, I take it, a very strong argument, at least in its negative sense. There are radical differences among institutions of higher education; it is absurd to think that a common set of requirements for a teaching license, set in a state capital and applied uniformly, would equally well discriminate the likely from unlikely teacher in the undergraduate population of each institution. Positively, this argument points rather to an ideal: that the entire faculty of every college and university should seriously study its own resources and limitations and establish its own policies for what kinds of school teachers it will train and how. It seems a little improbable that this academic soul-searching should actually take place, but one can surely see a strong case for the rightness of this policy, and careful planning for bringing it into existence could at least begin.

But the second part of EAT shows that Conant was not serious in that argument. If he had been, he could not propose long lists of course requirements for every kind and degree of teacher. The two ideas are simply incompatible. What Conant really meant by his argument to allow each institution to formulate its own policies is that the Establishment, with its amply demonstrated capacities for nationwide organization, should use the protected polity of the academic community to *register* its (i.e., Conant's) decisions and use the ceremonial offices of the college president as a way of enforcing them. Conant does not really want the internecine struggle between Academics and Educationists to be let loose as a jacquerie on each college campus. No, he expects all major conflict to be worked out through voluntary organizations—the whole congeries of meetings, conferences (particularly Governor's Conferences), co-ordinating committees, interlocking directorates—*before* it reaches the local campus. Therefore, one cannot take his remarks about the uniqueness of each college as a serious argument for deciding *there* the educational policies for teaching-training.

The second argument is really an extension of the negative side of the first. According to Conant, the state department of education can and should make sure that every college or university provide all prospective teachers with a carefully planned and supervised period of student teaching. The public interest in teacher-training is such that the state ought to prevent the harm that might occur to youngsters whose teachers have had no practice in teaching. But beyond preventing harm, what good can state control accomplish? Services—information, equipment, and suggestions—can well come from the state to the teacher-training institution, but the policies *guiding* the use of all resources, state and local, must depend on the institution actually doing the work. Only when this is made clear and explicit will the entire faculty and administration of every college and university take responsibility for teacher education.

There is obviously more rhetoric than substance in any such argument. According to this argument, if the college or university is the institution that is going to train teachers, then (aside from the student teaching requirement) the college or university ought to determine *how* it is to be done. That conditional appears quite valid. It can be justified on theoretical grounds from political science, and it appeals strongly to the common sense of men who have tried to follow policies they had no hand in forming (or who have tried to form policy for others to follow).

But notice that is a conditional. Why *should* we allow colleges and universities to have a monopoly on teacher-training? Or, more accurately, why should we allow graduates of colleges and universities to have a protected market for teaching jobs? There may be compelling reasons for this policy, but a careful reading of Conant's EAT does not reveal any reason *at all* for this monopoly. It may be intuitively obvious to some people that only college graduates should be allowed to teach children the rudiments of their culture, but I must confess to a certain blindness: it isn't obvious to me. It appears rather that the only clear and unequivocal beneficiary of this policy is the System, especially the Establishment which runs it.

Probably most of those who read and respond to literature like EAT are either in the System or so deeply affected by it that they would tend to see advancement, the System, and the educational progress of the nation as identical. For such persons, the distribution of power between Educationists and Academics becomes a (perhaps *the*) "crucial issue" of educational policy, and agreement or disagreement with Conant's particular proposals for compromise becomes one's significant "stand" on the "issue." From a slightly larger perspective, these are quite trivial, internal matters: as a colleague put it in another connection: "An institution is in a bad way which requires an energy expenditure of this order merely to rewrite its house organs."

How did it happen that James Bryant Conant became the spokesman for the System as a whole? That, clearly, is the source of his strength. A given Educationist may think that certain of Conant's recommendations go a little too far on the Academics' side, and an Academic may believe the reverse. But these are questions to be resolved *within* the System. Conant's strength is this: no one ever questions that he puts the interest of the System above the interest of any particular sub-System. Thus, he forces all parties to adjudicate their quarrels by appeal to the larger whole of which they are parts.

Notice that all Conant's arguments take the form we may call the conservative's conditional: If you want to keep Y running with minimum changes and maximum efficiency, then you ought to do X. When Conant formulates an argument in this form, it is usually valid. The trouble is that he has no sensitivity to the very tenuous, dubious status of the antecedent. But we should not expect him to: he is both creator and creature of the System he serves.

II. THE NATION'S SERVANT

No one ever consciously planned to elevate a Harvard chemist to the rank of Ambassador Extraordinary to American education. That was among the many future eventualities in Mr. Conant's career which did not figure in the decision to make him president of Harvard in 1933. Indeed, it has not been revealed what considerations were uppermost in the minds of the committee that recommended Conant to the Board of Overseers. That he was a scientist must have been of prime concern, for such a leader was distinctly needed at Harvard. But he was an organic chemist, not a physicist, nor an astronomer, nor even a geologist. Did this kind of reasoning influence the selection committee? At that time, organic chemistry occupied an extreme position on two different scales. It was probably the *most useful* of all the sciences, in the sense of pulling practical discoveries right from the laboratory to the production line. The synthesis of natural or altogether new organic compounds having specifically needed physical, chemical, or biological properties is probably *the* activity which establishes the popular image of the white-clad scientist going about the business of benefiting mankind. And a big business it is! The strongest lines between the academic world and the world of industry and commerce were anchored in the organic chemistry laboratories.

But in 1933 organic chemistry was probably the *least theoretical*

science, i.e., the branch of physical science least affected by the
then current revolutions in physical theory. It was touched neither
by the theory of relativity nor by quantum mechanics. Its basic
theory explaining the peculiar combinative properties of the carbon
atom dated back to the middle of the nineteenth century—the
theory of valence which altogether lacks the generality and imagination of evolutionary theory in biology, to say nothing of the
great theoretical structures in the more closely related fields of
physics, mathematics, and philosophy.[9]

This may seem to denigrate Conant's base in science, and that
would be misleading. The development of the physical equipment
and the mathematical techniques for the analysis and synthesis of
organic compounds is among the most impressive achievements of
our century and, to an outsider, among the least comprehensible.
But it is qualitatively a different *kind* of enterprise from that
going on elsewhere in the sciences; only in organic chemistry could
a man be regarded as a genius because he was ingenious.[10]

Did all this influence the selection committee? One may hope
that some day we shall have a biography which adequately explains
Conant's appointment to the presidency of Harvard. We shall
probably then see a group of men in need of confidence finding a
man who inspires confidence. For Harvard was in trouble in 1933,
as was every other institution in Western civilization. Harvard
needed a New Deal, and a New Deal needs a dynamic leader, one
who knows what programs he wants to institute and knows how to
use limited political power to institute his programs. The leader
of a New Deal must have respect for the imagination and rationality of the intellectual community, but he must make sure that
the intellectual penchant for theory and ideology does not stand
in the way of getting the job done. And, finally, a New Deal leader
must be deeply, fully, unqualifiedly committed to the preservation
of the institution he serves, willing to institute radical changes in
what is peripheral and incidental if those changes will help to con-
serve what is central and essential. When Conant at the age of
forty became president of Harvard, he was an ideal New Dealer.

Conant's major programs for Harvard can be divided into three
categories: (a) to provide encouragement and a sound financial
base for a vastly expanded research emphasis throughout the university, (b) to engage the faculty in a responsible and democratic

program of internal reform, and (c) to effect a merger between Harvard and the public schools of the United States. Concerning (a) and (b) it is enough to say that they were successful, in the case of (a) spectacularly so.[11] It is (c) that is our concern, for it was here that Conant's efforts effected a final consolidation of the System and that, in turn, reduced the conflict between Educationists and Academics to an affair of honor within the Establishment. The term "honor" is used deliberately. Given the continuous expansion of all educational activities, and the great growth of the System, neither the Educationists nor the Academics were going to suffer materially from loss of clientele. But there are many degrees of honor, and there are consequent struggles to attain the highest of them.

Conant's program for the schools can be described very simply. He wished to make the nation's oldest and finest university the capstone of the nation's educational System. The success of his program required at some points no more than a subtle shift of emphasis; at other points it required some quite definite dislocations. The fate of Harvard's Divinity School under Conant's presidency is an example of the latter. The System is universal and non-sectarian, while a divinity school is neither. The System operates under the epistemology of science: truth is open and growing, subject to public tests according to canons and procedures specified in advance; while truth in a divinity school is Truth—immutable and absolute. As long as Harvard was merely a provincial university, an institution serving one particular class and region with a quaint cultural and religious tradition, then the divinity school ranked with its undergraduate college and its law school as a central concern. But as a capstone to the System, the university which pre-eminently in the New World accepts *universal* canons of scholarship, Harvard has little use for a divinity school. The scientific study of religion, of course, must be pursued, in the appropriate departments of the graduate faculties, not in a school which has as its primary purpose the preparation of sectarian preachers for New England Protestant churches.

(*Veritas filia temporis est.* The first public act of Nathan M. Pusey after he succeeded Conant in 1953 was a convocation address to the Harvard Divinity School, where he promised his effort to restore the School to a central place in Harvard's activities. In his speech he referred many times to President Eliot's active antipathy to sectarian religion, but he did not mention his immediate predecessor's name even once. But it would be naive to think that Conant's policy had been altogether reversed. By 1953, Biblical and theological studies in the *best* Protestant seminaries had accepted and exemplified in high degree the ideals of scientific truth held in other departments of scholarship. The Divinity School was re-admitted to Harvard by Pusey—but substantially on Conant's terms.)

But making Harvard the capstone of America's educational System means much more than curtailing the Divinity School. First, it was necessary to overcome the financial and psychological barriers which stood between the talented public school graduates and admission to Harvard. Second, Harvard had to accept a proportionate responsibility for training teachers to serve at the secondary level of public schooling. Finally, Harvard had to take its rightful place in the leadership councils that gave guidance to all American schools. Again, Conant perceived clearly the tasks confronting him, and he moved surely and, in the main, successfully toward their accomplishment. The Harvard Scholarship Plan eventually broadened into the Merit Scholarship Program which today touches almost every secondary school in the nation.[12] Harvard graduates, dispersed across the nation, became recruiters not of football prowess but of academic talent. It probably did not hurt the cause that Franklin D. Roosevelt was both a Harvard graduate and the champion of the common man, a symbol of that national unity which Conant fought so hard to achieve in and through education.

The Master of Arts in Teaching began at Harvard under Conant's personal direction. Harvard had always trained teachers for private secondary schools—and for public high schools until certification requirements added more education courses to the undergraduate program than could be fitted into a "sound" liberal arts degree. The response of most state universities to this latter development was to expand the department of education to a college and give other-than-liberal-arts degrees to prospective teachers. Many of the great private universities, of course, simply gave up teacher-training altogether. Harvard's solution—to maintain the university's responsibility for the specifically *training* part of a teacher's education, but to move it to the post-baccalaureate level—

could not have been taken by state universities, which were required by law to provide opportunities for teacher-training at the
undergraduate level; it could not have been taken by financially
weaker universities, for the Master of Arts in Teaching is a very
expensive program; and it *would* not have been taken by any
university which did not feel the pangs of conscience at abandoning teacher training entirely. With its numerically small but qualitatively excellent MAT program, Conant's Harvard maintained a
capstone-like relation to teacher-training for the public schools.

The expansion of its graduate school and research activities gave
Harvard another opportunity to prepare teachers—this time for
other universities, liberal arts colleges, and teachers' colleges. Under
Conant's presidency, Harvard's graduate faculties were eminently
respectable in almost every field of scholarship, though they had
clear pre-eminence in few if any. The same could be said of
Harvard's professional schools, including the Harvard Graduate
School of Education. But so far as Conant was concerned, perhaps, the other side of the coin was more important: no field of
significant research or creative scholarship was ignored at Harvard;
no fresh breath blew anywhere in Academe without causing a
rustling in all branches of graduate and undergraduate teaching. In
sum, Harvard graduates who became teachers in the nation's
schools and colleges were, in principle, trained well to represent a
particular branch of scholarship and motivated to discover and to
develop intellectual talent in young men and women of all races
and social classes.

And, finally, Conant himself took his rightful place in the councils of educational leadership. During the thirties he wrote and
spoke often on educational topics, as anyone in his position would
have had to do. But Conant's words were, from the beginning,
quite distinctive. He did not quack the purely ceremonial and
humorless prose of the "typical" college president, nor the radical
bombast of such an atypical president as his contemporary in office,
Robert Maynard Hutchins. Conant avoided, whether by design or
intuition is not clear, the fashionable quarrels among educators
and intellectuals. He wrote for *Atlantic Monthly*, not *The Educational Frontier*. He addressed specific issues and specific groups,
but always in relation to the ideals of a threatened liberal democ-

racy which must maintain itself through and in defense of its free, open, growing, and pluralistic system of schools.

The rhetoric of his prose was much more that of the historian than the scientist. He often found elegant and unexpected parallels in the history of *thought* through which to illuminate present problems in educational *practice*. His speeches were unshadowed by affectation; his writings were remarkably free of ostentation, cant, or hypocrisy. His language had grace but not brilliance, his scholarship had more relevance than profundity. One sees in Conant's occasional writings of the thirties a merging of qualities of scholarship and personality that would make him indispensable during the war. Conant's essays were not polemics, they were pointers. There was no question, there was no questioning, that the direction toward which he pointed was the direction we ought to go. Conant never underestimated the desperate problems faced by the nation and its educational institutions during those years, but neither did he ever lose confidence that adequate measures would be found to solve them. Somehow, wherever Conant happened to be standing at the moment was just that point of ground to which the good and brave might repair.[13]

What banner did Conant hold aloft on that hallowed spot? It was emblazoned in red: "Education For A Classless Society." Then Conant was a Marxist? Far, far from it. If it were not so appealing it would be appalling, and vice versa: Conant was a classical Jeffersonian liberal in his notions of political economy. It was not only that he employed a Jeffersonian rhetoric in discussing education but that he genuinely believed excessive growth of big business and big government, the loss of private initiative and decline of local ownership in commerce and industry to be the evils which brought on the economic collapse of the country and had to be removed before genuine equality—in education and elsewhere—could be achieved.[14] His notion of Harvard's being the capstone of a nationwide system of education derived, in his view, directly from Jefferson's vision for the University of Virginia. But while Jefferson had proposed a system of educational selectivity which successively removed the less than academically talented from schools, Conant saw these selection procedures (and by 1940 he could identify them as "careful testing . . . conscientious and discriminating forms of educational guidance") [15] as ways of differentiating students into various programs, mostly *within* the same schools. The comprehensive secondary school replaced Jefferson's neighborhood primary school as society's tool for carving an American—a distinctive kind of human being, united with all fellow Americans in loyalty to the ideals of the nation but perfectly individuated and educationally prepared to fill that political, economic, and domestic role for which he is best suited by nature. This is an ancient American ideal, and Conant, perhaps more explicitly than any other educational leader of his time, perceived America's salvation as requiring a "radical reconstruction" *backward* to the system of political and economic individualism which gave rise to that educational ideal.

This is not to say that Conant saw it all clearly and finally when he assumed the presidency in 1933. But by the time of Pearl Harbor, when he was already a member of the Educational Policies Commission, Conant had a fully developed mental picture of what the educational System of this nation ought to look like. It included secondary education as the birthright of every American boy and girl, free and compulsory high schools offering finely differentiated programs to gratify the interests and develop the talents of each youngster. For the academically talented there should be a wide choice of colleges and universities which provide not only specialized advance training but also a general education sufficient to the needs of leaders of a democratic society. No economic or social obstacle could be allowed to come between the talented youngster and the finest education our civilization can provide. This open-ended democratic educational system will both preserve and justify the nation's heritage of economic and political freedom: preserve because it perfects the skill, commitment, and leadership necessary to the continuation of the nation's political and economic institutions, justify because it promotes the maximum development of each individual—the ultimate criterion for judging any social institution.

We know what Conant then believed and how he felt about these matters, for he stated his feelings and beliefs quite often. Perhaps they were stated most clearly in a series of four radio addresses prepared for the students of Harvard College very soon after America entered the war against Germany and Japan. In a sense, these speeches were Conant's own declaration of war and a statement of his war aims.[16] Surprisingly, he spoke very little of what he was fighting against. Conant's antipathy to Nazism was long-standing: he had created an international "incident" by snubbing the official representation of the Nazi regime to Harvard's Tercentenary celebration in 1936, and he had been among the leaders in helping to rescue and resettle German intellectuals who, for being Jewish or independent or both, had been persecuted by the Nazis. But beyond insisting that "unconditional surrender of the Axis Powers be the first war aim of the United States," he said little about our enemies. Instead he spoke of what we were fighting *for*, and that, most astonishingly, turned out to be "the abolition of inherited privilege." [17] He spoke movingly of the traditions of political and economic freedom we shared with the British, freedoms then undergoing their severest threat in history. But according to Conant, America had added to these shared freedoms another that is distinctive, freedom from "social classes." In three of these addresses, Conant went beyond the mild Jeffersonian liberalism so clearly expressed in his specifically *educational* ideas. Here he became a Jacksonian, an old Western Populist, an ardent believer that it was we, not our gallant Russian allies, who had built the foundations for a truly classless society. One can but wonder if the Harvard students who heard him shared his conviction that the war they were about to join was against "privilege." They probably had few political convictions, and it may not have been altogether without significance for many of them that the president of their university should declare social unity and equality to be their official goals. Or again it may.

But for Conant, a system of education providing for the equal self-development of every individual was America's moral contribution to the Allied cause, and in its name he led Harvard into the struggle. While her casualties were not as heavy as Leningrad's, Harvard's war record was distinguished.[18] Her president's was even more so. As Chairman of the National Defense Research Committee he led the most concentrated cadre of scientific talent the world had ever seen, and his influence in the nation was no longer restricted to the relatively unpressured issues of education but penetrated into the most urgent and controversial concerns of military and economic policy. Conant, whose only previous non-academic work had been as entrepreneur of a very small chemical plant just after he received his Ph.D. during World War I, moved easily and effectively into his expanded role. For he could perform the same service for his scientific associates that had become his forte among educators: he could point steadily to the national interest as a basis for reconciling very deep conflicts among particular individuals and groups. By never allowing himself to become identified with any one segment of the scientific world, much less with any parochial economic or political group, Conant became an invaluable mediator in the constant pressure and conflict of the war years.[19]

There are two points about Conant's wartime role that may have significance for understanding his later view of himself as mediator-general to American education. First, the normal political means for resolving conflict could not operate during the war. Often there was not time. And the open publicity necessary for democratic politics had to be curtailed in the interest of military security. Second, the conflicts were frequently the consequence of the revolutionary impact of science itself, and an understanding of the issues in relation to the national interest required technical expertise peculiarly combined with a sense of the American morale. But this means that the usual qualifications for a *judge* of issues are not strict enough. As is true of any revolution, the scientific revolution demanded a new legality. Conant's personal charm and modesty, his deep commitment to American liberties, and his truly extraordinary ability to grasp the essence of very complex issues may have concealed some of the revolutionary aspects of his role as representative of both science and the *common* sense of American justice in the decisions made by the councils in which he sat.[20]

But our concern is not with Conant's career as such but with the logic of his arguments in support of educational policies. One cannot be sure, but there seems some reason to believe that his experience in the broader world of national politics brought on a profound but subtle shift in his educational thinking. In November, 1945, he delivered the Sachs Lectures on Secondary Education at Columbia University.[21] At first glance his statements then seem little different from what he had said in 1936 or 1938 or even 1940. He still wanted plenty of free enterprise and economic competition; and he wanted the state to use its power to educate and to restrict patrimony in support of equal chances in the race for the goods of life. He still wanted every boy and girl to complete a program of secondary education finely differentiated for individual tastes and abilities, and he still wanted those young men and women who possess academic talents and interests to have access to higher education without encountering obstacles of birth, race, money, or neglect by teachers. But the reasons he gave for these beliefs and the conclusions he drew for educational policy had changed in a noticeable way. Let us consider three illustrative points, the last of which is the most important for Conant's later writings.

He no longer spoke of a "classless society." He shifted from his political terminology to a sociological jargon: he spoke of "social structure" and abjured altogether the word "class." Hence, he could claim that all societies, American and Russian included, had "structure." The only questions, really, were whether the social structure was open or closed, slightly or highly visible, complex or simple. He preferred and hoped America would come more and more to represent an open system of low visibility, one that was complex in the sense of having many different status systems rather than a single hierarchy of classes. This was not a retrogression, for, as shown below, Conant's Utopian Jeffersonianism of the late 1930's was an absolutely untenable position, logically speaking. But the 1945 position did represent a different way of talking.

He had come to be quite wary of any openhanded policy which might produce a large class of unemployed intelligentsia, that dreaded precursor of Fascism and totalitarianism in Central Europe. He had opposed the indiscriminate G.I. Bill, to which he much preferred selective support for a smaller number of men who would be expected to demonstrate academic aptitude during a one-year probationary period. In his pre-war writings Conant had urged that standards not be sacrificed to mere quantity, but he had never before seemed to fear "over-education" in itself.[22] In his Sachs Lectures, Conant showed the attitude of a man well practiced in democratic politics: his preferences having been overruled, he was willing to do his part to help the majority's plan succeed, but he would feel it an evasion of his duty *not* to express his fears for the venture.

Earlier, as indicated above, Conant had argued that the nation's system of education—open to all and finely differentiated for the benefit of individuals—was both a support and a justification for a democratic political and social system. By 1945 the notion that its schools constitute a nation's justification had disappeared. In its place we find the most clearly drawn statement that an educational system's function is entirely subsidiary to the economic and political system. He insisted that no study be "introduced into the school curricula" except that it "develop in each boy or girl (a) the maximum use of his talents in a vocation, or (b) the adult behavior we postulated as desirable in the citizens of our ideal republic. Unless we can demonstrate that the study of a given subject can contribute to these ends, we should eliminate it from the curriculum" (Sachs Lectures, p. 25). And lest he be misunderstood, Conant says it again: "Unless one wishes to start a discussion of education with certain postulates which may not be examined, I see no alternative to making every subject prove its worth; either it must be of value in connection with a vocation or it must contribute to the proper behavior of the citizen of our ideal republic of free men" (Sachs Lectures, p. 29).

These quotations indicate that Conant had taken the line of the "behavioral definition of educational objectives" with hook and sinker attached. In the chapter on B. F. Skinner, it will be necessary to argue some of the very difficult technical points that arise from that way of treating educational policy, but right now I wish only to indicate that in our *ideal* republic of *free men*, as opposed to Plato's Republic of slaves and pure souls, each generation must decide for itself what is proper behavior. Education can contribute to the richness and fullness of life, but it is scarcely a means of perpetuating one generation's notions of propriety in the next. With Skinner we will encounter a powerful version of this argument; from Conant it comes out only confused.

If, as profound minds have assured us, the essence of history is irony, there is no better case in point than the Sachs Lectures of 1945. Under Conant's inspiration, sometimes with his personal guidance and supervision, two documents of basic educational policy had been prepared during the war. One, by the Educational Policies Commission, was entitled *Education For ALL American Youth;* the second, by the Harvard Committee on General Education, was entitled *General Education in a Free Society* and was better known for a decade as "The Harvard Report." [23] The first was an attempt to present the case that every American boy or girl ought to attend secondary school and to examine the consequences for the high school's program of its becoming an extension of the common school. In retrospect, it appears a timid work, one which merely added some rather suspect statistics to the basic *kind* of argument which American policy-makers had used since the publication of the *Cardinal Principles of Secondary Education* in 1918: the argument which starts from a statement of what valued behavior we want our children to exhibit in their out-of-school and later adult life and then proceeds with a list of school *studies* which will produce that valued behavior. As will be argued later, since they logically depend on there being known connections between school studies and out-of-school, adult behavior, and since these connections are neither statistically demonstrated nor even plausible to common sense, all such arguments are suspect. Nevertheless, *Education For ALL American Youth* was the most complete expression ever made of that Jeffersonian idealism toward which Conant had been groping during the thirties. It was full of the mystique of equality and unity arising from an educational environment common to all Americans. It rang with the conviction that a school could protect the productivity of the labor force and the stability of the electorate while at the same time providing a model of the democratic, individual-regarding community yet to be achieved in the economic and political domains.

The Harvard Report was equally a product of that environment which nourished Conant's rather short-lived idealism. The basic concern of the Report was to free the great tradition of liberal education from the snobbish, class-ridden caricature of itself that had come to dominate "college life" in America. Surely the tradition of humane learning, probably the noblest product of Western civilization, has a function in a modern industrial democracy; but those whose special responsibility it is to guard that tradition must actively re-form the society's educational institutions. The very term "general education," used in preference to "liberal education," or "humane learning," shows the democratic spirit of the Committee. If Conant's Harvard was going to be the capstone of an open, public school system, its faculty had to think through exactly what was involved in providing for the intellectually superior representative of *all American youth* a cultural background equal to that of the most favored aristocrats. And for a brief moment in the institution's history the faculty was willing, albeit not precisely eager, to undertake that task.[24]

Conant, in 1945, accepted both these documents which represented his own just-past thought. He began his first lecture by saying, "I have had the privilege of sponsoring in one way, and certainly endorsing enthusiastically, two volumes . . . *Education for ALL American Youth* and *General Education in a Free Society*." And he closed it by a ringing declaration: "Armed with [these two books], I should hope to answer all critics of the future of our American schools." In between he denies being "aware" that there is any contradiction between what he advocates and "the spirit of these two documents, from which I have borrowed freely." We can believe this protest of unawareness, even as we recognize that, in the fact of its being made, that protest is quite revealing. For Conant's thought was by then very different from the spirit of those documents, a spirit that pervaded the best American educators when the very unity and essence of our nation was in danger and when education was more than a tool of politics and economics. It was a spirit which had not yet abandoned reason and replaced it with *raison d'état*; it was a pre-Auschwitz spirit, a pre-"unconditional surrender" spirit, and it was a pre-Hiroshima spirit. Conant's war service had taught him only too well to think in the nation's interest; it had entirely incapacitated him for thinking higher.

The crisis of conscience came later. After all, in the autumn of 1945 it was quite natural to identify the welfare of mankind with the national interest of the United States. But by the summer of 1948 things were very different. Where in 1945 there had been at least the appearance of harmony among the great powers, there was in 1948 overt conflict which stopped just short of actual war; where there had been national unity in the war effort itself, there was now domestic discord so deep as to splinter the Democratic Party and threaten the dissolution of traditional political processes. Where there had been a clear mandate to the schools to pitch in, rebuild, and catch up, there was now only a nagging and ambiguous question: what for? Is the war to be fought all over again? Is there a new depression just around the corner? Are we back in the same old groove that we fought to get out of?

Conant recognized the change and felt it deeply, so deeply that he saw in it an obligation to rewrite his earlier lectures so that they would speak to the new situation. The result was a new book in which old passages from the Sachs Lectures appear but in a very altered setting: *Education in a Divided World*, (hereafter abbreviated as EDW), in my opinion Conant's best work on education. For the first and last time in his career as spokesman for American educational policy, Conant perceived that the System he had helped to build confronted a moral challenge. Soviet Marxism proclaimed many of the same values which Conant had claimed as distinctive to the American educational System, particularly the value of equality of opportunity. As had never been true of German and Japanese enemies, behind the Soviet military threat lay an ideal which had demonstrated a strong appeal among the dispossessed of the world. No response to the military threat alone would suffice; the moral challenge must be faced as well.

But there are two quite different senses of the expression: "face the moral challenge." In one sense it means to confront the questions: Can we be sure that our economic and political (with its accompanying educational) system is the *right* one? For us? For the contested areas of Europe? How can we be sure? How sure can we be? In a second sense, "face the moral challenge" means something very different: What strategies should we adopt in order to prevent the Soviet ideology from gaining support among Europeans and disaffected Americans? Conant *almost* recognized the difference between these two questions, but at the point of genuine confrontation with the first, he failed in the strangest sort of way. His prose, which had always had its ups and downs in rhetoric, had at least been straightforwardly intelligible. But when he found himself forced to "enter the twilight zone that separates philosophy from theology far enough to come to grips with the question of the basis for our ethics," his muse deserted him.[25] His writing at this point constitutes one empirical case to support the emotivist school of ethics which claims that all ethical discourse is meaningless except as an expression of personal feeling.

Conant's problem here is admittedly very difficult. The basic Soviet philosophy—Marxism-Leninism—is supposed to be universal in the sense of expressing truths which all men must recognize by simple human reason. But for the average American, the most basic support for ethics is found in a religious creed and cult, which he regards as "true" for him but not necessarily true; the other fellow is entitled to think as he pleases on such matters. From the point of view of strategy, this situation makes it hard for us to put up a counter-ideology to meet the Soviets'. From the moral point of view, it makes it hard to find a common set of basic beliefs from which to argue the rightness of our political and economic system. For some three pages in this book, Conant tries, *really* tries, to find such a set of basic beliefs in what he calls the "common denominator which unites many Americans of otherwise highly divergent views." The search is, in *his* opinion, not without success: "Our practical democratic creed turns out on analysis to be the affirmation of the common basis of our many faiths." And a good thing it is, too, for "when we must meet an aggressive Soviet ideology . . . we endanger our political and social solidarity if we close our minds to the nature of the spiritual unity of this nation. (EDW, pp. 101-104)

Fine, but just what is that that we can affirm in common from an analysis of our many faiths? Conant, of course, does not analyze faiths, and he has little confidence in those people (of the Divinity School type) who do. Instead, Conant looks deeply into the American animal and finds that when an American faces truly basic ethical questions, he "will answer these questions almost instinctively in just one way." And *that* is what in actuality constitutes our "spiritual unity" if only "theological and philosophical warfare" would not "obscure" and "confuse" matters.

But the problem still remains. We cannot put the American's *instinct* or *spirit* into the argument against the Marxist's *theory*, in attempting to meet the "moral challenge," in either sense of the expression. Conant senses this, for he quotes several pointed passages from Koestler's *Darkness at Noon* to illustrate the "basic conflict between the followers of the Soviet philosophy on the one hand and the believers in the 'Christian and humane' ethics on the other." (It is instructive that Conant uses Koestler's label for ethics, "Christian and humane," and puts it in quotes.)

For its utilitarian values, Conant gives the highest marks to "a Hebraic-Christian view of human nature." For "you can build a free society" on it. It is *more* utilitarian than a merely utilitarian view, Conant argues. But is it true? Can Conant's own version of this tradition be made articulate and explicit, embodied in a concept of history and elaborated in a theory of social institutions? Can it be put into continuing dialogue with the Marxist view and all the many, many others which make up the rich panorama of Western thought? No, that is not its function. A man's life—his values and ideas in particular—"can be measured only by the way he faces his own problems, by the success or failure of the inner conflict within his soul." (EDW, p. 105)

This shows how badly Conant missed the point of Koestler's novel. It did not merely portray a choice of values; rather, its point was a monstrous crime—the crime of ending the dialogue of responsible inquiry by shooting one's adversary. The essential case in *Darkness at Noon* was in showing that even for these old intellectuals who spent their whole lives in argument and discourse, there was always something more to be said, some new insight, some fresh turn of phrase that would make the other mind see things in a new light. So long as full engagement of argument continues, there is hope.

In a lesser way, Conant is also guilty of Nekrasov's crime. The gentle New Englander does not shoot; he merely withdraws into his own soul, a place that has a strange kind of conflict, i.e., one which *is* either a success or failure. And there can be no doubt that Conant has withdrawn. He welcomes the confrontation of Marxism with its adversaries in American universities, for that is the only way for us to "win the ideological conflict . . . on a non-shooting basis." But Conant offers this meeting only because of his supreme "confidence that *our* philosophy is superior to all alien importations." (EDW, p. 173) How our philosophy—which is "instinct," not argument—can be demonstrated superior is never made clear, indeed it is never even discussed.

But if Conant's philosophy were made articulate and explicit, it would find itself confronting not only "Soviet ideology" but the many, many other schools, systems, and streams of social philosophy which constitute the unique heritage of Western civilization. Conant would have to argue, to search for evidence, to think carefully about abstract things, and he would have to look with critical eyes on the basic system of American economic and political institutions. He could no longer be merely a servant of his nation, however exalted. He would have to leave that privileged spot where he can speak with unique authority on "this system of universal education as an instrument of national policy" (EDW, p. 5).

Education in a Divided World represents the closest Conant ever got to a moral *argument*. Until then he had a whole congeries of notions, images, and slogans which he used in lieu of moral argument. So long as his only concern was to organize the System, to eliminate the anachronisms and inequities in the various historical institutions which had to be linked together to make the System, serious moral argument was unnecessary. The Cold War posed a challenge which went deeper. Conant went as deeply as he could—and then faltered. After that painful experience, it is not surprising that ten years later he confessed to "a sense of distasteful weariness" when "philosophical" problems are introduced into discussions of educational policy.[26]

Before leaving *Education in a Divided World,* however, I must pay tribute to Conant, the Cold War Warrior. Recognizing the need to avoid both "supineness and belligerency," Conant calls for "patience and yet more patience, strength and courage to handle strength, a belief in the importance of the historic goals of our free society, intelligence and courage to cope with problems of terrifying complexity." (EDW, p. 233) These were exactly the qualities which Conant was to display first as High Commissioner to the American Zone of Germany and then as our first Ambassador Extraordinary to the Deutsches Bundesreich. Never did he suggest that we blackmail the Soviet Union with our capacity to explode atomic bombs in their cities. Never did he suggest that we use our enormous industrial might to pressure an arms race against an economically weaker nation.[27] One may believe that the Cold War could have been avoided altogether and that, in any event, it has been prolonged past all endurance largely because of American intransigence. But one must admit, even so, that like any war, the Cold War calls out extraordinary virtues in its best soldiers. James Bryant Conant and George C. Marshall were its best soldiers.

III. THE ARGUMENTS

But where does this leave Conant's arguments for educational policies? As opposed to his very naive approach of 1945, he no longer believed that every study in the curriculum must justify itself by producing just those behaviors valued in the economic and political system. Presumably he relinquished that view in response to some of the criticisms he acknowledged receiving subsequent to the publication of the 1945 lectures. (EDW, p. vii) In any event, the view had been untenable: the research by which to demonstrate such a connection between study and behavior is simply not available and (for reasons hinted above and developed more fully in Chapter Five) could not even in principle *be* developed. But Conant has not given up the next line of defense: all arguments for educational policy are essentially utilitarian arguments. That is to say, one chooses certain values (and we shall have to see how *that* decision could be made) and then one argues that a certain program of education—organized in certain kinds of schools, available to certain kinds of students under teachers selected by certain procedures, etc.—will be an effective instrument for producing those chosen values. The above schema, which I will call S for short, seems commonsensical enough to gain *prima facie* plausibility, as the harder, stricter "Course-of-study-X-produces-behavior-Y" does not. But S becomes operational only when it is supplemented by the equally commonsensical idea of *how* study in school is connected with the values for which it is instrumental. This connection, call it C, is as follows: If you want the youngster to pursue value V when he is an adult, have him practice V in school when he is young. Or "train up a child in the way that he should grow, and when he is old he will not depart from it."

Within certain limits, S and C provide a framework for very intelligent discourse on educational policies. For example, Conant believes that there are certain values, *and not others*, to be gained from the study of science. He then devises a most carefully worked out program of studies with texts and materials which will permit students to *practice* those values he believes should obtain from the study of science. Other would-be policy-makers for science education—e.g., Jerome Bruner and Jerrold Zacharias—may disagree either with Conant's claims about what values ought to accrue from the teaching of science *or* with his claim that this course of study produces practice in those values or with both. This dispute can be carried on intelligently even in the absence of specialized research findings concerning the actual consequences in behavior of teaching particular youngsters under particular conditions. Note that C is not at all dependent on specialized research. Note also that S and C together *appear* to provide an adequate framework for theory and practice. Why, then, should we have specialized, technical research in education? The difficulty in answering this last question may explain the paucity of such research.

But S and C together make a house of cards which tumbles at the first breath of criticism. S is all right so long as the value scheme contains the same *kind* of values, i.e., values which can be ordered on the same scale. Thus S will work so long as only the instrumental value of schooling is considered. Conant's scheme of 1948 was fairly simple: the preservation of the American way of life in the face of its myriad of enemies. And for him the American way of life had three related sub-systems: (a) an honest, decentralized, federal *political* system, (b) a laissez-faire-as-possible *economic* system, and (c) a fluid, complex *social* system, probably in that order. If we can establish some such ordering of non-educational values, we can in principle order activities in school by their contribution to that system of values, providing a basis for intelligible discourse at least. The trouble is, of course, that once we put *distinctively* educational values—intrinsic, for-themselves values— in the schema, we have incommensurables, and the whole notion of ordering is lost. There is simply no single standard by which to measure the relative value of mastery of a complex proof in pure geometry on the one hand and learning the routines necessary to perform adequately as a service station attendant on the other.

Both of these activities *are* values, the first intrinsic, the second instrumental. There are many things one can say about both these values, e.g., that both are important in a total society, that both take some diligence and attention, that there should be no invidious distinctions between individuals because of particular talent or preference for one over the other, etc. A well-known John W. Gardner made a big deal of saying those things one *may* say about both sorts of values.[28] But none of that will help S. S depends on the logical possibility of comparing various school programs by their contribution to an ordered scheme of values. But mastering a proof in pure geometry, sharing the unity of sense, feeling, and form of *"Es war ein König in Thule,"* and values like that cannot be ordered on the same scale with learning the skills necessary to get a job, and to vote, and other values *like that.*

Hence, S will not do when complex problems of educational policy arise, where "complex" means requiring decisions involving incommensurable values.

It is noteworthy that in Conant's own use of this schema to justify his science program, he did not face a complex problem. Despite his efforts to weave it into his notion of a school serving exclusively economic and political values, his actual treatment of science is strictly as an intrinsic value. He says that he is treating science not as a branch of vocational training but as the essential ingredient of "secular education," i.e., that process by which a student comes to understand man—his work and his world. Here we are clearly on the side of intrinsic values, but Conant cannot let the matter simply rest there. He adds a section entitled "Science and National Policy" in which he adumbrates the familiar view that since our lives are now "profoundly influenced by highly technical scientific consideration," those whom chance has granted great political power ought to have an "understanding of science." One could imagine what would happen if that position were taken seriously and a course designed for the vocational training of potential future political leaders; topics might include: How to make scientists talk so that you can understand them. Economic factors affecting R & D operations in government, etc. Fortunately, Conant does not take that position seriously; having mentioned it, he quickly agrees "not to press the point further." [29]

Now C is no better off. C asserts that the connection between learning and valued behavior *is* the practice of the latter by pupils in schools. Conant often writes of the need for the *practice* of social democracy in the comprehensive high school in order that *habits* of democratic behavior will be instilled in the youngsters. This may look like commonsense psychology, but it conceals a logical fallacy of existential importance. The fallacy is that one cannot formulate a description of what the youngster practices in school which is also a description of the *value* he is to demonstrate out of school. The skill, for example, of running a wood lathe safely and effectively in the production of some object can be taught in school and accurately described. We can describe what the student practices. But is what we have described a *value* of the sort we need for S? Not at all. That skill is a value *if* it contributes to a man's employment and production in industry. The skill of running a lathe correctly is also a value *if* it contributes to a man's capacity to make "worthy use of leisure time," but the youngster in school cannot be accurately described as *practicing* a leisure-time pursuit.

Your initial reaction to the argument, which utterly destroys C if it stands, is probably to say something like the following: The argument seems to hinge on there being two utterly different settings—the woodshop in the school and the production line in a furniture factory—and two different kinds of people—schoolboys and workers. But the absolute distinction, you say, cannot be maintained: one can imagine an older boy who studies wood working in school during the mornings and in the afternoon works at the factory, doing exactly what he was taught earlier the same day. One can imagine a shop which serves the school five days a week as a place for teaching and is used on the weekends by a community service group as a factory to make furniture for the Old Folks Home. You might even continue by pointing out that modern educational theory attempts to break down the barriers between school and community, while my argument seems to want to build up barriers.

Your reaction is understandable, but it shows that you *just* missed the point of the earlier argument. Granted, the same boy may be doing the same thing in school and on the job. But the *value* of his doing it on the job is that he is *employed*, not that he is running a lathe without injury to himself. Or the *value* is that he is producing some object that has economic utility, can be sold at a profitable price on the market. Running a lathe correctly is instrumental to those values, but running a lathe in itself is neither employment nor productivity. No, if the boy *is* employed, *is* productive, and *is* taking instruction in woodworking at the same time—not an uncommon occurrence—one can describe his actions as achieving those economic values, but then the decisions on what training practices he is to engage in are *not* made as matters of educational policy but as following the economic strategy of the company that employs him. The decision to have him learn a certain skill might be justified by saying that the practice of the skill will increase his productivity and add security to employment, but only if he is practicing a skill which, other things holding true, *will* help to achieve those values. Some of the other things that have to hold true concern the technology of his industry, his own willing-ness to accept employment, a market in which objects produced by the application of his skill can be sold profitably, and so on. It may be a very wise decision in pursuit of the values of increasing productivity and security of employment (the first from the com-pany's point of view, the second from the boy's) that he take in-struction on company time. But even then the practices he engages in under instruction are not the values he and the company are seeking. These practices are only "practicing."

None of the points above deny that there are concrete instances of on-the-job training activities which are clearly both the practice *of* and practice *for* a productive skill. Those training activities have two different lines by which decisions are made. But on the educa-tional line, the *values* which are presumably to be achieved by the training activities cannot be described in the same literal language by which we describe the *activities themselves*.

If the argument against C holds for skill-training, it holds even more for the other sorts of values Conant sees "practiced" in schools. For example, Conant values social democracy rather highly. By "social democracy" he means the reverse of snobbery; he means a general tendency on the part of individuals to regard other individuals as having worth and dignity proportional to moral virtue, not occupation and economic success; he means an active willingness to seek association with individuals whose status and background are in contrast rather than identical to one's own. This is a value which we may try to achieve through our school practices, but it is not something that, literally, can be practiced by school children as a part of a curriculum or extra-curriculum. As teachers and administrators, *we* can practice social democracy, we can provide opportunities for children to practice social democ-racy, and we can reinforce their doing so with more or less subtle rewards. ("We can" is used in the logical sense of "can"; in the social world of most schools the practice of social democracy is *very* difficult.) But in those activities which are decided as educa-tional policy, youngsters cannot practice social democracy at all, for we mean by that expression actions of the sort mentioned above which people do voluntarily, by their own intention. All we can say about the inter-racial, inter-faith, inter-social-class activities that are a part of the school program is that *if* the youngsters exhibited these same social practices with full cognizance of what they were doing and full freedom to do differently, then we would say that they were practicing social democracy. It may well be, as Conant insisted in 1948, that the best way to insure a populace devoted to social democracy is to have the youngsters practice in schools those mixing-type behaviors which, if engaged in freely and for their own sake, we would take as exemplifying the value. But that value itself cannot be what students are practicing when they meet in their economically-racially-religiously-integrated social studies class.

(You can bend a twig to make a tree the shape you want, but what you want to grow from a child is not a pre-shaped bigger child but a self-shaping adult.)

Let us summarize these remarks in the form to be found in Conant's arguments at that point in his career as educational theorist when he was most seriously seeking a synoptic view of the System he had helped to build; he held to the simple schema S which may be diagrammed as follows:

S

Educational Practice   Ordered System of Values V

C $\longrightarrow$

where C, the connection between the educational practice and V, is: the practice *is* the value sought. I have argued that S is a logically feasible argument only if V contains but one kind of value at a time, and that it breaks down if you try to mix intrinsic values and instrumental values in the same ordering system. I submit that Conant's own work demonstrates the futility of this attempt when he is forced to say that the justification for teaching the humanities is the contribution this study makes to the mental health and consequent political stability of our citizenry. (EDW, p. 92) That sort of patent nonsense is unavoidable unless one is willing *really* to restrict his attention just to instrumental values, and Conant is much too much a humane gentleman for that. Indeed, he does not follow his own scheme when he considers matters that are really serious for him, i.e., science education.

I have also argued that C is not just a psychological or physiological premise asserting the persistence of youthful habits into adulthood. For those habits are values, in the sense of being what Conant and other democratically-inclined educators really want, *only* if they represent free and consciously chosen action. Despite the efforts of educational reformers to change it, educational policy lays down directions for action which students accept on some basis other than their own free and conscious choice. Hence, it cannot be that school behavior is itself the value sought. Thus C cannot be the connection it purports to be. To make clear what *is* the connection would require the examination of *many* psychological and physiological premises, and these might prove quite dubious when made explicit.

There are at least two ways one can rescue S and C. This form of argument is consistent and can be used for intelligible discourse if one is willing to talk only about desired behavior and one will accept simple, commonsense notions of how habits acquired in childhood persist in adult life. This is the form of argument typically used by those who view education "as an instrument of national policy," a Cold War weapon. Soviet politicians are very addicted to this kind of talk, and there are those in the United States who can conjure up horrendous scare-stories from the published statements of their Soviet counterparts. Since we have very little valid evidence on the connections between school activities and political attitudes, all such talk about "instrument of national policy" is suspect. There is no doubt that certain people make a good thing for themselves in perpetuating it. It is deplorable that the federal government had to rely on the title "National Defense Education Act" to justify perfectly routine aid to schools and colleges.

But that way of saving S and C is un-serious. A second way would be to recognize with Conant that "to be well founded an educational philosophy must be part and parcel of a comprehensive social philosophy" (EDW, p. 230). It is the task of a comprehensive social philosophy to reconcile the incommensurable claims of intrinsic with instrumental values, of individual rights with social responsibilities, of freedom with necessity, of equality in personal dignity with differentiation in social function and reward. Conant saw that such an intellectual foundation was necessary, but he could not distinguish the criteria applicable to "ideology," by which he meant the propaganda phase of the Cold War, from those applicable to "a comprehensive social philosophy," which has to be something quite different from political propaganda, else it is nothing.

Thus, Conant was able to provide neither an ideology nor a philosophy. As ideology, his naive Jeffersonianism had relevance and appeal only to middle-class Americans; one cannot imagine its being successfully exported to the working class of Algeria or Brazil as a competitor to Marxism. It does not even pretend to be a "comprehensive social philosophy," for Conant does not ever work out explicit doctrines to solve the intellectual problems in conflicting claims of authority, responsibility, hierarchy, and so forth. But without a philosophy or at the minimum an ideology to back it up, Conant's adherence to the S-and-C form of argument makes his discourse unintelligible in the context of rational debate over educational ends and means.

The difficulty here is quite analogous to that of building an intelligent economic policy for the nation on our commonsense ideas about economics. Conant follows exactly the same commonsense approach in economics that the S-and-C argument uses in education: as a typical Eisenhower Republican, he holds that government incomes and expenditures were drags on economic growth and should be held to the minimum consistent with military security; that only an economy which encourages unlimited personal greed can provide incentives for productive effort, and so on (EDW, p. 33). These conceptions, so deeply rooted in conventional wisdom, to use Galbraith's phrase, have to be rooted out before one can talk intelligibly about macro-economics. This task requires argument at the level of comprehensive economic theory. Analogously, the S-and-C model of educational argument hinges on premises which may seem obvious to conventional wisdom but become dubious indeed when made explicit in the context of systematic thought.

The impact of this last argument is *not* to be considered a plea for a "comprehensive social philosophy," in the sense that we use that expression to refer to the works of Marx, Herbert Spencer, or even John Dewey. To recapitulate: the S-and-C form of argument is consistent and intelligible *only* if (a) one takes a completely instrumental and behaviouristic view of values and a deterministic conception of the effect of schooling on later behavior, *or else* (b) one elaborates a comprehensive social philosophy which reconciles conflicting values, incommensurable *orders* of values, and freedom with educational determinism. It is obvious that (a) is incomplete and that (b) is neither stable enough nor sufficiently common in a free society to provide the basis for educational decisions.[30] From which I would conclude that we ought to give up the S-and-C model for educational policy. This model is all right as long as the actual practices of schools are determined in the main by tradition, modified by minor adjustments to the exigencies of the moment, as long as "arguments" of educational policy partake more of the nature of rationalizations than decisions, so long as we really do not *have to think* about educational policy at all. Once the need for thought becomes genuine, the S-and-C model becomes obsolete.

Conant, with his uncanny sense for such things, does give up the S-and-C model of argument. In fact, he gives up argument altogether. It is not necessary to follow his excursions into comparative education. There he seeks to justify the American comprehensive high school by showing that it performs socially valuable functions which are impossible to achieve in selective English and Australian schools, and that it also has the capacity in principle, although too infrequently in practice, to provide first-rate academic training for the talented minority.[31] Nor is it necessary to trace in detail the development of his distinctive views on the teaching of science as an aspect of general education. One may be dubious of the terminology of "tactics and strategy of science" as descriptive of desired educational content; it seems the military image has all to deeply impressed itself on Conant's mind.[32] But his thesis that science is best *taught* through the careful analysis of the great experiments, including *Gedankenexperimenten*, in its history since the sixteenth century seems quite valid and quite independent of his *very* naive conceptions of what science *is*, philosophically speaking.[33] As is so often the case, Conant's practical conclusions are far superior to the arguments he advances in support of them.

General arguments on educational policy simply disappeared from Conant's writings after his return from Germany to become the Carnegie Corporation's inspector-general to American schools. He has led an excellent team of fact-gatherers, and their publications give us handy and reliable education data from a selected sample of states and school systems in this country. He has made a large number of proposals and recommendations for bringing certain poorer and weaker elements in the System up to the level of performance seen in those elements which Conant considers superior. When his proposals fit existing trends, they are eagerly seized upon and put into practice by the designated members of the Establishment. This has been the case with many of the conclusions in his *American High School Today*. When his proposals do not fit at all, they are simply ignored. This has been the fate of most of his proposals for the junior high school. Where his proposals have touched on genuine conflicts of interest within the Establishment, as in the case with his ideas on teacher training, they have become the focal point for debate and controversy. Where his proposals have touched on an inherent conflict between the interests of the System and some outside political force, as was the effect of his views on compulsory racial integration in *Slums and Schools,* his ideas are simply lumped together with the conservative, Systemic side of things; and the conflict goes ahead within its proper *political* setting.

The more Conant studies and investigates and writes, the less he is an actor in the arena of educational policy and the more his writings become merely the occasion for action by others. The more recently he writes about "our success against the spread of communism," the more hollow it sounds, the less it indicates a serious attempt to offer a *reason* for doing one thing rather than another in education.

Just here, perhaps, we can understand how and why there is neither a clear form nor compelling reasons in Conant's latest policy proposals, e.g., those examined in detail in Section I of this chapter. For not even Conant can take the simple schema S seriously, even though that simple schema is all he has to work with; on losing that he loses the only form of argument for *general* educational policy that he has ever used. He can not formulate a comprehensive social philosophy in which the contradictions and anomalies of S disappear; neither can he explicitly accept the institutional structure within which S becomes an adequate schema, "adequate" only in the sense that no one points out its inadequacy. Lacking the will for the philosophical task, understanding present institutional inadequacies so clearly that he cannot merely accept things as they are, Conant finds himself writing on the trivia of educational politics even while his aim is infinitely higher.[34]

Conant's unwillingness to stay with schema S articulately and explicitly explains in yet another sense, the curious lack of form we encountered in Section I. Just to take the first topic considered there—look again at that list which Conant alternately labels "problems," "reforms," "developments," "significant phase of the educational revolution." *If* Conant would assume S, *if* he could assert the values V that the System should pursue, then he could rationally assert just how and where present institutional practices fail to *be* the values we ought to seek. In that case we would not get a list containing all these disparate elements, some of which Conant desires (e.g., advanced placement), some of which he despises (e.g., segregated schools)—all lumped together under conflicting labels. We could go through the other topics treated in this first section with the same effect: were Conant willing to assume S, he could pull together his scattered, irresolute comments into a form of argument. But *no* one can assume S any more. It's not genuinely a live option, as politicians are wont to say. We can't assume any longer that the interests of the national state *define* the values we should pursue in education. We can't assume that an unlimited growth economy *defines* educational values. We can't assume, even, that there is one institutional structure within which valuable educational practices can be achieved. None of the assumptions of S are tenable today. With his splendid sensitivity to the nation's "instincts," Conant knows all of that. He still offers his own projections as the ground to which the brave and the wise may repair. But he no longer means it.

CONCLUSION

Conant's career as educational statesman possibly illustrates some very profound and pervasive pattern inherent in the dialectic of the universe, but it is only a possibility. What is patent in his career is the following: Having assumed the presidency of Harvard

University in the very depths of the Great Depression, Conant gradually began to formulate a vision of an American System of schools, one in which any boy anywhere in the country realistically might aspire to enter Harvard, and no barriers other than the relative strength of his own energy and academic talent in competition with the other boys of the nation would stand between him and his goal. This vision of a System became a touchstone for Conant's major work as policy-maker. Following that vision he early rejected Fascism, he strove to bring public education up to the level of the best private schools, he formulated a conception of leadership consistent with social democracy, and he developed the open, public, and unfinished nature of scientific truth as a basis on which an open, public, and ever-unfinished school System could be built. His ideas were only beginning to take form when World War II broke out, and Conant lent his agile mind and loyal heart to the service of his country. Suddenly the Cold War was upon us, and Conant's talents were again called on to serve the nation's interest. When at last Conant could give up his duties as ambassador-extraordinary to the world community of scientists, to the competing economic interests in this country, and finally to the West German Republic and return to his vision of an American System of schools, his vision had somehow disintegrated. His very success in making himself a living embodiment of the national interest rendered him incapable of the higher thought necessary to articulate and expand an educational ideal. So he came back, and gathered facts, and offered recommendations, and attended conferences, and listened carefully, and wrote reports.

How instructive it would be if Conant had the talent of inwardness and could tell us how he viewed his own mental changes over the past third of a century! Unfortunately, he has not that talent. If he had, it would have appeared in his contribution to the Credo Series, a collection of the personal views of distinguished men, edited by Ruth Nanda Anshen. Conant felt embarrassment, as is clearly seen in his remark that any attempt to articulate his guiding principles would have to be regarded, "in the light of modern psychology," more as fiction than fact.[35] What we should like to know is just what fiction appears most factual to Conant right now, how that fiction differs from the one he believes he might have written on assuming the presidency of Harvard, on the eve of Hiroshima, on his first postwar visit to Berlin, on first taking up the unending task of examining and criticizing American schools. Instead of that interesting and possibly enlightening fiction, we get a truism—that there are two modes of thought, the empirical-inductive and the theoretical-deductive, both of which are important and deserving of balanced development in a nation's leadership class.

Besides that commonplace, we do get some interesting facts from the history of science. Indeed, from the genuine excitement generated by his recounting of Thomas Midgeley's invention of an antiknock gasoline, we can see the real set of Conant's mind. Perhaps the tragedy is that his college, his nation, and his own Puritan conscience pulled him to vocations other than teaching science.

ANTICLIMAX

How, then, is one to evaluate Conant's total contribution to the literature of educational policy? The answer is that one is not. Instead, one is to learn from Conant to see the *need* for a new polity, defined by new and higher standards of argument and discourse.

Earlier it was pointed out that the System grew out of a marriage between Educationists and Academics. Conant's role may be likened to a preacher at that wedding. He was responsible neither for the compelling forces which brought Academic and Educationist together nor for the constitutional incompatibility in their union. But in his ceremonial function, he did provide them social sanction, practical advice of a very helpful sort, and a vision toward which they jointly could strive. As a visionary, Conant is not compelling. Conant can see very young children from all races, religions, and economic classes coming together in primary schools, thence advancing on to comprehensive secondary schools in programs which ignore the student's origin in order to maximize abilities—academic and otherwise. Having achieved the highest education which their native talents permit, unrestricted by all extraneous factors, each of these young men and women leave the System to take on the roles and duties of citizens in a free democracy and workers in a competitive economy; that is, the System prepares educated members of our political and economic tradition which now finds itself in a protracted world struggle against communism. How sane and sensible this sounds, how like the world we read about in the newspapers!

How unlike anything real or serious. I have given reasons for holding that, in relation to this vision of things, Conant has not provided and could not provide rationally compelling arguments for educational policy. But is not Conant's vision itself singularly uninspiring? About it I say only what Jean Giraudoux had Helen say to Hector when the latter demanded that she forsake Paris and do the sane, sensible act of returning to Menelaus: "It may happen as you say, but I cannot picture it in my mind with color and clarity."

Notes

JAMES BRYANT CONANT

Works of Conant referred to in the text, arranged chronologically.

Our Fighting Faith (Cambridge, 1942)

Educational Policies Commission: *Education for ALL American Youth* (Washington, D.C., 1944)

Harvard Committee Objectives of Education in a Free Society: *General Education in a Free Society* (Cambridge, 1945)

(Sachs Lectures) *Public Education and the Structure of American Society* (New York, 1946)

(EDW) *Education in a Divided World* (Cambridge, 1948)

Education and Liberty (New York, 1951)

On Understanding Science (New York, 1951)

Science and Common Sense (New Haven, 1951)

American High School Today (New York, 1959)

The Child, the Parent, and the State (Cambridge, 1960)

(EAT) *The Education of American Teachers* (New York, 1963)

(SEP) *Shaping Educational Policy* (New York, 1964)

1 Two questions constitute one of the more battle-scarred frontiers of educational research: How long does it take to introduce new material into the high school curriculum? How (if at all) can that time be shortened? See Matthew B. Miles, (ed.), *Innovation*

in Education (New York, 1964), especially the editor's opening chapter.

2 Like all significant arguments in educational policy, Conant's ideas cannot be reduced to a simple syllogism. Apparently he intends to show that there are some features in advanced placement which, taken together, constitute sufficient evidence for the conclusion that we are at the end of one era and the beginning of another. Let us diagram a possible form of the argument as follows:

Advanced Placement	*Change of Era*
1. Any organization which cannot provide for nationwide planning of advanced placement programs is incompetent to serve as the major focus of nationwide school policy planning.	i. There is some era of school policy planning, E_1, which has among other characteristics the following:
2. The regional accrediting agencies cannot provide for the nationwide planning of advance placement programs.	ia. Regional accrediting agencies serve as (or in lieu of) foci for nationwide school policy planning.
3. Therefore the regional accrediting agencies are incompetent to serve as major foci for school policy planning.	ib. Regional accrediting agencies reflected only the opinions of the Educationists.
4. Independently of 2., "Advanced Placement Programs" implies "Planning to reflect opinions other than those of Educationists."	ii. It is a distinctive feature of our present era of school policy planning, E_P, that statement 1. (across) must be acknowledged and acted on.
5. Therefore (from 1. and 4.) any organization reflecting only the opinions of the establishment is incompetent to serve as focus of nationwide school policy planning.	iii. Therefore (given 3. and 5. across) E_P is not E_1.

Notice that what is given is a diagram, not an argument. In order to make it into intelligible discourse, one would have to do two things: (a) Provide (or else indicate where and how to secure) evidence to support controversial factual claims such as 1. and 2. Without evidence we really do not know what they mean or how seriously to take them. (b) Clarify the various grammatical modes in the premises. Some are simple empirical claims; some are apparently involved in chains of conceptual implication, e.g. ii.; some premises are historical in character, i.e., involving claims that certain things which were once true are no longer, e.g., ib.

All these different premises have a legitimate, indeed necessary, place in policy arguments, but careful reasoning requires that they be distinguished and used in combinations that *do* imply what it is claimed they imply. Let me reiterate that I am not describing anything erudite or esoteric, but rather a simple common sense notion of what is required for relevant reasoning on an important question.

3 Miles (ed.) *op. cit.* especially Henry M. Brickell: "State Organization for Educational Change: A Case Study and A Proposal" pp. 493-532.

4 Conant (SEP p. 32) heartily endorses the "report of promising practices" approach to educational change, a strategy much favored by the Fund for the Advancement of Education. See Brickell as cited in note 3.

5 See Miles (ed.) *op. cit.* especially pp. 317-328.

6 The word "fallacious" is here used in its strictly logical sense. Note again the criteria listed as (i)–(iv), pp. 73-74. Let us call them C. Note Conant's description of the state departments of education of California and New York (SEP, Chapter 4.) Let us call that description C-NY. Now the claim C-NY uniquely satisfies C means at least that C implies C-NY, if not that C-NY implies C. But C-NY is an empirical description of certain politico-historical facts, while C, especially (i) and (ii) are fundamental moral judgments. But any argument which claims that a set of moral judgments imply a politico-historical description is fallacious. Now if Conant means only that C-NY satisfies *him* better than anything else he has seen or imagined, *that* may be true, but its truth is *about* Conant, not *about* how we ought to organize ourselves for educational planning.

7 Not exclusively in the South either. It is not just coincidence that the repeal of California's anti-discrimination housing law was accomplished by statewide referendum. It was through judicial appeal to the Federal constitution, not through the state legislature, that California moved away from discrimination in housing. See Arthur Krock's column in the *New York Times*, Sunday, May 15, 1966, p. E15.

8   Only an intellectual, corrupted by bad philosophy or the so-called
    sociology of knowledge, would hold that the questions "Is this
    idea true?" and "Would the general acceptance of this idea
    further my self-interest?" are asking the same thing. The point
    of academic training is to bring a *socially* responsible method to
    bear on the truth of ideas, so as *not* to depend on individual con-
    science to distinguish between truth and self-interest. This point
    is developed in Charles Frankel: *The Case for Modern Man.*
    (New York, Harper & Bros., 1956) Chapter V.

9   John S. Waugh, "The Organization of Matter," in Lyman Bry-
    son (ed.), *An Outline of Man's Knowledge of the Modern World*
    (Garden City, 1960). Speaking specifically of organic chem-
    istry and its industrial and medical applications, Waugh says:
    "It took chemistry a long time to discover even the existence
    of these complex puzzles, and we still understand them only in
    the vaguest way. . . . Most of its generalizations have been em-
    pirical. . . . Clearly this is a laborious process, which requires a
    scientist with imagination and a capacious memory that can be
    tapped for obscure bits of information in response to the slightest
    hints." (pp. 252-253) Cf. Philipp Frank: *Philosophy of Science*
    (Englewood Cliffs, 1957) p. 45. Quoting Herbert Dingle, Frank
    writes: " 'The part played by chemistry in the growth of science
    has been a pragmatical, heuristic one.' " Frank goes on: "To
    speak briefly, chemistry is today a common-sense term, but not a
    scientific term." (The meaning of "common-sense" here might
    very well be Dewey's: knowledge organized to contribute to "use
    and enjoyment.") Conant's first book was a high school text
    *Practical Chemistry: Fundamental Facts and Applications to Mod-
    ern Life* (New York, 1922). The April 3, 1923, issue of the
    Harvard *Crimson* contains Conant's contribution to a series ex-
    plaining the reasons for majoring in various fields. Three-quarters
    of the article is devoted to the intellectual excitement in chemical
    research, and the last quarter (the part headlined by the *Crimson*
    editors) emphasizes the field's practical contribution to industry
    and advises a graduate degree in business school for chemistry
    majors.

10 Conant, concluding the Chandler Lecture, 1932, stated: "We
    may rest confident . . . that the fascinating art of organic chem-
    istry will yield only slowly to the devastating inroads of an exact
    science." (*Industrial & Engineering Chemistry.* XII, p. 374).

11 Conant was not without practical experience in finding support
    for research prior to becoming president of Harvard. Under his

leadership, the Converse Memorial Laboratory had become the nation's leading center for pure research "into the fundamentals of the chemistry of carbon." He was quite effective in convincing donors of "the importance of applications of organic chemistry to medicine or to technology," but he was insistent in his quotation from the inaugural address of Charles W. Eliot (another chemist turned president of Harvard): " 'Science, no more then poetry, owes its best warrant to its utility.' " (Quotations from *Harvard Alumni Bulletin* May 22, 1930; and *The Chemist* XXI, p. 5.)

12 Conant was entirely clear in his own mind on the major lines of the scholarship program as early as 1934: "In my opinion we should aim to have the scholarship funds of this country used in such a way as to enable the high school graduates of real ability to enter our universities irrespective of the financial status of their parents." (Address to the Middle States Association of Colleges and Secondary Schools, printed in the *Harvard Alumni Bulletin,* December, 1934.) Conant has never changed his mind on this matter, nor yet recognized what an enormous task he thus sets for miniscule scholarship funds. By 1938 he had succeeded in establishing Harvard's Merit Scholarship on this basis and was then calling for the nation to adopt a similar policy. See his "The Future of Our Higher Education" *Harper's Magazine,* May, 1938, reprinted in various forms.

13 Very early and very clearly Conant saw the qualities he ought to possess if he were to be adequately equipped for the tasks confronting an educational statesman: "He is honored, respected, and his opinions are heeded not because of any specialized intellectual powers but because of the integrity of his character, the wisdom of his judgments, and his skill in handling human problems." (From his address to the Middle States Association, cited above.) Conant did not intend this as a self-description, but it could well be taken as such.

14 Conant: "Education for a Classless Society: The Jeffersonian Tradition" *Atlantic Monthly* (May, 1940) pp. 598-604. Reprinted in various forms. This article, delivered first at the University of California in the spring of 1940, summarizes a great deal of Conant's political and educational thought of the 1930's and presages his later preoccupation with the conflict between native American "Jeffersonian" radicalism and imported European "Bolshevik" (later "Marxist" or "Soviet") radicalism. It is a well written paper, illumined with graceful similes and pleasant allusions. Its argument is simple and straightforward:

(a) The Jeffersonian tradition is severely threatened by social change. Indeed if things continue the way they have been going, the distinctively American vision of a classless society is as good as dead.

(b) But today we have a new social mechanism—"our newly erected system of public education"—which could be used to restore vitality to that American ideal.

(c) Therefore we ought to lend every effort to see that our schools are instruments of a classless society.

15 *Ibid*, p. 602.

16 Conant: *Our Fighting Faith* (Cambridge, 1942).

17 *Ibid*, p. 8.

18 A very understated version of Harvard's contribution in World War II is given by Conant's successor. See Nathan M. Pusey: *The Age of the Scholar* (Cambridge, 1963) pp. 25-26.

19 David B. Truman: *The Governmental Process* (New York, 1953) p. 435.

20 Conant was very sensitive to the last point. Many times in discussing science in the curriculum, Conant would point to the increasingly technical character of political decisions. Fortunately, as we shall see, his arguments on this line made little difference in the way he proposed to teach science. See his *On Understanding Science* (New York, 1951) p. 19ff.

21 *Public Education and the Structure of American Society* (New York, 1946) Referred to in the text as the Sachs Lecture.

22 It is hard for us to appreciate that "over-education" was only recently considered a serious problem in Western society. It may be considered an aspect of "over-production," a term that became a fashionable one to obscure the causes of the Great Depression. As is true of all economic goods, the amount and kind of education appropriate to a society are functions of that society's technology, rate of growth, and political equilibrium. Cf. Karl Mannheim: *Man And Society In An Age of Reconstruction* (London, 1951) pp. 98-106. Conant much earlier had come to doubt the wisdom of an indiscriminate expansion of education: "I am inclined to think that probably there are too many rather than too few students attending the universities of the country." (*Harpers' Magazine* May, 1938). At that time, a very small proportion of the age group was actually attending universities.

23 Educational Policies Commission: *Education for ALL American Youth* (Washington, D. C., 1944). Harvard Committee on the

Objectives of Education in a Free Society: *General Education in a Free Society* (Cambridge, 1945).

24 A colleague of mine reports that Conant was very subtle, very unobtrusive, and very effective in using the weight of wartime concern for the nation's interest to lever the Harvard faculty toward much needed reforms. To this same colleague, the idea that Conant's successor could or would emulate the feat is ludicrous.

25 Conant: *Education in A Divided World* (Cambridge, 1948) p. 101. (This book will be referred to in the text as EDW)

26 Conant: *The Child, the Parent, and the State* (Cambridge, 1960) p. 1.

27 In an address delivered at the 100th anniversary celebration of the Community Service Society of New York, April 28, 1948, Conant said: ". . . when the free world had once made up its mind to meet each type of military threat of the Soviet Union with a defense against that threat and no longer relied on the magic of atomic bombs, from that moment on, hopes . . . revived." Of course, John Foster Dulles' idea of "massive retaliation" meant precisely going back to reliance on "the magic of atomic bombs." Dulles' formula became official policy (c. 1956) only shortly before Conant resigned from his ambassadorship to the Bundesreich (1957). Conant made many speeches about the problems of using atomic power for the benefit of man, but he never spoke against making nuclear blackmail the cornerstone of our foreign policy.

28 John W. Gardner: *Excellence: Can We Be Equal and Excellent Too?* (New York, 1961) *passim.*

29 *On Understanding Science, op. cit.,* Chapter 1.

30 Cf. B. Paul Komisar and J. E. McClellan: "The Logic of Slogans" in B. O. Smith and R. E. Ennis (eds.): *Language and Concepts in Education* (Chicago, 1961) Chapter XIII.

31 Conant: *Education and Liberty* (New York, 1951).

32 Conant: *Science and Common Sense* (New Haven, 1951) p. vi. This same "tactics and strategy of science" became the focus of the beautifully done Harvard Case Histories in Experimental Science.

33 It would be far too digressive to pursue Conant's philosophy of science. It is probably very good philosophy of science to have come from an active university president and international statesman, and very naive if judged on other grounds. Conant always claims that he is *not* doing philosophy. He seems quite convinced

that one can handle the really technical questions in philosophy of science—e.g., What is the difference between a concept and a fact? Or how do time variables function in scientific statements?—by ignoring all the analytical work that philosophers have done. For him, the word "philosophy" means something like "personal commitment." He uses the expression "a philosopher in his most philosophic moments" as approximately synonymous with "a fool at his most most foolish." (*Science and Common Sense*, p. 237) One looks in vain in his bibliography for references to the standard works and arguments on the questions he treats. But most of this can be forgiven, for his writings contain the critical insights into the history of science that could come only from a man with Conant's breadth of experience in the world and depth of experience in the laboratory.

34 That statement, taken in one sense, is quite unfair to Conant for Conant's writings on educational politics have a sense of wider perspective and human compassion that is noticeably lacking in so many writings on this subject. Two of the books on educational politics appearing in 1964 are illustrative of just this point. Ralph B. Kimbrough: *Political Power and Educational Decision-Making* (Chicago, 1964) focuses primarily on the local school system, together with the local political system in which it operates. Nicholas A. Masters, Robert H. Salisbury, and Thomas H. Eliot: *State Politics and the Public Schools* (New York, 1964) is, as its title indicates, a study of state level politics, particularly Missouri, Illinois, and Michigan. The first is dreary beyond measure; Kimbrough is one more example of that awful tendency in the empirical social sciences to confuse metaphors—in this case "power" and "power structure"—with literal descriptions of human actions (not to deny that in the hands of gifted men, such metaphors can be revealing). Masters *et al.* are better writers, and their case studies, which do not have to be disguised, carry greater verisimilitude. But even so (and even though Masters himself did a great deal of the research on which Conant's *Education of American Teachers* and *Shaping Educational Policy* was based) their metaphysics is limited in a way Conant's never is. Conant *knows* that the particular struggles over local budget and administrative control are of interest precisely because they are part of a larger reality that involves the System, the Nation, and the course of human history. This wider perspective and an ability to hear the authentic voice of the other man shine, albeit dimly, through all his writings. But since he does not bring out this per-

spective and compassion explicitly so that others can criticize him on those points, he ends up in the same category with Kimbrough, Masters *et al.* In that category his work suffers by comparison with that of his intellectual and spiritual inferiors.

35   *Two Modes of Thought: My Encounters With Science and Education* (New York, 1964) p. XXVI. Ruth Nanda Anshen's essay on "The Credo Series" appears in this volume as pages VII to XXIV. A sentence quoted at random from Miss Anshen's essay will illustrate her style.

"*The Credo Series* submits that the universe itself is a vast entity where man will be lost if it does not converge in the person; for material forces or energies, or impersonal ideals, or scientifically objectified learning are meaningless without their relevance for human life and their power to disclose, even in the dark tendencies of man's nature, a law transcending man's arbitrariness." (p. IX). Following an introduction of this sort, Conant should have felt no embarrassment in exposing the fictions of his life, or anything else for that matter.

3

Theodore Brameld and the Architecture of Confusion

Why bother with Theodore Brameld? One could well argue that Brameld's proposals for educational policy and his arguments in support of them are no more relevant to the present educational situation than are Horace Mann's arguments from phrenology. The comparison is valid in that both today represent historical oddities having little relation to the actualities of changing educational policies. It is invalid in that Horace Mann's beliefs, however eccentric from the point of view of modern psychology, were once of genuine import in determining educational policy. Brameld's contemporary eccentricities are merely curiosities.

The argument against treating Brameld seriously could add that they are not very enlightening even as curiosities. It is not as though Brameld had built some splendid edifice of ideas, the architecture of which justifies careful study for itself alone, whatever its relevance or irrelevance to political reality. One can use that argument for giving serious attention to the great canon of educational philosophy from Plato through John Dewey. An attempt to study the structure of Brameld's thought resembles nothing so much as B'rer Rabbit's encounter with Tar Baby.

So why bother with Theodore Brameld? One cannot even maintain that his thought is influential in the philosophy of education, much less in the practice and politics of schooling. Primarily, Brameld's ideas represent only Brameld. Despite the emphasis given "the group," "consensus," "community of persuasion," etc., in his writings, he stands pretty much alone, being neither a part of nor an effective critic of the major trends in the evolution of American education. He has found few followers who would take on his self-assigned label "reconstructionist." Whatever his theory may hold, in practice Brameld is not an organization man.

But, in part, that is why Brameld is worth studying. In fact, if Brameld had not existed it would have been necessary to invent him; he is necessary in the same way that God and the Austro-Hungarian Empire were necessary. Like God, Brameld gives personal representation to spiritual forces which, considered as abstractions, are incomprehensible or, at any rate, incommunicable. Like the Austro-Hungarian Empire, Brameld provides the most improbable concatenation of contradictory historical residues, giving them at least the shadow of life far beyond their natural term. One cannot understand the language of the toughest school administrator talking about the most concrete, brick-and-mortar question, like washroom maintenance, without understanding all that Brameld pulls together in the crazy-quilt he calls Reconstructionism. Brameld has been in the forefront of every "forward-looking movement" of the past thirty years in American education, and he has never had the prolonged trial of administrative leadership to befog his theoretical ardor. Like the System itself, Brameld does not believe in disbelief: Anything he ever thought true he still thinks true; his oldest idea will be found somewhere in his latest writing— caught up, re-worded, and added to his newest belief. Without the personal integument Brameld gives them, we could never accept the co-viability of the elements in his (and the System's) intellectual inventory.

This neither asserts nor implies that Brameld's thought deserves to be treated as a chamber of horrors. On the contrary, among the elements held in uneasy suspension in Brameld's philosophy are some of the most valuable in the American tradition of educational policy. Our policy arguments would be far poorer than they are without these elements, and Brameld is quite right in fearing that the current trends in school politics threaten their extinction. (See *Education for the Emerging Age: Newer Ends and Stronger Means,* "Prelude," hereafter abbreviated as EEA.)* But Brameld's language so easily lends itself to caricature that it is very difficult to give a fair characterization of his thought. In trying to be fair to Brameld and to the genuine values he expresses, one is forced to adopt something like the medieval *disputatio* as the form for treating his works. In that spirit, then, the presentation of Brameld's thought consists of an overview of the philosophy which permeates his thought; a rather full exposition of his actual proposals for education; and an outline of the defensive tactics open to Brameld in the face of attack. It is easy enough but fruitless to point out errors in detail in Brameld's works; what is needed is a full comprehension of the way of thinking and arguing which he exemplifies. That *way* has to be caught up and transcended before an adequate polity can emerge.

I. A WAY OF LOOKING AT THE WORLD

Brameld's proposals for educational policy are embedded in a total philosophy of man and history. According to that philosophy, called Reconstructionism, the human species is now at a crisis point in its long struggle to satisfy basic physical and spiritual wants. Technological power now makes it possible for men to acquire the goods necessary for a fully human life, but that power can be used equally well to destroy life altogether. Indeed, present political and economic institutions throughout the world are based upon the destructive, exploitative uses of technological power. Unless those institutions can be reconstructed so that they serve the needs of all the people rather than the vested interests of a few, the inertial drift of the world toward war and despotism is almost inevitable.

But the impact of most revolutionary movements is as dangerous as the conditions they seek to correct. Force and fraud used against force and fraud can produce only more force and fraud; only the power of uncoerced consensus among free men can break the ever-narrowing spiral leading to the extinction of the human species. The search for free consensus has deep historical roots in religion

* References to Brameld's work appear at the end of the chapter.

and philosophy; Jesus, Socrates, and Buddha together with their followers scattered widely in time and space have held forth the ideal of a community of men based on freely given commitments. Today, however, this is more than an ideal. It is a necessity for survival. The great fact that we *must* have cultural reconstruction is penetrating the hearts and minds of men and women throughout the world. Armed with the democratic vision, drawing strength from the race's deepest desires for peace and freedom, the Reconstructionist takes his place in the battle against fear, ignorance, and narrow self-interest.

Reconstruction, like charity, begins at home; that is, only by constructing a new social personality in its young can a society move toward the profound cultural reconstruction needed in this age of crisis. The human animal is not born with the ability to participate fully and effectively in the processes of a free and democratic community. But the casual and unplanned socialization procedures found in homes and schools today neither teach those democratic skills nor build a desire to use them. On the contrary, as anthropologists can easily show, our usual methods of inducting new members into the culture tend to reproduce in youngsters the same competitiveness and anxiety characteristic of today's adults. These traits, indeed, constitute the psychological consequences of institutions based on economic exploitation.

Thus, in the philosophy of Reconstructionism, the various facets of education must be seen both as ends and as means. Reconstructionism holds that the highest value for man is the full realization of his natural potentialities; hence it follows that education is not only a means toward some further end, education itself is a constituent of man's highest end. To be educated in the fullest sense *means* to have learned to participate fully and actively in the dynamics of cultural reconstruction, liberating full powers of individual creativity and overcoming the anxiety of alienation. But the barriers to the achievement of this end are not all inside the individual; the present system of economic and political institutions militates against education in the fullest sense. Thus a reconstructed system of education is also a means, an indispensable means, to the more general cultural reconstruction which will permit the full flowering of personality.

Note that the emphasis is to be put on "a reconstructed culture," not just on "education." The new members of the culture must learn to project utopian goals, freeing themselves from the constricting, ideological modes of thought which dominate the mass media, most churches, and nearly all present educational institutions. They must learn to look upon their peers as fellow participants in the most dangerous and yet most potentially fruitful experiment in the history of mankind: to test whether history itself can be wrested from chaos and brought under conscious, deliberate control. Reconstruction first requires an educational revolution; for the present system of schooling forces each youngster to look upon his peers as rugged competitors for the privilege of exploiting rather than being exploited. Knowledge—the sciences and arts which constitute the highest cultural achievement of the race—has become merely a counter in the pointless competitive game of social and economic advancement. A reconstruction is necessary to restore knowledge to its rightful place in human life: Knowledge is the great resource left by previous generations to aid the next generation in its struggle to avoid being the last.

A reconstructed education is one which will enable the new members of the human race, without regard for present national boundaries, to share freely and collectively in the projection of utopian goals for all mankind, in the most careful testing and refinement of those goals in the light of evidence from all the arts and sciences, and, finally, in action to achieve the goals to which they have become committed by thought, study, and group decision. Far from being utopian in the pejorative sense of impractical or unfeasible, only a reconstructed education can possibly meet the challenge of our crisis age.

The next step, of course, must be to say more concretely what is to be *done*. The Reconstructionist, at this stage in his argument, refuses to be bound either by the present administrative structure or the legal and financial disabilities under which present schools operate. His task, for the moment, is to project an imaginative vision of what education could do to create better men and women and a better world for them to live in.

Brameld's proposals for education begin with a new system for universal, compulsory schooling. He would have us create a new secondary school as the central and dominant feature of the educational program. This four-year school, serving all young men and women between the ages of seventeen and twenty, would be organized around the study of our great social problems. Preparation for it would require a three-level elementary system, beginning for some children at age two, for the rest at age three-and-a-half. Higher education would be concerned primarily with the pursuit of research on the social problems treated in the secondary school, but it would also allow for the liberal and technical education of all who seemed capable of profiting from such study.

These proposals for the system itself contain nothing revolutionary, but Reconstructionism's proposals for what is to go on *within* the schools are strikingly different from current practices. These proposals do not fit neatly in the traditional categories of curriculum, administration, and teaching methods. Let us, nonetheless, summarize them in these standard categories so that we can turn to the more important matter: Reconstructionism's *reasons* why these proposals, or something similar, should be adopted.

Curriculum: Using the metaphor of the wheel, Brameld envisions for each year of the secondary school a central hub of study devoted to some issue or aspect of the politico-economic situation. Leading into the hub would be "spokes" of discussion groups, in which "Students pursue various issues arising from the central area of the year, with primary concern for their more individualized choices and interests." (*Toward a Reconstructed Philosophy of Education*, p. 216, hereafter abbreviated as TRPOE.) In addition, there is to be opportunity for specialized academic and vocational training, the amount and degree of specialization increasing in succeeding years.

The hub of the first year is devoted to establishing the proper motivation for this different *kind* of education, as well as to inducing a concern for "goals in the sphere of economic-political reconstruction." (TRPOE, p. 218) In succeeding years, the central concern will shift to the place of the sciences and the arts in cultural reconstruction, the role of education and human relations, and, finally, back to the original topic of goals, eventuating hopefully in a determined consensus and readiness to act to achieve the group's projected goals. Along with studies and group activities directly connected to this hub activity, the school will provide a wide range of opportunities for recreational, aesthetic, and intellectual pursuits, always encouraging students to relate their individual interests to socially significant group activities but never insisting that they do so at the expense of personal involvement and creativity.

Brameld says very little about curriculum design for the elementary school or higher education. But he recognizes that in order to be prepared for this kind of secondary education, youngsters would require years of experience in responsible and self-directed group activity. They would need to have known a great deal of freedom, and they must have learned, somehow, that adults are not merely taskmasters but rather fellow participants in the enterprise of learning-making-doing. It is equally clear, even if not explicitly stated, that young men and women who have been through a secondary school of the sort proposed by Reconstructionists will be unwilling to suffer the fragmented and confused curriculum of the ordinary undergraduate college; there also a reconstruction of curriculum to achieve purpose and social significance would necessarily follow.

Administration: Since the system proposed by Brameld is to be one of "schools of the people" (TRPOE, *passim*), it becomes an important part of Reconstructionist doctrine to propose changes in the system of control of education. Present legal and administrative arrangements provide only the *form* of democratic control; the substance of control lies with a minority class and with a bureaucratic structure which is quite unresponsive to the real needs of the people. Three basic changes are required if democratic control is to be achieved. First, the school board—the local, state, or regional agency with ultimate legal responsibility for determining school policy—must represent the actual, divergent political and economic interests to be found in the region served by the board and should represent them proportionally to the size of interest groups in the population. In this way, the chances are increased that a policy consensus established by the school board will represent an actual consensus of values in the population as a whole. At present, of course, the unanimity of a local school board reflects the values of a dominant minority and conceals the value conflicts in the community.

Second, the interested public must be brought into the process of educational planning, more frequently and more intensely than is possible within the official school board itself. A system of councils and committees should be established—media through which parents, teachers, students, and community pressure groups may have the opportunity to participate in the formation of plans and policies. Supplementing the legal authority of the school board, these groups would have power to establish policy for various aspects of the school's activities. Since members of the board would attend and participate in the deliberations of these other groups, the overall policies of the board would be continuously responsive to the beliefs and attitudes of the community at large.

Third, as the administration of the school is definitely restricted to the purely executive function of carrying out the policies set by the school board and appropriate councils, and the board itself is restricted to the purely legislative function of establishing policy, a new range of freedom for students and teachers will be opened. Students gain a collective responsibility for self-government and self-discipline; teachers become fully professional participants in the planning and execution of educational policies, not only by achieving autonomy in matters of professional expertise but also by entering directly into the community of persuasion to establish *policy* at all levels—local to international.

Teaching Methods: Brameld follows the lead of William Heard Kilpatrick and the Progressives in education in shifting the emphasis in discussion of method from teaching to learning.[1] But for Brameld and the Reconstructionists, learning is a normative concept as well as a descriptive concept. Purely behavioristic theories of learning describe only the externals of any learning experience; when educators must decide what kinds of learning to foster and nurture in schools, they must ask toward what *values* the learning is directed. Because social-self-realization is the supreme value in Reconstructionist theory, it follows that *learning* must be organized to contribute to and exemplify that value. There are four phases or characteristics of learning particularly appropriate to the Reconstructionists' theory.

Learning from the study of evidence: From one's own experience and from the experience of others recorded in science, literature, and the arts comes *evidence* relevant to the satisfaction of human wants. As an individual or a group proceeds with the most important educational function—clarifying values and deciding strategies for their achievement—learning from the study of evidence is always logically relevant. Skill, in the planning of learning, however, is needed to make the study of evidence emotionally relevant to the learner. The teacher must have a firm grasp of the dynamics of motivation and problem-solving, and he must be able to relate problems of want-satisfactions of the individual to the great cultural crises from which individual problems derive.

Learning from communication: While any classroom is to some extent the locus of communication, mostly *from teacher to student*, traditional theories of education have been content to leave that process unanalyzed, ineffective, and culturally otiose. Reconstructionists insist that the latest findings from psychology, linguistics, semantics, and propaganda analysis to be applied to promote the effectiveness of classroom communication, remembering always that communication is much more than mere talk. Communication affects and is affected by the "unrational" as well as the rational (TRPOE, pp. 176-178); communication involves non-verbal as well as verbal symbols; it conveys unconscious political and economic attitudes and ideals. All these aspects of the communication process must be recognized, not merely descriptively but normatively, in order that the process may be turned to the achievement of education's utopian product—social consensus.

Learning from agreement: Through participation in the process by which groups strive for consensus, a person learns not only objective facts about the world and the behavior of other persons; he also learns about himself. He learns to defend his own values and ideas, but he learns to recognize that his motivations are often complex and rooted in the unconscious. He learns to accept the discipline of majority rule, even when he finds himself in the dissenting minority, but he also learns the obligation of the minority to keep the channels of persuasion open. Both majority and minority must be committed to the ideal of uncoerced consensus.

Many significant improvements in the art of learning from agreement have been made in the branch of applied social psychology known as group dynamics. In order to use these improvements, the teacher must be willing and able to participate fully as a group member in the process of seeking agreement. Accepting no privileged role for himself and his ideas, the teacher must yet acknowledge an obligation to defend his "partiality," i.e., his personal beliefs and values which *may* differ from those of his students and, if the teacher accepts a Reconstructionist approach to cultural crisis, will certainly differ from the beliefs and attitudes of the dominant minority in this country today.

Learning from action: Commitment to majority agreement means or at least implies readiness to act in defense of the values of the majority. Youngsters of school age, of course, cannot themselves perform the direct political acts necessary to free the majority from the dominant minority, but there is yet much that they *can* do. Beginning with the rules governing the classroom and, as the child grows older, extending to the basic norms of the society as a whole, the community must tap the latent power for commitment and action in every youngster by encouraging full participation in the active life of the widening social world. For *that* latent power is our last best hope for a better world (or any world at all) tomorrow.

If these four methods constitute the core of Reconstructionists' theory of *learning*, it follows that *teaching* for the Reconstructionist is a matter of helping boys and girls and later young men and women to participate in these learning experiences in a balanced mixture appropriate to age and interest. For the very young, more time in school may be devoted to communication than to some of the other methods of learning, while at the secondary level a larger proportion is devoted to learning from the study of evidence. But no absolute dogma may be admitted here; if the teacher is fully committed to Reconstructionist goals and is willing to participate as a member of the group in seeking action to achieve these goals, then the choosing of methods of learning appropriate to the particular interests and needs of the group at the moment may safely be left to the group itself.

Political Strategy: It is clear that Reconstructionism differs from most philosophies of education in its insistence on the need for concrete goals and dedicated commitment to their achievement. But this is no "pie in the sky" philosophy; on the contrary, Reconstructionism also insists that evidence from all sources, particularly from the behavioral sciences, be studied carefully in determining means appropriate and effective for chosen ends. Assuming that the essentials, if not the details of the program outlined above, can be established by consensus as the goal toward which education should strive, two questions naturally arise: How shall we do it? What are the first steps? The Reconstructionist admits these are pertinent questions and attempts to find evidence on which to base an answer. Surveying the history of education, the present political scene, the cultural situation as revealed by the most profound scholars in anthropology and other behavioral sciences, the Reconstructionist educator proposes the following strategy and tactics:

A preponderance, but by no means all, of existing political power is held by a dominant minority in this country. This minority has deeply vested interests in the present economic and political system, in the continuation of the Cold War, in racial and ethnic discrimination, and, most importantly, in a system of education which projects the *status quo* onto the next generation. School boards in general reflect the ideological, backward-looking modes of thought of the dominant minority; so do many school administrators who have not learned to distinguish between service to the community and service to that segment of the community which presently holds economic and political power.

But if the forces opposing educational reconstruction are strong and well-entrenched, there are also powerful counter-forces emerging out of that inchoate majority—the working people of the nation —who will no longer be content to see their values subverted to the interests of a minority. And, despite its obvious imperfections, American democracy *does* permit the formation of majority consensus and it *does* provide means whereby that majority consensus can be politically effective. These facts give faith and direction to the efforts of the Reconstructionist in education. His long-run strategy is to merge with the movement of the majority, adding the Reconstructionist's educational goals to the utopian cultural designs reflecting the ultimate aspirations of mankind. More immediately, his tactics must be to ally the Reconstructionist movement in education to other forward-looking movements in American life, particularly to the labor union movement, the Negro civil rights movement, and the great international movements for world peace and disarmament.

But the first step, of course, is to create a majority consensus in the educational profession itself and a suitable organization to give political weight to that consensus. There can be no compromise on this last point: Organizations which are commended primarily for their genteel civility and acceptability to present authority figures can play little part in advancing educational, much less cultural, reconstruction. Affiliation with organized labor is an obvious requirement for an effective teacher organization; but it is not enough, for the Reconstructionist can never forget his ideal of the great consensus including the entire community, nation, and mankind. True to its educational mission, the teaching profession must strive to persuade even the entrenched business and industrial leaders to join that great consensus.

From the point of view of basic political philosophy, the Reconstructionist believes that the minds of men are free. As more and more men and women enter the cooperative effort to establish long-range social goals, as they learn to expound and defend their beliefs at the same time that they learn to listen to the exposition and defense of others, even the shackles of inherited prejudice and vested interest can be broken.

In the community as in the school, Reconstructionist educators do not shun the use of myth, slogan, and propaganda in giving impetus and direction to social consensus; but they insist that the avenues to inquiry and criticism be kept open at all times. In our age of crisis, we cannot wait until all the evidence is in before we commit ourselves, but we must never set barriers to prevent the introduction of new evidence into the process of social deliberation. Committed to his utopian goals, the Reconstructionist yet recognizes the need for new thought, new evidence at every stage in the emerging consensus. Still, he will *not* allow the conservative to win out by simply and forever reiterating his plea "for more evidence." Audacity based on solid evidence and wide commitment is a necessity in this time of crisis.

These, then, are the main elements in the Reconstructionist's proposals for schooling. They will be treated in more detail and in a spirit of critical detachment later. At the moment the presentation continues, in a purely expository fashion, to show the standard objections to this view and how Brameld answers those objections.

Any dynamic, radical philosophy will create its own opposition, and in this Reconstructionism is no exception. Some of the criticisms are thoughtful and well-intentioned even when mistaken; others are patently the consequence of strange psychological or political motives. Efforts toward consensus with the latter have little chance of success.

Since Reconstructionism has been expounded, attacked, and defended for some years now, one can see the major lines of rational argument and meet them. Four will be discussed briefly: the charge of totalitarianism, the charge of political naiveté, the charge of anti-intellectualism, and the charge of anti-individualism.

Since the long-run goal of Reconstructionism is to establish a total design for the culture, a consensus shared at the level of all mankind, critics may object that the approach is totalitarian. This criticism would be merely a play on words except that the critic can point out that Reconstructionism, like certain totalitarian philosophies and unlike the more individualistic American Progressivism, deliberately aims to create a social commitment in every youngster. Reconstructionism wants to see the democratic faith, exalted in myth and ritual, become a life-giving force joining all the peoples of the world in their common effort to achieve peace, freedom, and plenty. Affirmation, not negation, is the dominant mood of Reconstructionism. If the critic wants to attack the philosophy for *this* commitment to totality, he may, indeed, cry "totalitarian."

But then the issue must be sharply separated from totalitarianism in its usual sense. For the Reconstructionist rejects absolutely *any* interference with freedom of thought, *any* use of terror or force for political intimidation, *any* attempt to lessen the worth or dignity of any group in the nation—whether such violations of democratic liberties come from the Right, the Left, or (the more likely danger in this country) from the dominant Center. Every man and woman has the right, indeed the obligation, to participate fully in the consensus-seeking process; education's primary task is to make that participation informed, effective, and growth-promoting. Moreover, no one has any special political rights, especially no right to deny the rights of others, however few and unpopular the others may be. Even today, Reconstructionists can be found in the forefront of the fight to secure full civil and academic rights for Negroes, Communists, and others whose views or appearance set them apart from the majority. Thus the charge of totalitarianism must be considered at best misplaced. From some quarters, this attack is simply one more effort to obfuscate and defeat majority will.

There is a common meaning of "utopian" which implies inattention to the realities of life. Enough has been said already to indicate that the Reconstructionist's commitment to utopian goals does not prevent his being tough-minded and realistic in his appraisal of the political means necessary to carry out his program. The way is not easy, but an age of crisis demands faith as well as realism. The naive or sentimental utopian who would forget the means in order to contemplate his beloved goal is unintelligent, but no more so, in the final analysis, than the pseudo-realist who so concentrates on means that he forgets his goal. Reconstructionism recognizes the truth in the pragmatic claim that ends cannot be judged apart from the means necessary to achieve them, but Reconstructionists also remember what Dewey and his followers too often forgot: that means are truly *means* only if selected and fashioned to achieve some chosen end. Hence only Reconstructionism can offer an educational program which provides learning both for ends *and* means. When all this is said, it is clear that "utopian" is now a word of praise, not a condemnation. Indeed, given the growing "movement" in this country and its correlative movements throughout the world, the charge of naiveté is most appropriately leveled against those who would deny the political potency of utopian thought.

Less often in print than in conversation, one hears the charge that Reconstructionism may be acceptable as a social philosophy but not as an educational philosophy since it makes no special place for the cultivation of the intellect, a requirement in any genuinely *educational* program. This charge would be more valid if the critic were willing to define "intellect" in terms that are really relevant to the age of crisis in which we live. For the Reconstructionist never denies the importance of disciplined thought, by which *he* means skill in the use of generalizations and abstractions, the study of evidence from the arts and humanities as well as the sciences. On the contrary, his whole educational program is specifically a *design* to make these intellectual skills and habits integral to the self-development of every boy and girl, just as far as individual ability will allow. But the Reconstructionist believes that these learnings, if they are to be truly *learned*, must be motivated socially and psychologically.

Perhaps, then, it is nearer to the truth to hold that the Reconstructionist's educational program defines what it means to be "intellectual" in these times. It no longer makes sense to believe that knowledge is the passive acceptance of a pre-existent reality. Nor is it feasible to define knowledge merely as the outcome of individual problem-solving, as it all too often reduced itself in the thought of many Progressive educators. The Reconstructionist holds that knowledge is a social achievement, that it rightfully belongs to all, that it must be used in reconstructing the entire culture, that truth and reality change as men collectively transform their environment to make it better serve their values.

Thus the Reconstructionist's definition of "intellect" is provided a basis in ontology, epistemology, and axiology. His pedagogical suggestions for school policy recognize the necessity for motivation and "prehension" if the student's active intellect is to be aroused and directed toward worthy purposes. When attacked as being anti-intellectual, the Reconstructionist cannot avoid the suspicion that his critic is more concerned to preserve a class monopoly amidst the snobbish trappings of intellectual-*ism* than to extend knowledge and skill to all the people.

Anti-individualism: In refuting the charge of glorifying the group at the expense of individualism, the Reconstructionist can also demonstrate the open, growing character of his own philosophy. Perhaps in its earliest formulations, Reconstructionism was rightly subject to criticism on the grounds that it under-valued individuality. But in response to that criticism, particularly that stemming from a growing number of existentialists, Reconstructionism incorporated a new emphasis on the problem of meaning in individual lives. Both existentialist and Reconstructionist believe that man must choose his destiny, that the pre-existent, being-in-itself does not determine *man's* being but rather opens possibilities for men and women to achieve fully human stature through and by acting on personal decision. From the existentialists, Reconstructionism has learned as well to face the dread and anxiety of a world without absolutes—a world which in itself has no meaning nor purpose, only potentiality. Each human being must create his own meaning and purpose, even as he confronts his own finitude and ultimate non-being. The unity of mankind is not only a fact, physical, biological, and social; it is also a spiritual force sensed by each individual who shares the ultimately tragic human condition.

(*Education as Power,* pp. 80-85 *et passim,* hereafter abbreviated as EAP.)

Thus it is distinctive of Reconstructionism, among all the major philosophies of education, that it has the capacity to grow in response to reasoned criticism. Far from neglecting the individual, only Reconstructionism has recognized and incorporated into itself the great, tragic insights of existentialism, insights all the more necessary as each of us, ultimately alone and silent, faces the meaningless terror of nuclear holocaust.

In closing his case, the Reconstructionist reiterates his original plea: Ours is an open universe; here is an open, growing philosophy of education. It needs, it welcomes, creative, critical inquiry into all its social and educational dimensions. There are only two requirements for joining this great collective task: a profound commitment to making the future of mankind better than the past, a willingness to put one's most treasured beliefs and ideals actively into the community of persuasion, that they may there grow and change even as the spiritual commonwealth grows from their addition.

II. BRAMELD AND POLICY

It is not difficult to imitate Brameld's grammar and rhetoric, but it is difficult to do full justice to his thought when forcing it into any logical mold for policy argument because Brameld is profoundly uninterested in educational policy. The key symptom is his off-handed, parenthetical definition of the term: "('Policy' is here defined as any consensus about values—that is, want-satisfactions—generalized in political purposes of a given period and given culture, and embracing the widest possible group for which the policy is intended.)" (TRPOE, pp. 130-131) This is nonsense, of course. It is true, as will be shown, that central to many of Brameld's *recommendations* for educational policy are his beliefs about policy-making itself, i.e., that the process obey the canons of consensus and emphasize the satisfaction of common human wants, etc. But he cannot literally *define* "policy" according to his own as-yet-unrealized recommendation. His casual attitude toward his own definition is seen clearly when he writes later: "School boards ... are under obligation to formulate only such policies as reflect values agreed upon by the majority. That they have not been attuned to the values of the majority in the past is evident from the gap between too many of the policies they have endorsed and the educational needs of the people." (TRPOE, p. 277) If Brameld really intended his definition of "policy" to be taken seriously, the first sentence in the passage quoted would contain a redundancy; for to be under an obligation to formulate policy would be an obligation to reflect values agreed upon by the majority (the meaning, in part, of "consensus"). The second sentence would be a contradiction: If a school board has endorsed a *policy*, then, by Brameld's definition, it has endorsed a consensus about values ". . . embracing the widest possible group for which the policy is intended."

To show a contradiction between Brameld's definition and his use of the term "policy" may appear petty. In one sense it is, for one soon learns in reading Brameld to give up asking exactly what he means; it is hard enough to comprehend approximately what he has in mind. On the other hand, terms that are in any way central to his thinking are used by Brameld with carefully guarded consistency. For example, he defines the word "values" as interchangeable with the expression "want-satisfactions." The latter notion is itself quite fuzzy and vague, but the idea of value is important enough to Brameld that he takes the trouble to define and use the term "value" consistently. Policy simply is not that important to him, hence the nagging doubt that one has done Brameld justice when forcing his thought into the mold of policy argument. But since he insists that philosophy of education *is* philosophy of politics,[2] a critic cannot avoid treating his ideas as if they were proposals for policy. In Section III of this chapter, we will have a chance to ask what they are instead of policy.

However, if Brameld wants his recommendations to be considered as proposals for policy, then surely he is obligated to provide some reasons why they should be adopted. Strangely, he offers no reasons whatsoever. He does discuss the cultural crisis and educational responsibilities for meeting it, but that line of talk can provide reason for accepting these proposals as policy only if there is reason to believe (a) that the social and cultural diagnosis is correct and (b) that the proposed educational program is an adequate remedy for the ills. I shall argue below that Brameld's conception of crisis is absurd, but it is the complete absence of any argument on question (b) that gives the game away. Contrast Brameld's (a) and (b) with Conant, who argues (*The American High School Today*, p. 69):

(a)' Present two-year programs of foreign language are largely waste since students who complete them have not advanced sufficiently to achieve independent and continuing mastery of the language, and

(b)' Extending all foreign language programs to at least four years would greatly increase the number of students who master at least one foreign language; therefore,

(c)' It is recommended as policy that all programs in foreign languages be at least four years in duration.

Now Brameld claims, quite rightly I believe, that Conant's argument is incomplete: "And in the perspective of our age, we have every reason to wonder whether the vast total of curriculum time (at least 20 per cent) earmarked by Conant for foreign language study could not, for many of the ablest minority, be devoted much more rewardingly to the study of other matters—of, for example, the explosive problem of survival of the human race itself." (EEA, p. 59) For Conant does not merely recommend, contingently, that *if* we offer foreign language, we should offer at least four years of it. Conant recommends that for "the ablest minority" (by which he *usually* means those more than one standard deviation above the mean on any well-normed IQ test) a four-year sequence of foreign language study be expected. (Conant is too wise to say "required.") Then Brameld is correct: "we have every reason to wonder" *why* these high school youngsters should study French, Spanish, or German instead of studying "the problems of survival" or instead of playing pleasurable erotic games. Brameld is also correct (EEA, pp. 59-60) in arguing that Conant cannot appeal to the fact that increased ease and frequency of international contacts make a knowledge of a foreign language more *useful.* For one doesn't know at age fourteen *which* language he will use later. And as Brameld points out, we now have pedagogical tools such that we can teach a person a working knowledge of the particular language he needs right when he needs it—and much more efficiently than in a four year high school sequence.

Conant knows all this as well as Brameld. He (Conant) has two basic defenses for the inclusion of foreign language study in the curriculum (i) Only persons who early in their lives really *master* a foreign language will be able to understand the structure of language and to master subsequent languages as needed. (ii) Success in foreign language study in high school is an excellent measure of general academic talent; therefore studying a foreign language provides a source of data needed for effective guidance and counseling. (See Conant's *The Child, the Parent, and the State,* Chapters III and IV.)

Brameld does not discuss Conant's argument (i) as such, but from what he says on other things, it seems likely that he would call it an "essentialist" type statement, reflecting a "training of the mind" type psychology. Brameld does discuss (ii), claiming, again rightly, that "academic talent" is defined as success in a certain kind of curriculum while the question at issue is the justification of that very curriculum itself. Hence (ii) is a case of *petitio principii.*

This interchange between Brameld and Conant is introduced not to decide the rightness or wrongness of Conant's proposals for foreign language study, but to demonstrate two other points: First, Brameld *does* understand what it is to be a *reason* for a policy proposal; he *does* know how to spot the absence of reasons and how to insist that reasons be provided before proposals are accepted. But, second, Brameld does *not* apply that understanding and logical skill when advancing his own proposals. No one is ever quite so critical of his own ideas as he is of others'. But that is not as important as the fact that the *form* of argument employed by Conant positively invites asking for reasons in logical succession while the *form* used by Brameld really inhibits it. Let us see why:

Suppose, *mirabile dictu,* that a responsible educator should agree with Brameld's diagnosis of cultural crisis. This mythical educator might well ask Brameld, "Why should we institute a four-year secondary school for young men and women seventeen to twenty? Would not a three-year school do just as well? Alternatively, perhaps four years are not enough; shouldn't we make it at least five, or preferably six years in length?" Brameld, as a proponent of the four-year school, is not obligated to provide absolutely conclusive reasons for preferring the last four years of the second decade of life as the period of secondary education, but if he expects anyone to take him seriously, he must give *some* reasons, at least enough to enable his reader to see what kind of reasoning is appropriate.

What factors ought to control the length of secondary schooling? Is it an economic function of national wealth, need for manpower, need for technical skill, etc.? Should the decision be influenced by psychological factors—readiness, interests, talents, drives, motives, etc. Which? What about sociological or anthropological determinants? Are social class differences in when and how adolescents leave home relevant to the length of secondary education? Why or why not?

All this is so elementary that Brameld cannot be altogether unaware of it. Indeed, throughout his writings, one can find remarks attesting to his belief that philosophers of education should pay careful attention to the "behavioral sciences." One might expect that when Brameld recommends that secondary education take place in the years seventeen to twenty, he would tell us what evidence from what sciences led him to that square number. But no. Sensing the need to provide at least some sort of justification, Brameld uses two very different kinds of statements, mingling them so that the great logical gap between them is partly concealed.

Statement (1) "Nevertheless, given stimulating but by no means impossible conditions, boys and girls of about seventeen years can and should understand the elementary attributes of a system where economic planning, for example, has become indispensable." (EEA, p. 185) In the earlier edition of the same essay, "sixteen" appeared in place of "seventeen"; the rest of the sentence was unchanged. (*Ends and Means in Education: A Midcentury Appraisal*, p. 211, hereafter abbreviated as EME.) I am willing to grant the truth of Statement (1) with either figure; indeed one may substitute "seven" or "twelve," or "thirty-seven years and four months" and its truth would still be granted. Any reasonably effective teacher, faced with conditions which are at least better than "impossible," can teach, with a depth and intensity reflecting the age and ability of the students, the elements of economic analyses so as to show, "for example," a Keynesian explanation of business cycles. Statement (1) is, we may say, certified by common sense, and while any intelligent man would be willing to reject it if *very* strong evidence from research studies should be brought against it, one would not ordinarily quibble about it in the absence of evidence. But, equally,

Statement (1) is no reason for holding that sixteen or seventeen is a *particularly* appropriate time for studying the elements of economic analysis. Hence Statement (1) is no reason, nor even a miniscule part of a reason, for holding that a four-year, seventeen to twenty, secondary school should be adopted as policy.

Now let us consider another statement which is supposed to be a *reason* for the policy proposed:

Statement (2) "Students between seventeen and twenty years are, or at least are capable of being, young adults. They are on the threshold of citizenship, marriage, vocation. To them the issues of culture are or could be made very real. Moreover, if the elementary schools are reasonably successful in developing concern with important issues of contemporary society junior college students can and should be sufficiently mature to participate effectively in such units as we have described." (EME, p. 124; EEA, p. 169)

Is Statement (2) true? The part about being "young adults" is not obviously false, but it does not mean very much. "Threshold?" Some are already over the marriage and vocation part, while "citizenship" is rather vague. Others face very long professional training programs before these other roles can be undertaken. "Issues of culture made real"? Those acquainted with present schools will probably demur. The "Problems of Democracy" course so prevalent in the social studies program of the public high schools does not seem very "real"; in fact the whole social studies sequence has a relatively hard time in making itself "real," even to youngsters who stand "on the threshold." Of course, *if* the elementary school prepared them sufficiently, they would be prepared sufficiently; but that part of Statement (2), being a tautology, conveys no new information.

In short, Statement (2), in contrast to (1), contradicts common, everyday experience. It may be true, but we have to be shown its truth. It would take many experimental studies, holding variables under careful control, to convince the ordinary teacher, parent, employer, etc., that youngsters of that age would find discussions of cultural goals very real.

(It will not do for Brameld to point to his exciting days in Floodwood, Minnesota. [*Design for America, passim,* hereafter abbreviated as DFA.] Brameld is a man of extraordinary personal charm and vitality. He also possesses a genuinely religious attitude toward the ideas and practices he propounds. With all this going for him, *he* could succeed, I shouldn't doubt, in making Recon-structionism real to Afrikaaners. His experience will not count as an experiment.)

The common belief, one would judge, is that being "on the threshold" makes most young men and women very impatient with talk and very eager to get on with it. This common belief may not be correct; it may not even be as common as supposed. But in the logic of the case, the responsibility is on Brameld to produce a *reason* for choosing four years of secondary education, particularly the four years from seventeen to twenty. I conclude, therefore, that Statement (2), the heart of which is this term "threshold," will not serve as a good reason supporting Brameld's policy proposals. For Statement (2) just is not true; at least no evidence has been offered that would lead anyone to believe it true.

If one examines the context in which Statement (2) appears, it will be at least plausible to interpret Brameld as pleading that we ought to *make* the statement true, i.e., that we ought to recon-struct elementary education as well as the social and pedagogical conditions of secondary schools so that Statement (2) *becomes* true. In that case, the statement is part of the policy proposals, and the reader is still entitled to a reason why these proposals should be adopted. Let us grant for the argument that we could if we chose—and if we backed our choice with the money and human talent necessary to make it effective—create an institution in which "the issues of culture are . . . very real" to students of that age. But why should we do so? Statement (2), while pretending to be a reason for adopting Brameld's proposals, is just another proposal itself. A final statement should be considered.

"If the needed order must first of all be understood by those who are soon to be most responsible as citizens for blocking or backing its accomplishment, the heart of the new program should unquestionably center in the junior college." (EEA, p. 189) Is *this* a reason for accepting Brameld's proposals? Not at all. The passage constitutes an argument for putting the major emphasis on political education (to use an appropriate and neutral term for Brameld's proposed secondary education) at the junior col-lege level, rather than in the earlier elementary grades. For the junior college student is "soon to be . . . responsible as citizens . . . ," and, relatively speaking, the elementary school student is not. Assuming, as seems reasonable, that political education is more effective when coming just before the exercise of political rights, then it is more effective for junior college than for elementary school students.

But this argument does not constitute a reason for adopting a four-year secondary school for ages sixteen to twenty, but only for putting political education there instead of earlier, assuming the choice to be *either* junior college *or* elementary school. Notice how the relativity of this choice is concealed by Brameld: He writes "soon to be most responsible as citizens. . . ." Are young people aged twenty-plus most responsible for the needed reconstruction of our cultural order? One would not ordinarily think so. If the careful student of Brameld's writings is asked to find a *typical* argument that reveals the inherent fuzziness of "Reconstructionism" in general, one could find no better passage to cite than "soon to be most responsible. . . ."

Is it clear what it means to be a reason for a policy proposal? Suppose that, instead of what he did propose, Brameld had proposed: (a) a method for determining a group of people "most responsible as citizens for blocking or backing" needed cultural reconstructions, and (b) a program, specifically designed for that group, of political education similar to the "hub" of his proposal for secondary education. In that case, the fact of their being most responsible *would be a reason* for giving (b) to (a); together (a) and (b) would constitute a reason for proposing the establishment of a special school, even a compulsory school, for the group designated in (a). There might be even more compelling arguments *against* such a school, but that is not the question. What *is* the question is how Brameld might be provided at least *a* reason for his proposals. But as it stands, the form of his argument fails to make the distinction between his policy proposals and his reasons why we should adopt them. Perhaps we should conclude that the clarity of that distinction is a necessary, but by no means sufficient, criterion for a good argument on educational policy.

Brameld seems somewhat disappointed that there has been little discussion and argument in support of his curricular proposals. (EEA, p. 2) But what must an educational policy proposal be, what attributes must it possess, if it is to attract critical, constructive attention and incite changes in practice? Either one of two attributes will suffice. The combination of the two, a very unusual occurrence, makes educational history. A proposal may be interesting by virtue of its sheer novelty. An achievement of the imagination is not less a valued rarity in educational policy than, say, on the Broadway stage. In both cases critics analyze and dissect; imitators exploit the newly opened possibilities, often in ways not approved by the man who had the original insight. Dewey's educational thought possesses this attribute in high degree.

A policy proposal may attract critics and supporters by virtue of its extreme practicality. We may take it as axiomatic that American schools are always impractical: The direction and rate of change in school practices cannot possibly remain in phase with all the changes in other aspects of the society which the school supposedly serves. Anyone who has the technical skill and the perseverance to analyze *precisely* how schools are out of phase with even one aspect of society and also has the courage to propose policies which will pull the two together can gain a hearing among critics and administrators. If he is James B. Conant, he can find larger numbers who will follow his policies as if they were God-given dicta; if he is James S. Coleman, he will gain only a hearing,[3] at least initially.

Brameld's works, however, possess neither of these virtues. Even though he is treating, literally, the great issues of human life or death, his imagination does not open any genuinely new perspective on the human condition nor on the nurture of human values through education. On the other hand, his sense of prophetic mission prevents him from participating directly and effectively in helping school teachers and administrators do their jobs just a little better. Brameld falls between two stools.

Brameld's defects of imagination and compassion will be explored further below. But let us look now at a typical instance of his inability to think clearly on a practical matter, namely the problem of compulsory education. It is a problem, indeed one of the central problems that must be faced by anyone who wishes to propose serious educational policies. Compulsory education requires the use of police power for its enforcement, and there are genuine and profound conflicts of interest in the society on the length of time students should be required to attend school. By the time they reach sixteen, differences among individual boys and girls are much greater than they were at age six—differences in academic aptitude and aspiration, in physical and emotional maturity, in ability to secure (as well as need for) remunerative employment, in sexuality and plans for family life; these differences, all relevant to the utility of further education, will increase with each subsequent unit of age. When does it cease to be either expedient or morally justified to force *all* young men and women to attend school? To say the least, this question would seem to deserve some thought.

However, Brameld says only that "the important point is that the ceiling age for compulsory education, which has risen steadily for generations, should be placed at about twenty years. . . . In the years between seventeen and twenty—the crucial period in which most young men and women are crystallizing their plans for mature responsibilities—they should still have access to schooling. Therefore the Reconstructionist considers the period to be of key importance." (TRPOE, p. 212) This is really loose reasoning, even by Brameld standards. Is he arguing that because the terminal age for compulsory education has risen steadily for generations, it will necessarily continue upward indefinitely. Then why not place it "about" twenty-six, for purposes of, well, whatever purposes Brameld had in mind, in writing this passage? For one who "vigorously" insists that ours "is a culture which gives no assurance that it will, in the future, necessarily follow any of the roads it has followed in the past," (*Philosophies of Education in Cultural Perspective*, p. 386, hereafter abbreviated as PEICP.) it is unusual to receive this simple and unanalyzed extrapolation from past generations to future. It is odder still when one considers Brameld's insistence on the so-called normative element in educational thought. He seems to be saying that the trend observed in past generations is a *moral justification* for its indefinite extension into the future, though, of course, he could not mean what he says.

Perhaps the reference to past generations is just a small item of information to be taken only as that and not as a reason for either predicting or proposing that compulsory education be extended to twenty years. Perhaps the next sentence, referring to "young men and women . . . crystallizing their plans for mature responsibilities," is the *argument* to justify the "therefore" which follows. But in Brameld's words, what this justifies is their need for and right to "access to schooling." Is *compulsion* to attend a comprehensive secondary school the only way that society can provide *access* to schooling for youth seventeen to twenty? If not the only way, then among various alternatives is compulsion the best way, balancing gains and costs, considering both the value of freedom of choice for the individual and the need for a free political consensus?

Brameld is not interested in difficult questions like these. In fact, despite the avowal that compulsory education to age twenty is "the important point," he is really quite casual about the whole matter. In the original essay (1950) proposing the hub-and-spokes curriculum (EME, Chapter 22), Brameld said simply that "the junior college will probably include a larger and larger proportion of the young adult population," this prediction (which was remarkably prescient, as it happens) being a sufficient justification for making that institution the central one in the proposed curriculum design. Except for correcting the arithmetic (four years back from twenty is seventeen, not sixteen), the 1961 edition of the same essay involved almost no change; it included the quoted predictions in an unaltered context. But at the beginning of the 1961 version of the essay, Brameld advises the reader to consult Chapters Eight and Nine of his 1956 TRPOE, for "a more elaborate variation" of the curriculum design. It is in the 1956 work that he says that the important point is the extension of *compulsory* education. Did he change his mind between 1950 and 1956 and change it back before 1961? Or, more likely, despite what he says, is it not actually the case that Brameld simply does not care about the problem of setting a ceiling for compulsory schooling? And, if one were forced to guess on it, would it not be reasonable to suppose that his lack of concern accounts in large part for the fact that others care very little for what Brameld says on that topic and others like it? (PEICP, p. 177)

Brameld must and will be allowed a defense; but, before leaving the topic of policy argument, we should note that the same line of attack used against his position on the timing, length, and compulsion for secondary schooling can be effected against the curriculum proposals he offers. In no case do we find reasons advanced for specifically *this* proposal; instead we find the vague diagnosis of "cultural crisis" used as support of the total "design." Likewise, his proposals for administrative reform are unsupported by specific argument. Let us grant that a reasonable case could be advanced in support of the view that greater overall community involvement in the control of education is necessary or at least desirable. Would proportional representation by interest groups in the election of school boards meet exactly the sense of "greater community involvement" that had been argued for earlier? If so, how would it be worked out? Who would determine the relative proportions? What has experience with this sort of arrangement in other institutions, e.g., Fascist Spain and Italy, taught us? What and how strong are the legal barriers to its establishment? Until these questions are faced and answered, we simply do not know enough about what the proposal means. Brameld will not find the constructive criticism necessary to advance an educational point of view until *he* has done the leg work which must lie behind any serious policy argument.

At one point in the presentation of Brameld's own proposals one finds sober argument, that is, recognition of the seriousness of the issue, the specific reasons offered on both sides, and a clearcut conclusion supported by something more substantial than "Reconstructionists believe that. . . ." The sober argument concerns whether Communists should be allowed to teach, and Brameld came out on the affirmative side, and for the right reasons, and when the Cold War was still at its hottest. (TRPOE, pp. 321-322) His courage and conscience are not in question.

III. BRAMELD AND PHILOSOPHY

Brameld's defense might go something like this: "You have badly mistaken the purpose of my writing; I do not pretend to be an educational politician, seeking support for specific policy proposals, but rather an educational philosopher with quite a different role to play on the political stage. A philosopher who is deeply committed to the ideal of political democracy has an obligation to shore up the foundations of that ideal, now seriously shaken by wars, revolutions, and the spread of totalitarianism. Education is the pillar without which democratic political institutions must inevitably collapse, as has been recognized since the founding of this republic. With our age of crisis comes a slowly dawning awareness that a very special kind of education is necessary to democracy, an education built not on unanalyzed historical precedents but on philosophically defensible theories of man, society, and power. Reconstructionism is an attempt to formulate an encompassing philosophical foundation for democratic institutions. If there are weaknesses in that foundation, they should be pointed out. But it is grossly unfair and misleading to criticize those practical suggestions which were put forward with great tentativeness, labeled clearly as merely illustrations of the Reconstructionist's utopian goals as if they were projects, complete with budgets, to be put before a funding agency. Philosophy and politics are partners, but you cannot blame the former for not doing the job of the latter."

This gambit has promise, but it seriously weakens Brameld's position. At least half of a rather large book, the *Reconstructed Philosophy of Education,* is devoted to the proposals outlined earlier. If they are not to be considered as serious policy proposals, then we are wasting our time showing their lack of support in reason and argument. It becomes questionable whether anyone's time would be well employed reading that half of the book, for if the talk about the hub-and-spokes curriculum, the school as vanguard, and consensus and the rest is not proposing policy, then what *is* it doing?

The question must be taken literally despite its rhetorical form. Brameld may say that such talk is designed to suggest how Reconstructionists would view the problem of educational reform. He could counter the gibe about "half a book" by saying that the other book-and-a-half of this two-volume work presents an analysis of the four major philosophies of education in our cultural tradition, giving special attention to the newest and most dynamic of all four—Reconstructionism. Hence, he might say, one cannot isolate the suggestion about four years of secondary education and ask reasons just for that. One must grasp the basic ideas of Reconstructionism as a philosophy, then look at the present system and ask what next steps can be taken, not merely to create novelty, but to bring reality more in line with Reconstructionism's utopian goals. (EEA, p. 221; TRPOE, p. 211) That line of defense forces attention to the philosophy *per se,* to which it were preferable, now impossible, to remain inattentive.

The beginning is relatively inoffensive. In the little essay "Philosophies of Education in an Age of Crisis," published originally in

School and Society (1947), Brameld suggests that it might be possible to divide all the major attempts to think about education systematically into four categories. By an odd but useful quirk of fate it happens that these four categories—Perennialism, Essentialism, Progressivism, and Reconstructionism—coincide rather nicely with four recognized political attitudes—the reactionary, conservative, liberal, and radical. Therefore, philosophy of education might conceive of itself as something other than a mere ivory-tower pastime; it might take an active role in the clarification of these alternative political attitudes, particularly in respect to the connections between cultural and educational issues.

As one might gather from the title and from the usual character of Brameld's language, these ideas were not presented as mere suggestions but as a revelation of existing conditions. But discounting the apocalyptic language, one can see considerable ingenuity in this quatri-partite classificatory scheme. Anyone who has ever taught or taken a survey course in philosophy, especially in philosophy of education, must recognize that some classificatory system is essential, else one comes to parrot a stock of canned statements, beginning with "Thales believed that the cosmos is composed of water . . . ," etc. Brameld's categories had the virtue of novelty, while the traditional philosophical divisions—realism, idealism, empiricism, materialism, etc.—could scarcely be expounded without overwhelming boredom. Even more important, Brameld's scheme gave the teacher of philosophy of education a sense of being a significant factor in the course of events. One cannot deny that great options now confront mankind—war and peace, poverty and plenty, slavery and freedom, ignorance and learning. By following Brameld, the philosopher of education avoids being shunted onto the side tracks while the world hurtles toward an unknown future; on the contrary, he guides the mind that guides the hands on throttle, switch, and brake.

The philosopher of education cannot simply forget his hard-won knowledge of Comenius and Erasmus, but they are no longer just names to be associated with doctrines; they are now part of that great intellectual tradition in the light of which men must choose their political stand toward the future of education and culture generally.

Of course Brameld did not say all of that in the first little essay, but he said enough to interest a good many people. And very shortly thereafter (1950) he published a textbook which said all of that and much more. The title of that book, *Patterns of Educational Philosophy*, aptly describes the classificatory task which had been done for the teacher who adopted that text. But Brameld did far more than classify. Despite his scrupulous care to present each point of view fairly and persuasively, "Reconstructionism" was obviously Brameld's name for his own beliefs. Surely a man has a right to label his views any way he likes, and he has a right to classify the views of others in such fashion that the unique characteristics of his own are clearly revealed. He even has the right to extend his self-chosen label to others whose views are similar to or precursors of his own. But just as in civil life, a man's right to free speech does not mean that his neighbors are obliged to listen, so in philosophy: A man's right to coin a new term to label his views does not mean that anyone else is obliged to add that new designation to the list of recognized philosophical schools.

There is both a technical and a common sense meaning of "philosophy." Only if a newcomer has novel ways of solving classical philosophical problems or ingenious reasons for ignoring them can it gain recognition as a school of philosophy in the technical sense. Only the seer whose vision gives form to the nobest aspirations of his civilization merits respect as philosopher in the popular sense of the term. Brameld's Reconstructionism is simply a bad joke if treated as a technical philosophy, while Brameld's vision of school as a vanguard of social salvation is a social studies teacher's day-dream. In neither sense would "Reconstructionism" merit serious attention as a philosophy.

But as a pedagogical crutch for teachers of philosophy of education, many of whom at that time had had little formal training in either philosophy or education, Brameld's texts served a useful function. Other writers of textbooks often picked up the term "Reconstructionism" and added it to the glossary of labels to be memorized by prospective teachers. There seems to be a theory that making clear the meaning and use of terms like "Reconstructionism" is the key to thinking systematically about education. Later we will see how that theory is wrong, but first let us try to work within it.

The term "Reconstructionism" can be understood only in contrast to "Essentialism," "Perennialism," and "Progressivism." Each of these, according to Brameld, designates a philosophy consisting of systematically connected answers to the questions of ontology, epistemology, and axiology. Each is likewise a phenomenon of culture; that is, each is a product of a distinct stream of the cultural history of Western civilization, and each represents a general attitude toward the cultural crisis of the present age. Finally, each is also a set of beliefs about education, for education inevitably rests on beliefs about reality, knowledge, value, and culture; conversely, any significant belief about these final things must inevitably eventuate in educational programs to extend that belief to the next generation.

If one ignores the pomposity of "ontology," etc., if one is not too put off by the tone of superiority which accompanies Brameld's "cultural evaluation" of these "philosophies," if one reads with a blind eye to the political loading in Brameld's treatment of the Catholic Church, Robert M. Hutchins, and "the pre-existent" (whatever that is), and if one is willing to tolerate an unconscionable ambiguity and vagueness in writing, then one can discern a rough logic in Brameld's major thesis: *There is some kind of congruence between philosophical doctrines and proposals for educational policy.* For example, if a man, George, should assert, as a matter of philosophical doctrine, that there is a world of transcendent ideas far superior in reality and in value to the fleeting world of sensory experience, we should confidently expect that (*if* George had any children and *if* he had any ideas about the education of those children) George would want his children's education to put them into contact with that world of ideas. Indeed, if George should affirm that he believed in the existence (or "pre-existence") of such a transcendent world and then should deny that his belief made any difference to his concerns about education for his children, we should either regard George as a monster or else question what he could *mean* when he said he believed in the existence of a world of transcendent ideas.

Likewise, if Harold should assert *his* belief that the only truly valuable thing in the world in the pleasure of immediate experience and insist, at the same time, that his children undergo the rigors of an old-fashioned English Public School education, we should classify his asserted belief about values as merely an academic point of view, adopted for the sake of an argument, perhaps, but having little to do with Harold's *actual* beliefs and values.

It is very difficult to construct a watertight formal argument in which premises expressing beliefs about reality, knowledge, and value logically *imply* conclusions asserting that education ought to be of such-and-such. But rough congruences in thought are discernable; their absence is even more easily discernable.[4] A study aimed at discovering historical patterns and continuities in such philosophical-educational arguments is well worth doing, even if (as by Brameld) done rather badly.

Two corollaries of Brameld's major thesis have the same rough logic to them. First, ever since Dewey pointed out that the mental-physical dualism in Hellenic thought is of a piece with the two-class system of Hellenic society,[5] we are all ready to acknowledge the reciprocal influences of philosophical thought and cultural context, though again an exact statement of this connection between philosophy and culture is *very* difficult to formulate. General formulas which have been proposed—Marxist, Weberian, Freudian, Whiteheadian, etc.—are easily forced into rather meaningless vagueness if not outright falsity when enough specific counter-examples are thrown against them. But one would be quite foolish to assert that there is *no* connection. Again, it is worth the effort to show, albeit roughly, how *other* cultural forces affected and were affected by educational-cum-philosophical thought.

Second, these rough-and-ready congruences in thought, roughly-and-readily connected with other cultural forces, are not merely historical curiosities but do have a rough-and-ready involvement with current *political* attitudes toward education and social reform.[6] There is no single fixed relation between philosophical doctrine and political attitude; philosophical doctrines used to justify revolutions in one generation justify crushing them in the next. But for any given time and place there are probably converging tendencies between philosophical doctrines and political attitudes. At least a plausible case can be made that such tendencies exist: For example, those who today believe that science (as opposed to Divine Revelation) is our most important source of knowledge about human and social concerns are likely to have a liberal and experimental attitude toward the use of legislative action in relief of economic problems [7]—or so we are inclined to think.

In sum, the idea of "patterns" in educational philosophy is not only a pedagogical crutch; it is also a reasonable starting point for serious study. It might enable a scholar to show both historical causation for, and current political relevance of, philosophical-cum-educational doctrines.

But how is *Brameld* to conduct this study? He does not favor historical study "for its own sake"; what he wants really is to get at the connection between *present* philosophical beliefs and political attitudes. This suggests an empirical, sociological study. But a relatively small proportion of the population possesses either philosophical doctrines or political attitudes of sufficient distinctness to justfy treating them as objects of study. Thus Brameld speaks often of "beliefs about reality . . . knowledge . . . values." The expression is very strange. What does one say when confronted with the question: "What is your belief about reality?" A man may know a great deal, including how to distinguish real objects from unreal, true statements from falsehoods, valuable things from worthless ones, without having any particular beliefs about reality, etc. It would seem an impossible problem for the usual methods of sociological inquiry to determine how most people's (possibly non-existent) beliefs about reality, etc., influence their (probably very indistinct) attitudes toward political and economic reform. Brameld's essay into empirical research in Puerto Rico showed how impossible this sort of study is. (*The Remaking of a Culture*)

But there is a class of people called philosophers; hence it might be possible to isolate a population in which well-formulated philosophical doctrines exist alongside conscious and critical political attitudes. In such a population one *could* use standard sociological instruments to study how philosophy and politics are related. The results would probably be disconcerting, even though possessing little significance politically.

Or one might analyze carefully the *writings* emanating from this population, interlinearly if need be, to see how the philosophical doctrines affect or reflect political attitudes. The job is more easily done for past generations than for the present generation; intellectual history has no finer passages than those which reveal how shifts of philosophical doctrine were crucial, both as cause and effect, in the life of politics.[8] And it *could* be done for the present scene, were the critic and analyst sufficiently attune to his time—

sensitive of ear, sympathetic of heart, and tough of mind. If one were choosing a scholar on those criteria, Brameld would not be one's first choice, although, when he treats ideas which are close to his own, Brameld does demonstrate commendable sensitivity, sympathy, and toughness. The more important deficiency is this: Brameld is neither critic nor analyst. He is, instead, a partisan in the very struggle he seeks to define. It might be possible to combine these roles, to be at once the judge and litigant, better perhaps, the dramatist and protagonist. It might be possible, but Brameld does not succeed. To see how he failed we must look in some detail at the four "philosophies."

"Progressivism" is Brameld's word for the philosophy—technical, social, and educational—of John Dewey and his followers. Brameld's exposition of that philosophy, while suffering from the limitations inherent in textbook treatises, is decidedly a superior performance. He shares Dewey's sublime conviction that philosophy is *the* human enterprise of greatest existential importance. Like Dewey, he can frame the most portentous description of the most trivial event. He can borrow Dewey's voice to sing "democracy" with an honest passion that disarms the most caustic critic, and, with Dewey, he can infuse his talk about what goes on in classrooms with all the significance the universe possesses.

Yet there are weaknesses as well. While Brameld says that Dewey was concerned to provide a radical reinterpretation of the technical problems of philosophy, he does not make it clear to his readers just what such a reinterpretation might involve. In his treatment of Dewey begins a tendency in Brameld's thought which will end in making "Reconstructionism" a ludicrous title for nothing: Brameld neglects to mention that Dewey *argues* for his rejection of classical metaphysical question with their predetermined answers. Brameld leaves the distinct impression that one can say anything he *chooses* in response to, for example, What is reality?

In some sense, of course, one *can say* anything one likes in answer to any question, unless the questioner has provided some method for punishing frivolous answers. In technical philosophy, unargued treatises are punished by being ignored. The vanity presses publish dozens of them each year. There is nothing in Brameld to show his reader that Dewey's philosophy was different *in kind* from mere dreaming. Dewey had academic status, world-wide respect, and devoted followers; those marks distingush him from the retired sea captain who has invested his life savings to publish his collected scribblings on the nature of the universe. But from Brameld we could never discover that there is an essential difference between Dewey's works and those of our imaginary captain, much less what that difference might be.

A second weakness in Brameld's treatment of Progressivism becomes obvious in the first few paragraphs of his so-called cultural evaluation of this philosophy. For "Progressivism" is immediately swallowed up in something quite vaguely called "liberalism, old and new." Liberalism, according to Brameld, in one or both of its guises, is responsible for two world wars, a great depression, loss of faith and "dynamic," the general restlessness and spiritual malaise that besets our aging democracy. Nowhere do we get any sense of how Dewey's *arguments* specifically are the cause of the trouble, except for a most enigmatic reference to Dewey's failure to accept the Marxian "class struggle." (PEICP, p. 193) Brameld makes no mention of Dewey's political philosophy in *The Public and Its Problems,* a major work which is not even cited in Brameld's bibliography. Compared to the careful scholarship and detached objectivity of Morton G. White's *"Yes and No,"* the final evaluative chapter of his *Social Thought in America* (the study of Dewey, Veblen, Beard, and Holmes, which is also absent from Brameld's reading list), the "cultural evaluation" given by Brameld is unrelieved and uninformed special pleading. Brameld does *mention* one or two points that could have had substance to them, e.g., the disgusting use of Deweyan language by school administrators who never intended that their power or position would be threatened, and the disturbing fact that some of Dewey's most intelligent followers worked to deprive Communists of the right to teach. But Brameld does not provide substance for the points; he does not fill in the intellectual or historical context. He uses these facts as a debater, i.e., to win points on a judge's score card, not as a scholar who seeks understanding of a major social phenomenon.

If we follow Brameld, then, as a debater, it is not difficult to find the case he is trying to prove. This case, which has little or nothing to do with the *actual* views of Dewey and his followers, may be put in three propositions as follows:

Cultural Evaluation i

Premise 1_i) Ours is a crisis-culture, demanding democratically flexible plans to achieve clear norms and goals if we are to avoid annihilation and achieve the tremendous potential of industrialism and democracy.

Premise 2_i) Progressivism (a) does not explicitly assert 1; and (b) therefore can not provide what 1 asserts is demanded.

Conclusion 3_i) Therefore Progressivism is wrong (at best) and (in hands other than Dewey's) immoral.[9]

Brameld's problem in advancing this case is to fashion the first statement so that it is not utterly absurd and at the same time keep it distinctive enough that the "Progressivist" will deny it. Brameld refers to the difference between Reconstructionism and Progressivism as one of "emphasis," "a shift in the center of gravity." Another way to put the point is to note that Brameld's language is apocalyptic, a form of speech despised by Dewey and generally, albeit not universally, by the other pragmatists who wrote on educational matters.

Is this difference in rhetoric, in linguistic preference, the only difference between Brameld and his predecessors? One could never answer definitely on the basis of Brameld's "cultural evaluation." In respect of the only concrete divergencies cited, such as the failure of some Progressives to support the rights of Communists in the teaching profession, Brameld insists (rightly, I believe) that their action was a departure from, not a consequence of, the Progressives' more fundamental beliefs.

Perhaps, then, the difference between Brameld and the Progressivists *is* in rhetoric; still it *could* be the case that the difference in rhetoric makes a further difference in behavior, as follows: Beliefs expressed in terms which reflect Brameld's chiliastic vision of the world crisis are more likely to be maintained in unpopular and inconvenient situations than beliefs expressed in Dewey's moderate, often equivocal, prose. This is an interesting sociological hypothesis, but Brameld presents no evidence for it. If this is all the "cultural evaluation" amounts to, and if there is no research showing the consequences of expressing beliefs in the alternate forms, then we are left with a purely aesthetic choice between the linguistic style of Dewey *et al.* on one hand and Brameld on the other.

However unlikely as it might seem that one could *ever* prefer Dewey's style of writing to another's, it happens.

Or, looking at it the other way, perhaps the difference *is* more than linguistic. In reading Brameld's proposals for teaching method, administration, etc., one gets the distinct feeling that neither Dewey nor Kilpatrick nor others of similar bent would have advanced them precisely as Brameld did. But even so, does this mean that Brameld's "cultural evaluation" case is sound? Not unless it is clear how and why Dewey and his fellow thinkers deny Premise 1, and that, independently, Premise 1 is true and Dewey's denial false. But we get no argument nor evidence on these matters. Brameld says (PEICP, Chapter 5) that Dewey made a "painstaking" analysis of Marxism and rejected it, then (PEICP, Chapter 6) this rejection is used as a point against Dewey, with no intervening exposition of Dewey's analysis and no effort to refute it!

This question-begging in respect to Dewey versus Marx is no more crude and obvious than any other: The whole of the "cultural evaluation" is an example of *petitio principii* to delight the heart of any writer of a textbook in logic. But the example has its amusing side: When Brameld himself comes to talk about political phenomena in the control of education, he appeals to the concept of "interest groups," a theoretical approach more akin to Dewey's notion of multiple "publics" than it is to the Marxist view of "class struggle." He ignores Dewey's normative search for the "Great Community" which foretokens Lyndon Johnson's rhetoric. It is always safe and true to say that we need a conception of politics deeper than the "voting behavior" which we have learned to measure and predict with reasonable accuracy. But that a Marxist two-sided "class struggle" provides such a deeper conception is more than even Brameld can accept when he attempts to portray the actualities of American politics.

Instead of argument, analysis, and evidence in favor of his Premise 1, Brameld offers us a simplistic metaphor. Progressivism, he tells us, was the right sort of philosophy to have when our culture was in its adolescent stage—requiring freedom to search and try—but inappropriate to the stage of maturity, when we need carefully delineated plans and full commitment to their achievement. (PEICP, p. 147) Even as a figure of speech, this metaphor is awkward and unilluminating. It is no substitute for argument. But it is typically Brameld.

Essentialism: If one decries Brameld's treatment of Progressivism, one must still admit that it is his best piece of work. "Essentialism" turns out to be a catchall category which includes (a) all educators who believe that education is primarily an affair of transmitting knowledge and values from one generation to the next and (b) all philosophers who have tried to provide answers to the classical questions of philosophy. The latter, those who have contributed to the "philosophic beliefs of essentialism," "include the names of Plato, Aristotle, Plotinus, Hegel, Kant, Schopenhauer, Hobbes, Locke, Berkeley, Hume, Spinoza, Jonathan Edwards, Josiah Royce, Ralph Waldo Emerson, W. E. Hocking, A. N. Whitehead, Bertrand Russell, G. Santayana, Ralph Barton Perry, . . ." and on and on for another twenty-five or so incongruously connected names. One might think that this vast profusion would make of essentialism a hopelessly chaotic melange. One would be right. Brameld's ingenuity is astounding: Is it conceivable that an academically trained philosopher could so immerse himself in his own fantasies that he sees the major argument against the correspondence theory of truth in its alleged support for existing economic institutions? Brameld does so with such a casual disregard of scholarship that one finds eventually an unintended humor in his writings.

In form, the "cultural evaluation" of Essentialism goes like this:

Cultural Evaluation ii

Premise 1$_{ii}$) Ours is a crisis culture demanding novelty, change, new directions, and a bold pioneering approach in both philosophy and education if we are to avoid annihilation and achieve the unprecedented potential of our contemporary industrial democracy.

Premise 2$_{ii}$) Essentialism is *essentially* a conservative philosophy. (Of course, some Essentialist philosophers are radicals and revolutionaries, and some Essentialist educators are noted for their bold innovations, but *essentially* Essentialists are conservative.)

Conclusion 3$_{ii}$) Therefore Essentialism is an inappropriate philosophy for our culture.

It finally does not matter what a thinker caught in Brameld's

"Essentialist" net says or advocates: Brameld can always claim that the cultural effect of his doctrines, "more often than not," is to support the economic, political, and social status quo. (PEICP, p. 278) As expected, no historical evidence is offered for that statement.

Busy proving that all realists (by which strange terms he means all materialists except Karl Marx and his followers) and idealists—objective and subjective—wrote in support of the exploitative system of capitalism, Brameld neglects entirely the actual *cultural* bias in the conservative emphasis in contemporary educational thought and practice. This bias has its roots in social-status systems, in the economics of technological change, in a political system where mass, electronic, one-way communication is replacing face-to-face interaction as the dominant mode of contact between politician and constituent. But Brameld will not be distracted by trivia of that sort; his attention is firmly fixed on the cosmic deviltry of the "pre-existent." Given the basic form of his argument, he could come to no other conclusion.

Perennialism: There are two ways that one can approach that almost unaccountable, but genuine, phenomenon which Brameld aptly labels "Perennialism." As a political voice, the Roman Catholic Church in America has not been the most progressive element in our national life, but neither has it been all evil. In political terms, the Catholic Church is not one thing but many, not a fixed entity but a rapidly changing feature on the political landscape, a great shifting cloud rather than a mountain. Anyone who intends to work effectively on a political issue in which the Church has a stake, e.g., in the financial support and control of schools, had better recognize the existence and the particular, momentary configuration of that cloud.

Two strategies in dealing with Catholicism are bound to fail: (a) To regard the Catholic Church as just "another religion like any other," having no special political significance as such. To work for federal aid to public schools without even acknowledging the existence of the Roman Catholic bloc is politically unwise, as the supporters of that aid finally and fortunately learned in time to pass the 1965 Elementary and Secondary Education Act; (b) To regard the political position of the Church as eternal and immovable, set in Rome and promulgated by the hierarchy under pain of excommunication for all dissenters: a belief from which it follows that the Church is an institution totally incompatible with political democracy. Many voters denied the candidacy of John F. Kennedy on that ground, indeed nearly enough to cause us to lose one of the most interesting presidents ever to occupy the office.

No, the Church in America is composed of men and women, laymen and clerics, who in their political life think, feel, argue, reason, and reach conclusions on which they are willing to act, not just like everybody else but in ways which are (sometimes subtly, sometimes crudely) conditioned by the fact of constituting the present of an institution with a long past and, *Deo volente*, even longer future. Since the Church in America is a mass institution, variations within it are mass phenomena, i.e., accounted for by such mass variables as age, sex, race, ethnic background, educational attainment, income, social class, and class aspiration. Since the Church is everywhere composed of individuals, new arguments, attitudes, and thrusts are constantly appearing within it.

Some people, among them atheists like myself, believe the political life of the nation would be poorer if it should lose the active presence of the Roman Catholic Church in its manifold guises and aspects. Others believe that the monarchical-hierarchical structure of the Church makes it ultimately incompatible with a political democracy. It is doubtful that a precise, rationally arguable question can be formulated concerning the place of Catholicism as a whole in the American political scene. In any event, that question would have little interest for educational policy. What is of interest, indeed of crucial significance, is the fact that on many issues of educational policy there are Catholic interest groups, possessing some, but by no means unlimited, political power, arguing in a distinctive but by no means uncommunicative fashion. It would be useful to have an up-to-date and realistic appraisal of the varied, often conflicting, Catholic efforts in education, without the hostility of Paul Blanshard.[10] It would also be useful to have a careful analytic study of the analogical and "natural law" arguments typically used by Catholic spokesmen in the political arena. Now if we add a contextual element to account for the "spread," i.e., the fact that various Catholic educational and political interests are shared by non-Catholics and the fact that Aristotelian or Thomistic arguments on education are used, for one reason or another, by secular writers such as Robert M. Hutchins and Walter Lippmann, we can see that a serious study of "Perennialism" in America today would be a valuable one indeed.

Brameld's study almost qualifies. Perhaps because he shares what may be called a crisis mentality with many writers whom he labels "Perennialists," Brameld treats their position with admirable restraint and a scholarship which, if totally dependent on secondary sources, is at least a cut above the travesties visible in his treatise of the "Essentialists." But because he so badly misunderstands the nature of argument as such, his study of Perennialism finally emerges a mangled mess. Brameld insists that any argument cast in Thomistic language is, whatever it may actually *say*, an ideological cover for some political move directed to the re-establishment of the economic and religious system of the thirteenth century. This makes it very easy for him to conclude, in his "cultural evaluation," that "Perennialism . . . (at times almost despite some of its advocates)" (PEICP, p. 360) is incompatible with democracy, whether expressed in political, psychological, social, or pedagogical terms. Thus Hutchins' efforts in behalf of a democratic world community are belittled by Brameld as merely re-echoing Dante. We are left with neither a careful, analytic study of the Thomistic argument—the argument from natural law and analogy —nor a realistic appraisal of the political significance of those movements—Catholic and non-Catholic—which cast their arguments in Thomistic terms.

There has been a renewed scholarly interest in the appeal to "nature" in political and moral argument.[11] As I shall show later, Paul Goodman is an ethical naturalist, in something very similar to the teleological sense. But the use of Thomistic phraseology to express a Thomistic natural law argument on educational policy is a different phenomenon altogether from the revival of naturalism. Neo-Thomism is an attempt to formulate philosophical problems in language uncorrupted by Cartesian dualism, Humean skepticism, and Hegelian dynamism—in short, language uncorrupted by modernism. In its sophisticated forms, Neo-Thomism is quite analogous to Igor Stravinsky's efforts to find a historical musical idiom uncorrupted by accretions from Mozart, Brahms, and . . . Stravinsky, or the formally congruent movements in painting, poetry, and drama. In a strict sense, all such efforts are futile; it is impossible to receive the cultural forms of an earlier era except through ears, eyes, and minds formed in the present. But in a looser sense, one can understand the striving of an artist or philosopher who finds himself in a blind alley, his cultural resources exhausted or so tangled in contradiction as to be useless for his own creative urges, who then strives to work his way back to a main avenue from which new possibilities are visible.

Thomism was a particularly appropriate historical resource for those seeking to escape the assumptions in contemporary educational discourse. It was esoteric and yet, with the advances made by twentieth century scholarship, accessible. St. Thomas' own writings were set in a tradition of continuing argument, giving vividness and vitality to the expression of his thought. And, finally, Thomism appeared in a historical setting which, while it had many problems of its own, seems happily free of the particular evils that beset the twentieth century. The only other resource having anything like these advantages is the Platonic-Aristotelian tradition. And, not surprisingly, that resource has been heavily tapped by contemporary educational theorists.[12]

Brameld's "cultural evaluation" of this phenomenon does show some sensitivity to the social and psychological needs which give impetus to the return to the thirteenth century. Ignoring all the contemporary scholarship which emphasizes the richness, variety, and dynamism of the High Middle Ages, Brameld adopts the Henry Adams "Age-of-Faith" attitude toward the social milieu out of which Thomism emerged and thus explains its appeal to the modern soul best by anxiety, instability, and confusion. There is *something* in this view: It becomes dangerous and misleading only when taken literally.

But literally is precisely how Brameld takes it. Consequently his evaluation of Perennialism comes down to showing that it does not provide an appropriate rationale for popular democracy. The argument might go like this:

Cultural Evaluation iii

Premise 1_{iii}) In this age of crisis there are two fundamental criteria for any system of educational-philosophic thought: It must provide a basis for cultural wholeness. And that basis must itself be consonant with democracy.

Premise 2_{iii}) Perennialism provides a basis for cultural wholeness, but "the whole elaborate system of premises and deductions which constitute the Platonic-Aristotelian-Thomist *Weltanschausing* . . . [is a] definitive and finally undemocratic framework of beliefs." (PEICP, p. 377)

Conclusion 3_{iii}) Therefore Perennialism fails on a fundamental criterion and is an inadequate system of philosophic-educational beliefs for our age of crisis.

To anyone with any sense of historical reality, such talk about an "elaborate system of premises and deductions" is merely quaint. It strains the argument to put it in logically valid form. The basis for 2_{iii} seems to come down to this: Because Thomism (or Aristotelianism or Platonism) arose in an undemocratic society, anyone who uses Thomistic (or related) arguments in support of policy proposals, however democratic those proposals may be, is not to be listened to because he is really undemocratic. This is absurd, of course, but unfortunately no other interpretation of what Brameld actually says is possible. (PEICP, p. 377)

Thus Brameld falls again between the same two stools. He does not provide a realistic appraisal of the political strength of the various factions within the Roman Catholic Church in America (and their non-Catholic allies) in respect to different policy questions which confront education today. He seeks to attain the level of philosophy, as if there were a real essence behind the confusing appearance of politics. But no sooner does he begin to show what some of the philosophical questions are (Are there such things as self-evident propositions as asserted, e.g., in the Declaration of Independence? Is there a natural law which has normative as well as, or instead of, descriptive force? Can one use, or better, within what limits can one use an analogical argument (e.g., the art of teaching is like the art of medicine in respect of relying on external means to stimulate internal, growth-promoting processes) in support of policies in education and elsewhere?) than he answers them by applying a political criterion—do they *presuppose* a popular democracy? The answer is obviously no, for Perennialist arguments were used before there was such a thing as popular democracy. But surely the philosopher's question concerns the validity and truth of these arguments, not the presupposition by a political system. Thus from Brameld's treatment of Perennialism—a movement perspicaciously identified and labeled by him—we get neither political analysis nor philosophical analysis. We get the opposite of analytic, i.e., synthetic in the sense of ersatz, artificial.

Reconstructionism: Precisely that artificial character is the dominant one in Brameld's own creation—Reconstructionism. In the case of all the other so-called philosophies, there was a breath of genius somewhere in the background, and it could not be *entirely* stifled, even though badly muffled by Brameld's treatment. But when Brameld attempts to construct an ontology, an epistemology, and an axiology to replace pragmatism, realism, idealism, Thomism, and every other "ism," the result is as one would expect.

A close examination of Brameld's own contribution will show him to be a Christian Scientist or possibly a disciple of Norman Vincent Peale. Ultimately, the expression "Reconstructionists believe that . . ." comes to mean "if we all work together and think positively we can make it so that. . . ." Thus the question of ontology: What is the nature of being itself? If it is asked at all seriously it *must* mean: What is it in the world that resists human will? But the Reconstructionist believes that culture determines reality, that our culture is now at a crisis point, and that it is squarely up to us to *decide* whether we shall have war or peace, slavery or freedom, poverty or abundance. (TRPOE, Chapter 3)

To be sure, this attitude is courageous and progressive, but what is it in the world which *really* resists human will? We can give examples: The wave length of sodium does not seem to respond much to our will, individual or collective. But surely we can give some characterization of reality other than merely listing all the properties of physical objects. And some non-physical entities, e.g., the laws of logic, $A = A$, seem to have this property of obduracy to human will. So, the seeker for an intellectually defensible ontology might argue that we should pursue more deeply this question of what it is *to be*, as opposed to be desired, or felt, or thought to be. Even if the metaphysical quest for true statements about reality as such is taken seriously, it may well prove to be futile in the long run; all proffered solutions are probably doomed to contain paradoxes or contradictions. But the quest is surely not completed by the mere assertion of the power of progressive thinking.

Exactly the same considerations arise in treating Brameld's "beliefs about knowledge" and "beliefs about value." In ordinary language if you ask a person to state his beliefs about knowledge ("I represent the Gallop Poll, sir. Would you please tell me what you believe about knowledge?"), you might, if you are careful or lucky in choosing a respondent, hear such answers as "I think it's a good thing." Or, "The kind you get in college is no substitute for practical experience," etc. But the philosophical quest is quite different; epistemology is an effort to discover the general character of knowledge, i.e., those propositions which are true whether or not any particular person happens to believe them. Again, there is no guarantee of success in this enterprise and no particular instrumental value in pursuing it. But philosophers from Socrates to Brameld, not inclusive, have pursued it anyway, each offering arguments against the answers of his predecessors and for his own. But Brameld gives no arguments and no answers. Instead, he comes out with "social consensus in truth seeking" about cultural goals as the touchstone of knowledge. Brameld has a most useful skill in writing at the level of the almost-incomprehensible. Just when one is ready to admit total defeat by a particular passage, a glimmer of understanding will usually emerge. This is especially true in his treatment of epistemology. (TRPOE, Chapter 4) After puzzling through his discussions of "prehension," "the unrational," "ideology and utopia," one comes to see that this chapter (on knowledge) contains the same non-answer to its philosophical question as the chapter on reality contained to its. This is a time of crisis; men must choose their cultural goals; whatever beliefs about cultural means and ends can unify the group mind are its knowledge, etc.

There are certain obvious and standard objections that may be raised against such a view of knowledge. A philosopher would take some relatively trivial example by which to test the Reconstructionists' doctrine: Thus he might say, "Suppose a group were cast adrift in a life boat, in the middle of the ocean. They agree that sailing a course toward a particular star is their best strategy for achieving their agreed-upon objective, namely safe arrival on land. Is this situation analogous to a culture in crisis? Does agreement imply knowledge? Is there a concept of truth such that a proposed answer to the question whether land can be raised on a particular heading is true or false quite independently of any group's agreeing on it? Etc."

It is apparent that Brameld could not be required nor even expected to provide a careful and conscientious treatise of such questions. To do so would extend Brameld's work far beyond his intention and competence. But in the absence of serious argument, the bland assertion that Reconstructionists believe so-and-so is completely uninteresting. There are interesting problems in showing how and whether consensus figures as part of the meaning or as a criterion of truth and knowledge, considering the various kinds of propositions which may be said, in various senses, to be true, and the many uses of the word "know." When Brameld quite rightly ignores those problems in his presentation, he leaves the Reconstructionists' "beliefs about knowledge" void of significance, or rather possessed of only the significance that might be extracted from a pollster's report of Brameld's answer to the question, "What do you believe about knowledge?"

The Reconstructionist's "beliefs about value" *do* tempt one to make an analytic response, for they constitute the kind of commonsense confusion which got the whole philosophical enterprise going in the first place. Brameld's chapter on values reads very like the dialogue between Cephalus and Socrates (in Book I of Plato's *Republic*) as it might have been written by Cephalus who never quite grasped what was going on. The question is raised as to the nature of justice or value, and answered by giving instances of just acts (Cephalus) or valuable things (TRPOE, pp. 115-116) like *"sufficient nourishment . . . adequate dress . . . etc."* Splendid. But a nagging question remains, for we discover that what is valuable for one person would not necessarily be so for another; and we can see that words like "sufficient" and "adequate" really beg the question, for each means, in context, "in amount that promotes value." So we still need some definition of "justice" and "value." Cephalus responds by saying, in effect, that all right-thinking men know what justice is, and if Socrates does not, so much the worse for him and then marches off to perform his civic duties. Brameld says that what makes these things valuable is that they satisfy wants; hence, "want-satisfaction" is synonymous with "value." But there are difficulties here, for what satisfies wants for one person may create inconvenience for another. (Genghis Khan:

"I want to defeat my enemies and to take their wives and daughters for my pleasure.") This difficulty can be avoided, for *if* we have full democratic processes and *if* all these good things are properly projected in a total cultural design, inspired with appropriate myths and poetry, then all right-thinking men, i.e., all men except the selfish minority who are reaping profits from the present system of human exploitation, *will* know what are the right values and how they may be secured. Then Brameld marches out to write a chapter on the theory of the school "as social vanguard."

We should be warned against the temptation to take up the argument where Cephalus or Brameld left it, for the way may well turn out to be a false one. There may never be a definition of "justice" which is genuinely definitive, and the search for a single unified theory of value may well prove fruitless. Cephalus and Brameld may have wisdom as well as right on their side; one can sympathize with the man who leaves a bootless armchair discussion and goes forth to do his duty. One may even understand how his parting shot at those who remain behind can be regarded by the forthgoer as a winning blow. But to convince oneself that it is not really a winning blow one has only to read the rest of the *Republic* or to think about the absurdity in trying to reduce the complex problem of values to a simple formula of "want-satisfactions."

When Cephalus forsook the philosophical discourse, it was to offer sacrifice and prayer in the communal festival. We do not have the liturgy from that ancient Attic rite, but we might wager that it possessed more dignity and grace than the handbook of Reconstructionism which contains such gems as, "They [values] are attached to specifiable goals which, after open communication of all relevant evidence concerning their nature and desirability, are agreed upon by the largest possible number as necessary to the group if frustration is to be prevented and the group's wants are to be fulfilled." (TRPOE, p. 145) We may presume from this and other passages that Brameld wishes to promote a political system which does permit argument on the desirability of social objectives. But the only criterion which he proposes to distinguish the *desirable* from the merely *desired* is involvement in an agreed-upon cultural design, supported by deep commitments of the majority of mankind. Then *before* such agreement is reached, there is simply no way of making this distinction. One could not argue, for example, in the following terms: "I know the voters of this city do desire another multi-million dollar stadium for spectator sports, but I don't think it's desirable, for these reasons." The philosophical problem is precisely that of elucidating criteria to distinguish "desirability" from merely being desired, criteria to distinguish relevant evidence from irrelevant, etc.

In the projection and refinement of social goals through democratic political processes, we must argue not merely whether certain objects and actions will satisfy wants but, even more, whether certain wants ought to be satisfied. The language through which policies are proposed and debated must be rich with subtle distinctions among moral values and aesthetic values, animal-need-satisfaction values and spiritual values, personal values and social values, instrumental values and intrinsic values. Values are celebrated in myth, poetry, and liturgy. But values must be deliberated within a rational and sensitive polity, and, for the serious deliberation of values, the language of Reconstructionism will not do.

If Reconstructionism is utterly factitious as philosophy, it is fictitious as a theory of pedagogy. It advances no theory of learning and no theory of teaching. Scattered through the chapters expressing Brameld's "Educational Beliefs," one find occasional pieces of sound advice: Children have irrational motivations which the teacher would do well to try to understand; if teaching is carried on in groups, as it usually is, the interaction of the group is a significant factor in determining the quality of learning, and if the teacher can achieve a role *within* the learning group instead of being merely an outside force, the effectiveness of teaching (especially teaching directed toward ends other than merely transmitting information) will be increased.

Masked by Brameld's opaque language is a sensitivity to issues more profound still. Everyone must recognize that youngsters have to be taught to stop at red traffic lights and to "proceed with caution" at green lights. But just what is involved in this teaching? How is it different from teaching that green oak leaves in the spring mean the start of growth, while red leaves in the fall mean termination? Or different from teaching the mere information say that certain tribes paint their maidens green and matrons red? How can we teach youngsters about traffic lights so that they not only obey the rules but also recognize that such rules are conventions, not arbitrary, to be sure, but not fixed by nature either. Brameld senses that there *are* profound questions of this sort to be dealt with in a theory of pedagogy, but he does not show that he knows *what* they are, much less how to deal with them. (TRPOE, pp. 203, 253)

Likewise, Brameld *senses* that there is something quite profound in the idea of learning to learn from one's own experience, especially for the electronically-nourished generation who are constantly fed pre-chewed pap from the experience of others. But he seems to have no sense of what a philosopher is supposed to *do* with an idea like that, namely to provide a conceptual and theoretical framework for it. Note that in the absence of such a framework this "idea" is mostly rhetoric and metaphor. "Learn to learn from one's own experience" has a nice sound to it, but from the experience of whom else, pray, is one to learn (or learn to learn)? Just what makes an experience belong to one person? Can the *same* experience be transferred from one person to another? Those are the theoretical questions which gave rise to Dewey's doctrine of learning by problem-solving. (It's *my* learning if it occurs in the context of *my* solving *my* problem, says Dewey.) There are deep theoretical difficulties in Dewey's doctrine;[13] but that cannot be said about Brameld's, for the latter never quite grasped what Dewey was up to; hence he never felt obligated to provide an alternate theory of his own.

The absence of *thinking* by Brameld can be seen in the gaping holes in what he claims is a treatment of "learning theory." From the very beginning his so-called normative theory misses the point of the psychologists whom he purports to replace. Perhaps it is more important to treat the problem of learning as answering the question: "From what kind of experience *ought* children learn?" rather than answering the question: "What theoretical scheme (strict sense: axioms, deductions, confirmation by experimental evidence, etc.) best accounts for the phenomena of learning wherever and however they occur?" It is obvious that answering the first is no substitute for answering the second, but it is also true that *practically* we have to answer the first even though the second has yet to be (probably can't be) given by psychologists.

It is, nonetheless, wrong of Brameld to speak as if Reconstructionism provided an intelligible theory of learning, in the usual sense of an answer to the second question above, when in fact all he provides are answers to the first question. But that sort of mistake is less mischievous than in the answers actually given to the question of what learning experiences children ought to have. Basically, Brameld's answer is unexceptionable: Children ought to learn from their own first-hand experience, from face-to-face interaction with other people, and from symbolic communication through media other than talking. This last would be primarily reading for many people, but not for all and not exclusively for any. This three-fold classification of the sources of learning is merely common sense, but Brameld is not willing to leave it at that. He insists on elevating the second of these (interpersonal discussion) to the position of a metaphysical touchstone of truth. And he reduces the third to "the study of evidence" (TRPOE, p. 216) as though a classroom were a laboratory or a courtroom.

The tendency toward such nonsense is inherent in the original question. If one is *not* seeking a theoretical, scientific explanation of learning, the sensible alternative is not "From what kinds of experience ought children to learn?" The sensible alternative is: "What ought children to learn?" For the answer to the "kinds of experience" question, is, simply, from whatever kinds of experience they *do* learn effectively. There are limitless classifications of kinds of experience, and there is no reason, apart from a specified context, to prefer one scheme to another. The context in which Brameld purports to talk is curriculum policy. If we have already decided that children ought to learn, just to take a Reconstructionist example, the proper internationalist attitude, then presumably we will want them to have some pleasurable experience with foreigners, see some films, read some books, hear some music, etc. But one could not say in advance of a curriculum policy what kinds of experiences children ought to *learn from;* though one can say, on grounds of humanitarian sympathy, what kinds of experience children ought to *have,* namely experience of warm acceptance by parents and other adults, experiences of success in dealing with genuine difficulties in the physical world, etc.

In sum, Brameld has no theory of learning. What purports to be such is, in part, merely commonsense classification of the sources from which people do learn things. And, in part, his treatment of learning is just more curriculum policy put forth without any reasons for its adoption.

We may draw the same summation for Reconstructionism as a whole. What is professed as philosophical treatment of reality, knowledge, and value entirely misses the point of philosophy. The "beliefs" it propounds are either policy proposals or empty air, and since no arguments for the proposals accompany them, the two come very much to the same thing. This painfully extended survey of Reconstructionism was undertaken only to discover whether there were *reasons* for the policy proposals in the so-called philosophy; as it turns out, the philosophy is nothing but more unargued policy. (Whatever Brameld may believe, it is not *argument* to preface an *obiter dictum* with "nevertheless many Reconstructionists believe . . ." or "the crisis of our culture demands that we. . . .")

Thus we have no reasons at all to take seriously the strange policy proposals found at the conclusion of Brameld's essays on philosophy-building. Brameld's works will undoubtedly be of interest to the historian of educational thought, particularly to the student of the discipline of moral judgment or of group dynamics.[14] But the fact that Brameld's thought has historical importance is no reason to take it seriously as proposed policy.

IV. BRAMELD AND THE SYSTEM

And so we must return to our original question: Why bother with Theodore Brameld? Is it that, despite certain demonstrated inadequacies, Brameld's philosophy contains a valuable point that needs making? Is it that Brameld's philosophy demonstrates certain diabolically interesting features about the System itself? Are these two questions related? Affirmative on all counts.

Consider the first question: Does Brameld have a point worth making? The answer is Yes, certainly. Our century *is* a century of crisis. Western civilization still suffers from war and the hangover of wars, depressions, and an established precedent for genocide. Over-hanging every effort to secure peace and justice on this planet is the Damocles' sword of nuclear holocaust. And each time we seem to have made a little progress in escaping the threat of the Big Bang, our attention is caught by the ominous whimper of too many newborn babes. We doubt that our projected solutions to the world's problems are intellectually sound; we distrust our own resolve to do what we know ought to be done; and, even when mind and will are strong, we come against the inherent limitations of our power: Western civilization with its science, its nationalism, and its ideals of democracy and justice has bequeathed to the world more problems than capacity to solve them.

But the United States has succeeded in protecting itself from the full impact of world crisis. We have used our unmatched military power and economic affluence (a symbiotic alliance) to build a protective screen between us and the rest of the world. We are made anxious and fearful by what we hear from the other side of the screen, but our anxieties and fears only serve to make us more dependent on global military and economic power as our sole protection.

As American society as a whole is carefully protected from the revolutionary currents flowing over the world, so the majority of our youth are protected even from the social revolutions—particularly the racial and sexual revolutions—occurring in this country. This is mis-education, as systematic and devastative as if it were deliberate. In fact, since economic and political mis-education tends to be of considerable benefit to certain *very* powerful groups in this country, there is at least that much reason to believe its prevalence is not entirely an accident. This point can and cannot be repeated too often: *This is Reconstructionism's point-that-needs-making.*

But let us look again at the System. It was almost inevitable that someone should seize upon the fortunate fact that prospective public school teachers have to be educated in colleges and, while there, are likely to have either the opportunity or the obligation (depending on the state in which they wish to teach) to take a course in philosophy of education, to construct a funnel through which some consciousness of historical crisis could be poured into the schools. A series of accidents made it possible for Brameld to be that someone. It was the Depression, actually, which fixed Brameld's institutional status as philosopher of education. Receiving his Ph.D. from Chicago in the early 1930's, he found only in teacher-training, and that belatedly, an opportunity to practice his training as philosopher. But in his educational efforts, Brameld discovered a power and a mission unknown to most of the academic philosophers forced into teacher training by the exigencies of the job-market. Brameld could awake in his students—those in teacher-training and those in adult education and in high schools as well—a consciousness that America faces momentous decisions, and from that awakened consciousness he could evoke a commitment to democratic political ideals.[15] What could be more natural than a man's teaching what he believes, especially as it turns out that he has great talent for teaching it? It is only the next step that he propose as policy that all education revolve around the kind of teaching he does so well.

Let it not be overlooked, moreover, that it took genuine courage to make philosophy of education the vehicle to carry the message of social consciousness. Marx had said that the point of philosophy is not to interpret the world but to change it; still that was not the viewpoint of most academic philosophers, even in the thirties. Brameld affirmed his conception of philosophy forthrightly: "In the oldest and richest sense, the philosophic enterprise is simply the attempt of human beings to be conscious, honest, and consistent about the things they believe to be true." While there is historical sanction for this view, one seldom finds philosophers including among the "things they believe to be true" specific doctrines about, for example, the need for teachers to affiliate themselves with the trade union movement. As one examines Brameld's career, it is evident that his courage in defying the safe, academic conception of a philosopher's role was not without its costs.

But what about the larger power structure? How was Brameld allowed to preach democratic socialism in the context of that most conservative and sensitive sector of American education, the regular teacher-training system? He probably would have been forbidden in a state teachers' college, and even the major private urban universities in which he taught—New York University and Boston University—are not themselves entirely free from outside pressures, as several left-wing professors have discovered to their peril. Despite this, Brameld was never without an academic home, and his books were published and sold successfully throughout the McCarthy era. It is not that Brameld was never under attack; he was attacked quite viciously and underhandedly. But the point is that he survived and, by some objective measures, throve, despite the attacks.

Sometimes institutions behave in wiser ways than would men. Suppose the entire teacher-training system of the United States were subject to decisions made by a *very* sophisticated computer, programmed with a vast knowledge of the political and economic structure of this nation and a wealth of insight into the social psychology of schools as institutions. Suppose this computer were set to make decisions on teacher-training courses with the object of minimizing the chances of any fundamental shifts in the power (control) relations in the school. This computer might very likely decide that Brameld-type philosophy of education courses should be taught in *all* teacher-training programs. They fit so well into the *status quo* that they seem designed precisely for it.

In the context of world politics and the relative freedom of communication in this country, it would be impossible to shield our prospective teachers from all left-wing thought. Since the nation as a whole has decided that teacher-training shall take place in an academic environment, the chances are increased that the most talented and articulate individuals in the population from which teachers will be drawn will be also the most politically aware, most likely to have out-of-center views, left or right. Now if this political interest can be brought within the regular program of teacher education, it can probably be neutralized in its concrete effects. One can imagine no therapy more effective for a young member of the John Birch Society or the Socialist Workers Party than to be forced to express his "beliefs about reality, knowledge, and value" in the presence of a professor of philosophy of education and a classful of students, most of them young ladies seeking a teaching certificate as a form of insurance. The young radical who persisted in seeking a teaching career after that experience could be counted on to submit to anything.

And this fits exactly the pattern of administrative control structural to the school as a social system. Teachers, considered professionals, are supposed to have "beliefs" on every aspect of school life, and provision is made by all democratic administrators for teachers to voice those beliefs at approved times and places. But teachers have little power except in matters related directly to the classroom itself. Thus the language of belief is effectively distinguished from the language of action. The point can be seen in one example: Teachers are supposed to "believe in" the inherent worth and dignity of each individual, the "supreme value of social-self-realization" as Brameld expresses it; but the academic high school is designed to promote ruthless competition for high grades and places in prestigious colleges with the teacher serving as impartial referee, an auxiliary to the standardized testing procedures that really make the decisions. Thus one can scarcely imagine a more effective training to teach the prospective teacher to distinguish language used for some serious purpose from language used merely to express "beliefs" than a good course in Brameld's philosophy of education. Unless a teacher learns to make that distinction easily and unconsciously, he will find that teaching in the public school is a form of schizophrenia. This is one reason our computer would want to require that every prospective teacher study Brameldian philosophy of education.

But there are others. The proposals he advocates sound so very revolutionary, but a second look shows them to be merely harmless extensions of the *status quo*: They represent, in fact, the easiest sorts of compromises by which the school system can expand to meet the new demands put upon it without changing any of the present power relations. In detail:

The extension of the age of compulsory schooling to twenty years would obviously extend the control of the school over the lives of students in a decided way. Given the need for technical training in our society and the fact that two years of junior college is the least economically rational expenditure for education, it is clear that unless political power can be used to force young men and women to stay in the public school system they will seek training elsewhere or simply leave school altogether at the earliest opportunity. Brameld's solution of the drop-out problem is to raise the age of compulsory attendance. There could be no easier solution, i.e., none requiring less change in the power relations.

The changed form of political control advocated by Brameld is, again, simply an extension of present tendencies: first, to "professionalize" the legally elected local board of education, making it rise above partisan interests to see the value of education in the most general sense; and, second, to broaden the base of community groups concerned with education so that the largest possible number of citizens have some degree of participation in school affairs. Both these trends have the net effect of increasing the actual power of the local superintendent. It is only when actual conflict of interest can be legitimized and represented in a political context that the power of the administrative structure is threatened. And there *is* actual conflict of interest between the school as an institution and many segments of the population, including the school population. But in Brameld's view there is no *legitimate* conflict between the indefinite expansion of the public school and the interests of any group within the public. What is required is "audacious and aggressive leadership" to enlist the full cooperation of all citizens in expanding the size and scope of the school system. That is a familiar and pleasant sound in the ears of the Establishment.

Brameld is strangely silent on the very controversial questions of autonomy in the classroom and of job restrictive tendencies in the "professionalization" of teaching. So, of course, he ignores the connection between the two. By "autonomy in the classroom" is meant the following: Efforts to change the quality of instruction must proceed through the voluntary cooperation of the teacher. Even school systems that are terribly autocratic in administration will tend to maintain at least the fiction of classroom autonomy: The teacher may be *ordered* to police the washroom between classes, but he cannot (at least not so easily) be ordered to allow more time for group discussion in his course on "World Cultures." The latter may be suggested to him; he may be encouraged to do so; he may even be required to attend an after-school "workshop" devoted to the proper use of group discussion. But since there is no really effective way of forcing compliance, an order to allow, for example, at least fifteen minutes per class session for group discussion is futile.

The consequences of this fact are many, among them the necessity for teachers to be educated in college. The System must operate with inadequately supervised employees; it must either select or train them so that minimum standards of performance are assured. The requirement of a college degree may have quite variable or even no effect so far as training is concerned, but it works beautifully as a selective device: A college student also performs a whole series of rather meaningless tasks under inadequate supervision, and it is quite easy to determine which students can meet minimum standards under these conditions. Those who can are likely to satisfy *that* criterion for public school teaching. So the teaching profession has been raised by law into an exclusively college-stamped membership, and thus has been able to secure economic and political significance beyond other comparable white-collar workers.

Now one might think that a Reconstructionist would at least question some of the job-restrictive tendencies inherent in the present status of the teaching profession. Even if he had not considered some of those tendencies, he *must* have thought of the difficulties in changing the content and methods of teaching in a system which leaves the classroom an autonomous sanctuary for all sorts of reactionaries, but Brameld says nothing which could indicate the slightest disapproval of the present system (or lack of system) in changing teaching. By avoiding the word "teaching" and concentrating on the idea of "learning," he reinforces the present power structure of the teaching profession, which is, incidentally but obviously, nicely tied up in symbiotic competition-cooperation with the administrative structure of school systems, state and local.

Not even Brameld's imaginative and well-stated case for a federal education authority, a proposed public corporation to operate under a new department of education, really contradicts anything in the existing power system. While he would advocate a renewal of measures like the CCC and NYA of the 1930's (an advocacy at least partially met by the Job Corps and the Neighborhood Youth Corps), a careful reading shows that he sees these measures not as alternatives but rather as auxiliaries to the all-in-one-school proposals made earlier. In fact, as he outlines it, the "consensus" would grant to the regular school System organized at the national level—with wide latitude for varied curricula down to the local level—an authority far greater than at present it possesses, an authority to regulate *all* educative media, including "newspapers, radio chains, and other instruments of public enlightenment" (TRPOE, p. 302), with a matching expansion of the educational budget. In fact, Brameld's approach might well be considered the final point in the century-old movement toward an educational System.

It is not really to be wondered that the Establishment, or our imaginary computer who makes decisions in their interest, can find room for Brameld's philosophy of education in the training of teachers. For this "philosophy," if it had any effect at all, would tend to trivialize social protest and to justify unlimited expansion of the System. That's why Brameld's point-that-needs-making *can* be made too often.

Personal Afterword

It should be obvious that Mr. Brameld and I share many things in common. One of those things is a wise and gentle friend who responded to the present treatise of Brameld's works with the following wise and gentle remonstrance: "With all the real villians at loose in the educational world today—the cynics, the self-seeking, the time-servers, the haters of youth and life—why single out a genuinely good man for such an attack?" I offer the following as an admittedly weak answer and excuse for not removing this chapter from the book:

It is always the heretic within the fold rather than the infidel without who poses the greatest threat to the values of the faithful. But that is not argument. A defense would go like this: (i) Among those who argue proposals for educational policy *within* the System, Brameld is regarded as *the* spokesman for political and pedagogical radicalism. (ii) But expressed in Brameld's language, radicalism is neither intellectually satisfying nor politically potent. On the other hand, (iii) radical ideas capable of generating and guiding a massive devolution of the System *are* desperately needed right now in the polity of education. From these premises, it would follow (iv) that an attempt to free radicalism from Reconstructionism is not only justified but necessary.

This chapter set itself to demonstrate that and why premise (ii) is true. It has not done (iv), but the ground is cleared. Later we shall have to ask what sound new structure might be constructed on that ground.

Notes

THEODORE BRAMELD

Works of Brameld referred to in the text, arranged chronologically.

(WE)   Workers' Education in the United States, Fifth Year-book of the John Dewey Society (New York, 1941) Brameld was editor of this volume and contributed an essay "Toward a Philosophy of Workers' Education."

(DFA)   *Design for America: An Educational Exploration of the Future of Democracy for High Schools and Junior Colleges* (New York, 1945) An outgrowth of the author's experience teaching his own materials on an experimental basis in Floodwood, Minnesota.

(MPSS)   *Minority Problems in the Public Schools: A Study of Administrative Policies and Practices in Seven Systems* (New York, 1946) Report of an on-the-spot study, financed by the Rosenwald Foundation.

(EME)   *Ends and Means in Education: A Midcentury Appraisal* (New York, 1950) A collection of essays published during the decade of the 1940's.

(PEP)   *Patterns of Educational Philosophy* (Yonkers-on-Hudson, 1950) A basic textbook in philosophy of education, continuing the original systematic statement of Reconstructionism and its relation to other 'isms.

(MEAT)   "The Meeting of Educational and Anthropological Theory" in George D. Spindler (ed.) *Education and Anthropology* (Stanford, 1955) pp. 216-237. Report of a conference of anthropologists and educators focusing on how anthropology can serve education. Contains transcripts of discussions, Brameld's appearing *passim.*

(PEICP)   *Philosophies of Education in Cultural Perspective* (New York, 1955)

(TRPOE)   *Toward a Reconstructed Philosophy of Education* (New York, 1955-56) A two volume revision and enlargement of the 1950 textbook (PEP).

(CFE)   *Cultural Foundations of Education* (New York, 1957) A philosophical analysis of the concept of culture and its implications for education.

(ROAC)   *The Remaking of a Culture: Life and Education in Puerto Rico* (New York, 1959) An extensive field study based on the theoretical position developed in (CFE).

(EEA)   *Education for the Emerging Age: Newer Ends and Stronger Means* (New York, 1961) Contains some material from the earlier (EME), but substantially a book of later essays.

(EAP)   *Education as Power* (New York, 1965) Lectures on American education and culture delivered in Japan and Korea, plus some other lectures and addresses.

(UEI)   *The Use of Explosive Ideas in Education: Culture, Class, and Evolution* (Pittsburgh, 1965) These ideas explained and their implication drawn for educational thought and practice.

1   Cf. William H. Kilpatrick: *Foundations of Method* (New York, 1926) p. 268 ff. In Brameld's TRPOE, the terms "teaching," "instruction," "pedagogy," and "didactics" are absent from the index; "method" appears only under "learning." In EEA (p. 11), Brameld speaks ingenuously of "learning machines," as if verbal legerdemain would change the fact that programmed instruction is a didactic device, a basic concept wholly unaccounted for in his philosophy.

2   "Philosophy of Education as Philosophy of Politics" is the title of one of the few essays reprinted essentially unchanged from the 1950 EME in the 1961 EEA. The same idea is presented with different trappings in the title essay of EAP.

3   See James S. Coleman, *et al., Equality of Educational Opportunity* (Washington: U. S. Department of Health, Education, and Welfare, 1966).

4   See Hobert W. Burns: "The Logic of Educational Implication," *Educational Theory* XII, 1 (1962) pp. 53-63.

5 John Dewey: *Reconstruction in Philosophy* (2nd edition, Boston, 1948) pp. IX-XI. For a truly magnificent example of showing in detail how cultural change and philosophic thought were connected in ancient Greece, see A. W. H. Adkins, *Merit and Responsibility* (Oxford, 1960).

6 This kind of rough-and-ready congruence is visible in James E. Russell: *Change and Challenge in American Education* (Boston, 1965). In his capacity as Secretary of the Educational Policies Commission, Mr. Russell tells us that he was forced "to rethink just about every idea I ever had on the subject of education" (p. 2), and that rethinking took him into the realms of philosophy, politics, poetry, . . . "just about every" field of human thought.

7 An analytical survey, somewhat of this sort, is found in Seymour Martin Lipset, *Political Man* (Garden City, 1963) Chapter Ten, "American Intellectuals: Their Politics and Status." In no study reported is there a clear effort to treat philosophical doctrine as a major variable. It would be difficult, but it should not be impossible, to devise an instrument to probe philosophical beliefs. Sample question:

Consider the sentence P: "God exists." According to you,

T–F a. P is a proposition confirmable by the same kind of scientific tests as the proposition that celestial galaxies exist.

T–F b. If a. is false, P is meaningless.

T–F c. P can be meaningful and true even if a. is false.

T–F d. P is necessarily true; if P were false there could be no such thing as science.

T–F e. P is meaningful, but it cannot be objectively true: P expresses something other than a proposition.

T–F f. P is not a well-formed sentence because "exists" is not a predicate by itself.

It should be obvious that the number of persons who would have well thought out beliefs on such question is very small; it comprises a group politically insignificant compared to those who would give a simple yes or no to P.

8 A lovely example is Garrett Mattingly: "Changing Attitudes Toward the State during the Renaissance" in W. H. Werkmeister (ed.), *Facets of the Renaissance* (Los Angeles, 1959).

9 The case for Brameld's cultural evaluation is sound enough in logic. It can be put, quite informally, as follows: "There is a social crisis having these features. . . but Dewey and his followers either denied that there is a social crisis or at least, in appropriate con-

texts, failed to assert and describe the social crisis. Therefore, Dewey and his followers are either lying or mistaken.

10 Paul Blanshard: *American Freedom and Catholic Power* (Boston, 1949).

11 Henry David Aiken, *Reason and Conduct* (New York, 1962), Chapter XII, "A Revival of Ethical Naturalism."

12 See, for example, Harry S. Broudy, *Building in Philosophy of Education* (New York, 1954).

13 See J. E. McClellan, "Dewey's Concept of Method," *School Review*, Summer, 1959.

14 There is no good history of either of these movements, both of which were central in the discussions of educational theorists in the postwar decade, both of which had been avant-garde for educationists in the thirties. A good collection of the classical papers as well as a survey of current research in group dynamics is found in Edmund Amidon and Jack Hough (eds.), *Interaction Analysis* (Temple University Bookstore, 2 Vols.) The attempt to establish a methodology of moral judgment analogous to scientific methodology owes its recent impetus to R. Bruce Raup, George Axtelle, Kenneth Benne, and B. O. Smith. Raup and his colleagues, who met and discussed the issue for many years, finally publishing their conclusions in the twenty-eighth *Yearbook* of the National Society of College Teachers of Education, 1943 (revised edition published by Harper in 1950, recently reissued by the Teachers College Bureau of Publications.) The literature of educational theory abounds with references to the *Yearbook*; See John L. Childs, *American Pragmatism and Education*. (New York: Henry Holt; 1956) pp. 298-311. A good study of how these movements came to have the central place in educational theory which they achieved, and the connection (or better, lack of connection) between these currents in theory and school practices has not been done.

15 This talent in Brameld can easily be discerned in his DFA. Another essay by Brameld which indirectly reveals something of his power as a teacher is his "WE." Here we see a faith in education, in intelligence, and in ideas which could reflect either a pathological delusion or experience in teaching far superior to that of ordinary teachers. The evidence from Brameld's students and colleagues (often hostile witnesses) is overwhelmingly on the side of regarding his extraordinary success in teaching (particularly in the earlier years) as the sources of his extraordinary faith in education.

4

Jacques Barzun: Is It Enough to be an Anti-Anti-Intellectual?

A person would naturally suppose that educational policy has something to do with (a) education and (b) policy. One might have many ideas about (a) and none about (b) or vice versa, yet one would not be said to have any particular ideas about educational policy. When we encounter Jacques Barzun, however, a new phenomenon emerges: He has much to say about both (a) and (b), and *still* we are inclined to doubt that he has very much to say about educational policy. Now if I can maintain that conclusion, I should be able to say something rather important about the meaning of "educational policy." But, even if the conclusion of this chapter does not prove persuasive, the road leads through the corpus of Barzun's writings and for that reason alone should prove entertaining. Indeed, a measure of inconclusiveness must be expected from any encounter with Barzun's thought: He seldom fails to be (just a shade) wrong and never to be interesting.

I. THE NAME "BARZUN" AND WHAT IT STANDS FOR

When treating the works of Theodore Brameld, one could be sure that, whenever Brameld wrote something, he believed what he wrote and would continue to believe it. When discussing Jacques Barzun, one can be sure of neither. Barzun often writes what he feels rather than what he believes. And what he feels at one time may be different from what he feels at another—an emotive tendency Barzun shares with the rest of humanity.

But such variability—not inconsistency, much less self-contradiction—tends to disconcert the serious critic of Barzun's works. Consider, for example, the question whether our efforts at mass schooling can, or conceivably *could*, produce education, in the full and honorific sense of the word "education." It does not take a profound thinker to recognize that that question is basic to many other questions of educational policy. What would Barzun say on the subject? It all depends. He might deliver a panegyric to mass democracy and its expression in education:

> What is going on in American manners is our characteristic process of education. We start with raw materials and the first licks must be adapted to the simple thoughts of large numbers. We begin "democratic" and then turn "scientific," which means becoming shamelessly self-conscious and mechanical. Gradually the grossness purges itself. We must not forget that what we have undertaken, no other society has tried: We do not suppress half of mankind to refine part of the other half. We let it spread out in daylight to do the best it can. So one may question whether it is fair to complain at once of popular crudity and of popular efforts to correct it. (*God's Country and Mine*, p. 181; c.f., p. 206, hereafter abbreviated as GCM.)

Or, he might say with great bitterness, on a different occasion:

> "Some . . . advocate mass education . . . 'without lowering standards. . . .' What they fail to imagine is the demoralizing effect of large numbers *as such* upon any work of the mind." (First Report, p. 20.)

Notice that these are not necessarily contradictory statements. One could well believe that large numbers *as such* do have a demoralizing effect on any work of the mind and still believe that that demoralization is a price worth paying for a unique historical effort toward popular refinement, or at least that it is better—all things considered and over the long run—to demoralize *certain* works of the mind than to suppress half of mankind. One could well believe both of Barzun's statements, but if one does believe both, one must accept that questions of the sort we began with are theoretical and complex, which is to say they are dialectical and analogical. At the risk of being pedantic, if you begin with a question like "Can any program of mass schooling be genuinely educative?" your answer cannot be a simple yes or no. An adequate response must pose conflicting answers set in a historical process; it has to borrow some simpler model of thought (e.g., the economic: X costs a great deal but still less than Y) in which these conflicts can be resolved; and, finally, it must discard the simpler model lest that simplicity itself become an obstacle to understanding complexity. Progress through a schema like that is what I mean by a theoretical mode of thought.

But as the name "Barzun" is actually used it does not designate a system of complex, dialectical, and analogical thought. On the contrary, the name evokes here a witty aphorism, there a flash of style and courage—marks of the self-conscious man of action rather than the contemplative scholar. Foreign interpreters of American life, particularly, seem unable to state their observations without citing Barzun. Thus when one contributor to the *Times Literary Supplement* issue on "The American Imagination" (anonymous as always in the *TLS*) needed an "acid" critic of American colleges, he used Barzun; when another needed an example of the American intellectual's inability to resist making a good thing out of "culture," again it was Barzun that served as exemplar.[1] When Herbert von Borch attempted to explain to his German readers the "Reconciliation of the Intellectuals" in American life, he attributed the expression to *Time* but borrowed the defense of it from Barzun.

> The rift between intellectuals and society has narrowed in consequence of a mutual rapprochement. *Time*'s star witness for the position of American intellectuals is Professor Jacques Barzun, who teaches history at Columbia. Actually, Barzun is highly critical of that position; what matters to Mr. Luce's editors, however, are the statements they can quote by Barzun . . . as evidence of a reconciliation.
>
> The intellectuals of America, Barzun says, have today "won recognition in tangible ways beyond any previous group of their peers." Grumbling is out of date. Intellectuals who still grumble,

Barzun says, "forget that the true creator's role, even in its bitterest attack, is to make us understand or endure life better. Our intellectuals do neither when they entice us to more self-contempt." The reference is to something that is already past, for by the end of the second world war, Barzun says, "it was no disgrace, no provincialism, to accept America and admire it. . . . America was quite simply *the* world power, which means: the center of world awareness: it was Europe that was provincial." [2]

This identification of Barzun is like calling Lyndon Johnson an employee of the federal government. But it matters no more to von Borch than it did to the late Mr. Luce exactly why Barzun is critical nor what he is critical of. There is the quotable quote and 'Barzun' to serve as its label.

The bitterest dregs are yet to be drunk. We must hear from a would-be reformer of kindergarten education:

I believe that primary education in this country is a holding-back procedure—the first official imposing of the anti-intellectualism (to use Barzun's term) that is queering our children's chance to develop the kind of ability they need to cope with our complex world. [3]

Aside from the questionable judgment and rhetoric in Simmons' statement, the fact that it could appear in one of our better slicks reveals (i) our capitalistic tendency to give proprietary title to public property and (ii) that the splendidly naked surname "Barzun" identifies not a complex thinker but an attitude-cliché toward American culture and education. But it is a sad fact, or perhaps an amusing fact, that no one uses that attitude-cliché called "Barzun" more deliberately, effectively, and (I presume) profitably than Barzun himself. When Barzun feels outrage, "Barzun" can be signed to a piece of outrageous writing. The barbed wit labeled "Barzun" can be turned against Barzun's enemies, and Barzun's friends find a firm defender whose buckler is emblazoned "Barzun."

Perhaps the relation between "Barzun" and Barzun is more subtle still. Perhaps Barzun can bear the burden of his offices and the heavy yoke of serious study all at once only because his daimôn is also named "Barzun." We may leave that question to his analyst. The task immediately at hand is to analyze the major elements in the attitude called "Barzun" as Barzun expressed it. Without intending anything very significant by the terms, the major elements of that attitude may be classified as philosophy, politics, and profession.

Philosophy: Despite surface resemblances, Barzun is not a classicist, neo- or otherwise, nor is he a humanist in the technical sense of the term. Classicism, as a doctrine, is defined almost entirely by negation, specifically as a negation of Romanticism.[4]

The classicist's credo derives most directly from Irving Babbitt's *Rousseau and Romanticism*, a scathing indictment of contemporary society for having lost its root sense of order and limitation. It requires only a sharpening of focus to make this specifically an indictment of the contemporary school for having lost its sense of limits and attempting tasks that lie outside its inherently restricted purposes.[5]

A great deal of what Barzun says about contemporary education sounds like that, but his objections arise from very different premises. Indeed, a large part of Barzun's scholarship has been devoted to restoring the Romanticists to their proper place in the history of ideas. This chapter does not provide any detailed treatment of this aspect of Barzun's work, but its mere existence is sufficient to establish the point that Barzun cannot be designated a classicist.[6]

Nor is he really a literary humanist as that term has come to have a technical meaning, although there is, again, a similarity: The literary humanist stands against theological and scientific absolutism, and so does Barzun. But subsequently the literary humanist will erect a particular canon of literary works into a new absolute, while Barzun will continue to echo William James' "Damn the Absolute." For Barzun as for James, there is no final Truth to be learned by studying a particular set of books, great or small. Human wisdom cannot be decanted from a Great Mind to a lesser mind. On that point there is a difference, radical and uneliminable, between Barzun and the literary humanists.

Not a classicist nor a humanist, Barzun is but too faithfully a Pragmatist. As will be argued later, this is a source of some strength and more weakness in his attitude toward education. The immediate point is that in the stress of educational politics, Barzun may appear to be wedded to ideas that Educationists, almost by reflex, label "undemocratic," "reactionary," or "socially divisive." But, remember, politics makes bedfellows, not marriages. Barzun's philosophical claim to Pragmatism and democracy is as good as any Edutionist's, showing that philosophies derive from life and not vice versa. (We are still treating "Barzun" as a complex of attitudes and moods. There are certain technical points which arise in Barzun's version of Pragmatism; these are considered in later sections of this chapter.)

Politics: There is in nearly everything Barzun writes an intense awareness of power and relations which are conditioned by personal and political power. But ideationally, Barzun is non-political. Very seldom do the categories of politics—interest groups, classes, civil rights, and the like—function as analytical concepts in Barzun's writings. He quotes Berlioz as having called politics "that tall skinny wench with shifty eyes, a pale face and a hard heart." (Berlioz I, p. 528) Is this also Barzun's attitude? He never says so, exactly, but from what he does say (e.g., GCM, p. 85, "Government is a mystery, a miracle. . . .") one can infer that he also treats politics as a dimension of life to be described metaphorically rather than analyzed theoretically. That attitude toward politics, of course, will result in a very unusual view of educational policy, as we will examine later.

Perhaps, the distinctiveness of Barzun's attitude toward politics may best be revealed in contrast to that of Arthur E. Bestor, Jr., who is also a historian of repute and was for a number of years a highly sensitive and self-conscious critic of educational policy. One senses directly in the writings of, for example, Conant and Brameld a total exteriority, i.e., an absence of any particularly critical view of self in the discussions of exterior things like curriculum and administration. But such exteriority is attributable neither to Barzun nor to Bestor. Perhaps the discipline of historical research has made both these men conscious that motives and purposes are, in the very nature of things, questionable; else historians had not spent so much effort questioning them. Every judgment reflects a judger as well as an object judged. Bestor displayed that consciousness most clearly in *Educational Wastelands*, less so in *The Restoration of Learning*.[7] Bestor was interested in changing things, and he believed, as Barzun apparently does not, in the "primacy of institutional structure."[8] This means for Bestor that an effort to modify educational practices is a political struggle to change the men and machinery that determine school practices. A book, an essay, a speech—all are actions in the struggle. Such a conception of self and work is obviously alien to a reflective scholar; it creates a tension which divides the self. In one of his last contributions to the policy argument, Bestor showed a diminution of vigor and resolve which may indicate that the tension between scholarship and politics proved greater than he wished to sustain.[9]

Barzun is happily free of *that* tension, though not, of course, of all tensions. He does not regard his writings as weapons in a general conflict for control of educational institutions. Consequently he is free from the tiresome moralizing that infects so much educational literature; one will happily not find in Barzun's writings the crisis mentality, the constant "We must act now!" But free from the need to moralize, Barzun is also free from the need to be constructive. His writings are frequently petulant and socially irresponsible simply because he does not, as did Bestor, set out to change the institutional arrangements of American education.

Notice that Barzun is *ideationally* non-political. Practically, he takes sides in education politics with evident delight. But Barzun does not treat local skirmishes as merely tactical maneuvers in a grand struggle to establish a new system of power. Each encounter is its own justification. Hence, he can enter on one side or another in an educational struggle without committing himself to the ultimate goals of either protagonist. "Damn the absolute!" "All education is inherently inadequate. . . ."

Do not be deceived by this: Barzun does not unconsciously delight in combat for its own sake. That mode of being lacks the high self-awareness that Barzun displays in all his works and words. No, for Barzun, an ideationally non-political attitude toward politics, including educational politics, is the only stance justifiable to intellect:

> A "system of democracy" must be either a piece of empty verbalism or the plan of imposed unity. In pointing this out, Intellect is doing its proper work; in cobbling together the proposed system it would be usurping the role of will and making itself a dangerous substitute for satisfactions which democracy denies. To put this more generally, the greatest danger of Intellect is that it so readily breeds intellectual*ism*. (*House of Intellect*, p. 155, hereafter abbreviated as HofI.)

Of course, it is not so simple as that. How and why we will see later.

This brings us to the point that Barzun is at once a professional critic and powerful administrator. He does not have to regard his critical writings as weapons of war; they are rather the visible manifestation of the critical way of life, one that since the time of Socrates has been an honorable if not exactly a lovable calling. Today its practice brings not the hemlock but "wealth . . . and manifold distinctions." (GCM, p. 57) It also brings, at least to Barzun, administrative responsibilities in the exercise of which he shows his devotion to Will and hostility to Intellectualism.

To these matters we must return with more concreteness later. But in what follows the reader must keep in mind that Barzun, by virtue of being a professional critic *and* a highly successful university administrator, simply will not fit any one of the usual categories into which we divide critics of schools. The platform prose of a typical college administrator is distinctly out of character when Barzun writes it, as he is forced occasionally to do. The difference between the ordinary college spokesman and Barzun is predominantly a matter of *metier*.

Even more striking is the difference between Barzun's criticism and that of say a salesman or admiral, not that there is anything wrong with the latter occupations, nor that their practitioners are necessarily ignorant about education. It is simply that criticism of education is, among other things, an aspect of a more general *art* of criticism, one that Barzun has practiced for more than thirty years with a deliberate individuality, both distinctive and distinguished, which is why Barzun's writings deserve our serious attention. The importance of his criticism does not lie in widespread influence, for precisely as that influence has been widespread it has also been diffuse and ambivalent. No, the importance is in seeing the strengths and weaknesses of one *way* of criticism.

What is Barzun's way? Let us borrow Charles Frankel's threefold classification of intellectual activities: history, criticism, and theory.[10] It is absurd to make invidious comparisons among these "speculative faculties" (the apt expression which Frankel takes from John Stuart Mill); each of them plays an essential role in the efforts of men to understand themselves and their world and to modify both enough to make life possible.

But precisely here begins the most fundamental conflict between Barzun and the Educationists. Barzun, for his part, deliberately rejects theory, the third figure in this triad, even as he manages a most ingenious synthesis of the first two in a literary form he calls cultural criticism. In contrast, for good or ill, American Educationists are committed to theory as the primary, if not the sole, basis for educational policy and action. If I am correct on this point, it means that Barzun's criticisms of American education are far more radical than those complaining of a course in cosmetology or too much emphasis on sports. The whole of the Educationists' logic of educational argument is at issue.

To appreciate this most fundamental feature of Barzun's work—its deeply pragmatic bias against theory—we shall examine first *The House of Intellect*, then the larger scheme in which it stands, and finally Barzun's head-on attack against theory in *Science: The Glorious Entertainment*.

II. A HOUSE IS NOT A HOME

Educationists are likely to find *The House of Intellect* infuriating and to toss it into the pile containing other books that cause the same emotion. But those who begin it will probably finish it, for many besides Educationists feel the lash before the last chapter. Who can resist a bit of gloating when the anonymous writers of *Time* are castigated, when executors of philanthropic legacies receive the comeuppance they so richly deserve? Only an employee of the Foundation can fail to be amused by this:

> The intellectual life is expensive and it deserves solid comfort, but if due relations obtained, fundational offices would not look like the headquarters of a billion-dollar trust where the student's over-coat and hat seem a blemish, and where the long meditations of young executives are guarded by murmuring vestals trained to be kind to scholars. (HofI, p. 101)

No one who travels, or teaches, or lives with a spouse (or without one), or plays records, or writes, or reads, or does research, or tries to get in or out of power will fail to find his own foibles discovered and ridiculed, nor will he fail to find that his own special hate has received similar treatment. Whether one is a masochist or a sadist (or a normal, healthy combination of the two) one will find pleasure in reading *The House of Intellect*. This must include a rather large proportion of the reading public, for Barzun's book stayed in the best-seller column of the *New York Times* for twenty-one weeks in hardcover and maintains a prominent visibility on "quality" paperback shelves, a visibility not totally dependent on its vile pink cover.

This way of talking about *The House of Intellect* is not so flippant as it may at first appear. For the book is not, nor does it pretend to be, a unified argument. It is a set of aphorisms and vignettes ties loosely to the theme that Intellect is having a difficult time with its three great enemies—philanthropy, science, and art —while the intellectuals, who should be defending intellect, are either aligned actively and profitably with its enemies or else are off to a Northeast-Southwest Conference in Somaliland and oblivious to the whole controversy. It is this notion, as Barzun harries it, that has gained for him the foremost rank among the defenders of Intellect against its many foes.[11]

But what is Intellect, thus upper-cased? It is something like the alphabet; a tradition of more or less arbitrary conventions, the observance of which makes possible freedom and power in shared thought. Art, which seeks to escape the conventional altogether; Science, which destroys the common conventions of Intellect by its specialized language systems; and Philanthropy, in which love of man-the-species precludes any judgment of his makings and doings —this demonic trinity is corroding "the tradition of explicitness and energy, of inquiry and debate, of public, secular tests and social accountability." (HofI, p. 26) The term "trinity" is appropriate: These elements are consubstantial in their institutional epiphanies.

"House" in *The House of Intellect* is used as one might speak of a fraternity house or a brothel: "an establishment requiring appurtenances and prescribing conventions—with house rules and an income for its upkeep." (HofI, p. 56) As conventions disintegrate and rules evaporate into a formless informality, the house becomes a home; the company of scholars is lost entirely in the "Family of Man."

All this, of course, is not argument; it is imagery. One cannot argue, refute, rebut, nor, in the purely cognitive sense, even agree with Barzun's imagery, no more than one could argue, etc., with Picasso's "Guernica." This is not to say that *The House of Intellect* cannot be criticized; the purpose of this section is to do just that. But not all criticism is argument. We already noted that a simple categorization of Barzun's ideas is inappropriate. Equally so is to ask the naive questions: "What is his main thesis? Is it true or false?" His books are systems of images that *ipso facto* can be neither true nor false.

The series of vignettes that constitute *The House of Intellect*, then, must be taken for just what they are. "A book should be judged on the scale of its major qualities," says Barzun, quoting the late Albert J. Nock (HofI, p. 249), and surely this is the least consideration to which Barzun is entitled.

What, then, *are* the major qualities of *The House of Intellect?* Its qualities, in part, are passions. Unfortunately they do not remain at the level of major passions: Anger is here, sometimes controlled and profound, but it too often degenerates into mere nastiness and rancor. Pride also has difficulty in maintaining nobility; as snobbery it is ignoble. Wit forced is mere cuteness, and of that there is more than a little in *The House of Intellect*.

Two virtues, however, ring true throughout the book: courage and dedication. No group nor individual escapes Barzun's ire merely because that group or individual is powerful. Even this virtue, in the minds of the ungenerous, might evoke no admiration, for surely Barzun need fear no more the frown of the great. As Provost and Dean of Faculties, at Columbia University, having completed a memorable three-year term as Dean of the Graduate Faculties, having been appointed to the Seth Low Professorship in History, with unannounced effect on his administrative responsibilities, Barzun's stature perhaps exceeded that of "professorship" as he speaks of it in another connection:

> It is difficult for citizens of a federal union to appreciate how much power and financial advantage result from membership in the national Institute of a centralized state. A professorship in a great university only begins to approximate this degree of leverage while creating the same ambiguity as to actual merit. (Berlioz I, p. 13)

In Barzun's case, the approximation is probably rather close.

Still a mean and servile spirit does not become otherwise just by animating the seat of the mighty. The courage shown in *The House of Intellect* is no less than that shown in books written when Barzun was merely a somewhat unconventional professor of history.

Dedication is shown in two ways. First, the self-conscious crafts-manship of the artist shines through every line of his writing; it shines even through the distortions and ill-will that occasionally mar the book. Second, there is an ideal, albeit a negative one, to which Barzun is dedicated, one that goes beyond merely using words well. This ideal stand in opposition to the virulent cant and hokum that infect not only our language but also our feelings and actions which increasingly become tied more to language and less to non-linguistic reality. This negative ideal can arouse great passion, but only in a narrow range—disgust, revulsion, rage, and sustained hatred. It requires a positive ideal to turn these into maganimity and hope. This Barzun has lost. Sensing the need for it, he violates his own calling as historian and speaks of a mythical past as exem-plifying what he no longer has the will to create in the future. When he writes, and this is truly typical, that before about 1890 we had a "communicable idea of the purpose of schools" but after that time "it began to yield to the indefiniteness of mass educa-tion" (HofI, p. 90), he betrays not only historical inaccuracy but a failure of vision and nerve, a subjective need to see lost in the past what objectively needs to be visualized for the future.

The major qualities of *The House of Intellect* are passions com-bined with the virtues of courage and dedication. Let me say at once that sustained anger effectively directed against the "flatulent Newspeak" (HofI, p. 95) that so surrounds us is noble and neces-sary. We forgive ourselves and our friends, even our enemies, for writing and speaking the most blatant nonsense simply because we think it must be well intended. That is magnanimity carried to the point of vice. Those too insensitive to be infuriated by the degradation of language may ponder this: Without the disciplined control of language, we protect ourselves against advertisers and publicists only by a cultivated inattention to *all* words, an inatten-tion that leaves us incapable of taking an active, informed part in the direction of our affairs, public and private.[12] If the progressive degradation of language does not arouse your ire, your capacity for selective attention has already been lost.

But this campaign for clean language is not so simple as it sounds. For the only way the System can *surely* cease producing cant and hokum is to get rid of the Educationists altogether. And this, in a most disturbing manner, is implicitly what Barzun advocates that we do. The Educationist's way of argument has been lost when we no longer attempt to base educational policies on explicit, scientifically valid theory.

By precept and example, Barzun deprecates the theoretical faculty of human intellect when applied outside the "pure" sciences. This prejudice in Barzun is not restricted to matters of education; it appears wherever he encounters theoretical formulations of ideas. To show that this is the case, we must look, albeit hastily, at some other aspects of Barzun's thought. In Section V we return to question the place of theory in educational policy.

III. FORM AND STYLE

Barzun's academic home is the discipline of history, but his writings are not histories of the sort usually emanating from college professors. He writes, instead, in a form he calls cultural criticism, "clearly not pure biography, history, or criticism; it is a selection and fusion of all three. . . ." (*Darwin, Marx, and Wagner*, p. ix, hereafter abbreviated as DMW.) The three elements appear in approximately equal and integrated proportions in *Darwin, Marx, and Wagner*. In *Berlioz and the Romantic Century*, obviously a labor of love, the biographical element becomes dominant, although, as indicated in the author's preface, "this book is not a biography in the ordinary sense."

Barzun's discussions of education appear in several works having the same general form of cultural criticism, though in these works biography drops out almost entirely, replaced by commentary of the sort one finds in the best travel books: a vivid evocation of sounds, smells, shapes, and textures. In accuracy to the nuances of spoken language, Barzun's commentaries are superb. Sometimes, as in the essays reprinted as *The Energies of Art*, aesthetic or literary criticism emerges as central, but it never excludes history, biography, and commentary.

Though the elements included and their proportions may vary from work to work, cultural criticism as Barzun writes it has *form*, in the approbative sense of the term; it never disintegrates into a mere *pasticcio*. The lineaments of this form were clearly set as

early as 1937 in *Race: A Study in Modern Superstition;* they underwent no significant change after 1939, when Barzun published *Of
Human Freedom.* In thirty years and dozens of books since, Barzun
has used that perfected form and stamped it with his own conception of the nature and function of thought. Its strengths and weaknesses as a medium for educational discourse stem from that conception.

Quite as distinctive to Barzun as the form of his writings is their
style. And, again, the style is a conscious creation. The canons of
Barzun's style are described partially but charmingly in *The Modern Researcher.* Anyone who learned to obey those rules would
write clear and idiomatic English, pleasingly rhythmical and free
from affectation. Even so, however, no mere follower of those
precepts would write as richly, variedly, and elegantly as Barzun.

Some of the more gracious adornments of Barzun's language may
be described *post hoc,* but not even the Provost would dare pre-
scribe them for the aspiring Ph.D. candidate. For example, the
same technique which Vladimir Nabokov used with some restraint
in *Lolita,* and with utter abandon in *Pale Fire,* Barzun uses less
flamboyantly but no less effectively: the technique of uncovering
the buried metaphors in ordinary English words.

In his earlier works, Barzun's use of this technique is rather obvious: "No sooner has 'economic man' been split off by the econo-
mist than the same in-dividual (aptly so-called) acts in his capacity
as 'sentimental man' or 'Chinaman' and defeats the investigation."
(*Of Human Freedom,* pp. 175-176)

Later the same device is used more subtly: "Most productions of
Shakespeare, the traditional Molière at the Comédie, and the
Greeks in purple-edged nightgowns are unbearable travesties. . . ."
(HofI, pp. 264-265) This respect for metaphor saves a language
from the kind of debasement that would make the expression
"travesty of justice" equivalent to "the Dean denied my request";
a necessary (but by no means sufficient) condition for its practice
is enough knowledge of Latin to recognize that "travesty" and
"transvestite" have a common parentage.

More original is the deliberate use of allusions that arise when a
word is shifted from one part of speech to another. Concerning the
passions shown in Berlioz' *Memoirs,* Barzun writes, "reared in ar.
age that admired the Napoleonic virtues, he did not think it neces-

sary to show how they differed from a maniac's behavior." To this he drops a footnote. "But it is necessary now when we prefer the artist silent, cool and cucumbrous. . . ." Barzun can swallow a line as deftly as Shelly Berman.

From a commonplace figure of speech to the New Testament: "and although we twentieth-centurions are great seekers after irony, finding it, often, by fiat. . . ." (EofA, p. 196)

The same technique can be used with a more corporeal intent. Here he is quoting William Heard Kilpatrick: " 'I learn what I live . . . and I learn it as I accept it . . . I learn it in the degree that I live it . . . I learn what I live. . . .' " Then Barzun adds his kicker: "This incantation is powerful—the seat of learning is the liver." (HofI, p. 92)

But his distinctive style and form do not entirely protect Barzun from the failings of his academic background. Like most historians, Barzun is given to needless name dropping, sometimes, it seems, with intent other than to inform. Is it really necessary, or indeed accurate, to attribute to Chesterton that common line: "Everything worth doing is worth doing badly."? (*Music in American Life*, p. 70, hereafter abbreviated as MinAL.) And in the same book, why refer to the slave in Plautus for the thought that one can be so constituted that he regards nothing human as alien to him? (MinAL, p. 14) Ordinarily the line ". . . nihil a me alienum puto" is credited to Terence; it undoubtedly and unmistakenly appears in Terence's Hauton Timorumenos, I, i. line 25. Did Plautus, Terence's senior, say it first? If so, where? In this context (MinAL) Barzun is advancing the very interesting claim that the universality of human nature is seen by a slave, while those virtues which distinguish man from man are visible only from above. That is also a very controversial claim. Instead of *arguing* his claim, Barzun makes an unusual citation in Latin comedy. Now why? Just a simple mistake? Then maybe his claim about the universality of human nature versus the specificity of virtues is also a mistake. Or the attribution of the quotation to Plautus may be Barzun's way of asking that we change our usual citation for this common quotation. But surely that cannot be the case. What does it matter in the context of "a personal expression of views on music" (MinAL, p. 15) whether Plautus, Terence, or Menander himself was the first author of that thought? Indeed, in the context of a personal expression of views, why not just accept Barzun's views on the universality and specificity of human traits? These last two questions tend to seem more natural, in this context, than the suspicion of error and mistake; criticism is thus disarmed. The old doctrine of "false in one, false in all" is now curiously reversed; as we learn to overlook small lapses in particular details, we lose our healthy skepticism toward the overall drift of things. I cannot regard this consequence as entirely unintended. Let it be noted that this develops the faculty of inattention which Barzun rightly excoriates on other occasions. Barzun cautions us not to "jib at incidentals," then he fills his books with incidentals that invite jibbing. Soon we cease to jib altogether.

Is this feature of Barzun's writing a fatal or a minor defect? It depends on the aim of any particular passage, really. So long as criticism is of revolving shelves in refrigerators or coin boxes on Broadway buses(GCM, Chapter 12), the details are unimportant. We will agree that everyday articles could be designed better than they are. When it comes, however, to whether Charles Darwin or Samuel Butler was on the right track in promoting the study of biology, the details are of the essence. (DMW, pp. 107-126) What is essential is not the context of literary warfare in which they write, fascinating and instructive as that context is, but rather the relation of Darwin and of Butler to the gradual filling-in of evolutionary theory, proceeding apace right now in micro-biology. Because of his profound lack of interest in systematic theory, Barzun, in his chapter entitled "After Darwin: What Is Science?", ignores this completely. He writes as if contemporary biologists were a debating society concerned with the resolution that "Mind, feelings, ethics, art: all these things once again [have become] real instead of being the dreams of automata, accompanying the physico-chemical changes called digestion, respiration, reproduction, and death." (DMW, p. 109)

Barzun's scholarship is meticulous, his story of the nineteenth-century intellectual crusades is engrossingly told. His interpretation of its significance is incredible.

Barzun's profound hostility to Karl Marx leads to less disastrous misunderstanding, for Marx, despite his incalculable impact on the world, has not been in the mainstream of major theoretical developments in Western thought. His contributions to economic theory *were* slight, just as Barzun says they were.[13] (DMW, p. 159) But, truly, it is beyond belief that anyone who really cared about what he was doing would dismiss the whole matter of value theory by quoting Whately's "men dive for pearls because they are valuable; pearls are not valuable because men dive for them." In what sense are pearls valuable without the labor of the diver? Is there not something in the idea that a thing has value because a human being puts *effort* into seeking or making it? Is there not something in the utility theory, that one expends effort only because of an *interest* in some object? Barzun, in describing the impact of the theory of marginal utility on the classical (not distinctively Marxist) labor theory of value, was standing at the fountainhead of a great *theoretical* question in Western thought: What is value? From Meinong and Ehrenfels through Perry, Dewey, and Prall to current game theory, this question, arising out of economics but transcending that field, has aroused some of the most profound theoretical work of the past century.[14]

But Barzun does not care about any of that. His concern with Marx and Darwin was to label them as mechanists, anti-humanists. His concern, which has practical, historical consequences, is directly opposed to the theoretical concern which, in itself, has none whatever. Again we see his adherence to Pragmatism and its doctrine that ideas which do not make a difference in action are pseudo-ideas.

Barzun wished to make the case that mechanical interpretations of Man and his place in Nature were post-Romantic aberrations. This concern is most properly that of cultural criticism. What more relevant question may the critic ask than how a cultural movement accounts for Man's mind and spirit? If the historian of economics ignores this question in treating of Marx, then the task of cultural criticism is to insist that it be raised. To treat *Capital* as if it were an informal essay on the nature of man is to reveal the work in an interesting light. To treat it only as that is to show blindness—the blindness of a partisan.

Barzun has long been involved in a guerrilla struggle to restore the Romantic spirit and the age in which it flourished to their proper place in men's esteem. According to Barzun, that place is not a lowly one.

Romanticism contained all the leading ideas that we ascribe to Darwin, Marx, and Wagner: evolution, natural selection, the contradictions of capitalism, class struggle, scientific sociology, dramatic music, and "popular" art. . . . Nor was it devoid of realism, though this was an inclusive realism that embraced feeling and fancy as well as the world of matter. It preferred the concrete to the abstract, but recognized ideas, dreams, romance as having reality, too. (DMW, p. 330)

I must admit that Barzun has convinced me. I now wince when I see the term "Romantic" used as a general predicate for laziness, immorality, and mild insanity. May the Berlioz revival win many converts to a true appreciation of this gifted man and his gifted contemporaries!

IV. IT IS AMUSING, BUT IS IT ENTERTAINMENT?

But even when Barzun is looking directly at nineteenth-century intellectual history, he is seeing the cultural malaise of twentieth-century America. There is no escaping it. Cultural criticism, Barzun's very form of thought, is necessarily directed toward one's *own* culture. Barzun's style is the style of engagement; he is engaging in the transitive sense of that verb—engaging others in the struggle against shuffling, inarticulateness, and apathy. And yet his natural audience—those whom Goodman would call the community of scholars—remains mostly inattentive. His form is not theirs; his style is pleasant and amusing, "engaging" only in the trivial sense. The intellectuals are fully involved in theoretical discourse alone; all other uses of language are, in the final analysis, playful, holiday-type talk. So, at least, it must have seemed to Barzun. One can see in the direction of Barzun's writing that eventually he would have to deal forthrightly with science and the place of theory in policy arguments. For as long as the academic community is involved in theoretical discourse, Barzun's non-theoretical language and values will be regarded as non-serious. And sure enough, the attack finally came—directed according to predictable strategy. Science, says Barzun, is not really serious at all; it is entertainment. That attack must be considered carefully, for it bears centrally on the question of the intellectual foundations of policy arguments generally, including those of educational policy. I use the word "attack" in a figurative sense, just as Barzun unwittingly uses the word "science" in a figurative sense. *Something* is stealing rigor from language, will from action, and joy from life, and Barzun labels that something "science." It is similar to whatever bore the same name in *The House of Intellect,* but since it must bear all these burdens of sin, its base is broader. To reveal the demon and exorcise it—that is more apt than "attack" as a description of *Science: The Glorious Entertainment,* (hereafter abbreviated as SGE).

But what a terribly disappointing performance. I do not know what it is that steals tautness, volition, and gaiety from existence, but it is literally true that these qualities have been stolen from Barzun's writing. There are at least two possible explanations, one of purely personal interest and one of theoretical significance. It may be that "Barzun" has been captured by the manifold enemies the name has evoked—a brilliant episode in the guerrilla warfare endemic in the Groves of Academe ignominiously ended. Perhaps it is comment on self, rather than "man," when Barzun writes in the coda to this work:

> Instead of reserving his freedom, of being severe with techne while also loving it; of being skeptical but gay about the prospects of humankind; of being full of wonder, yet self-possessed, at the inexplicable success of mathematical and scientific thought; instead of these acts of intellectual courage, he prefers to think he is being driven, if not to his own destruction, then toward his ever-greater pain and confusion.

How confidently we expect just that freedom, that loving severity, that skepticism and gaiety, that self-possessed sense of wonder in everything that Barzun writes. But this time our expectations are unfulfilled, and we are naturally inclined to look for some mishap to Barzun.

But the second explanation for the loss of tone in SGE is probably sounder and certainly more significant. It is impossible to frame a persuasive argument against theory in the literary form called cultural criticism. I do not care what disastrous cultural and spiritual consequences stemmed from, for example, Darwinism; these consequences are irrelevant to the question whether what Darwin said was true or false. Barzun made that mistake earlier and we forgave it; for it *is* distinctly the task of cultural criticism to show what are the consequences of major intellectual movements, and to confuse truth and consequences there is a natural error. But the same law applies at the level of meta-theory, and, at that level, also, cultural criticism is totally irrelevant. Let me use an example to explain what I mean by "the level of meta-theory": It is a question to be decided by research and argument whether the concept of stimulus generalization in reinforcement theory can account for learning to solve novel problems in geometry. I do not know the answer to that question, but I have a fairly good idea what kind of evidence and reasoning it would take to convince me one way or another. I take *that* question to be at the level of *theory*, in this case psychological theory.

But suppose one asks whether, *in principle*, any such distinctively human phenomenon as learning geometry is to be counted among the legitimate concerns of psychological theory. This latter question does not lie specifically within any particular theory but is, instead, a question about psychological theory in general. Hence, it lies at the level of meta-theory.

But what kind of *argument* would provide a convincing answer to a question at the level of meta-theory? Suppose Barzun and his retinue of graduate students collect a thousand items from the *New York Times* showing that theoretical terms and concepts from psychology result in a debilitated confusion when applied to practical affairs like advertising, law, and employment. (Cf. SGE, Chapters 8 and 9) Suppose we are convinced that these items represent no mere coincidence but rather a relation of cause to effect. Such an argument might convince us that, as a matter of *policy*, we ought not to use theoretical terms and concepts from psychology in practical affairs like advertising, law, etc. But two points have to be made perfectly clear about that (not quite) hypothetical case:

It does *not* provide an answer to the meta-theoretical question with which we began, namely whether, in principle, a phenomenon like the learning of geometry *can be* accounted for in psychological theory. Only an argument at the level of meta-theory could provide a convincing argument here. Such an argument would take as its data a careful analysis of what, in principle, psychological theory is and is not; it would then relate these data to some *theoretical* distinction between human action and non-human events. Out of the confrontation of theory and data would come an answer to the "in principle" question; we can never say in advance what the outcome of such a confrontation will be: sometimes automatic confirmation of the theory, sometimes abandonment or amendment of the theory, sometimes a rejection of the data as unreliable or irrelevant, sometimes something of each. That is the way the dialectic of theoretical argument proceeds.

Even on the policy question to which they *are* relevant, the items gathered by Barzun are not without theoretical presuppositions of their own. How can we distinguish a mere coincidence from a relation of cause and effect between two sets of social phenomena? Perhaps the awkward shuffling, noticeable among business managers, marriage counselers, college deans, and other such practical persons, is *caused* by their diet, while the debilitating confusion of their talk derives from the caused-to-be awkward shuffling. That hypothesis is ridiculous, or nearly so, only because of our basic, ordinarily unexpressed, *theories* of how human action, physiology, and language are related. But suppose one wanted to formulate an accurate, believable statement of the complex relationships among language, thought, and action. Would *that* be a simple matter? More importantly, could our policy argument be any stronger than whatever presupposed *theory* about the relation of language, thought, and action our argument contains? Without some attempt to formulate the theory which would give them significance, items in any number, lifted by Barzun from the *New York Times*, are simply idle chatter.

This, then, seems the more significant explanation for the diminution of energy, wit, and compassion in *Science: The Glorious Entertainment*. The book set itself a serious task of scholarship, but its author lacked (for reasons we must explore) the appropriate form and style to perform the task set. Seriousness, as such, please note, does not preclude any of the intellectual virtues one is accustomed to find in Barzun's writing. But nothing, I submit, can be more enervating to a serious writer than total incompatibility between the form and content of his work.

Two questions remain to be explored briefly. (A) What reasons can be offered for the judgment that *Science: The Glorious Entertainment* is a terribly disappointing work? (B) What general conclusions about the nature of policy argument can be drawn from Barzun's essays? The latter question leads into the last section of this chapter.

To show all the errors of detail and of general interpretation in *Science: The Glorious Entertainment* would require a book larger than the original; for it takes argument to *show* that an error is an error, while it takes only a hasty pen to commit one. But the basic form of error in SGE is easy to outline: Max Black has given it a neatly derived name, "The Fallacy of Misplaced Imprecision." Black coined the phrase in his celebrated review of Sir Charles Percy Snow's doctrine of the "Two Cultures." [15] His mild strictures of reproof against Snow apply with even greater stringency against Barzun's "One Culture, Not Two," the second chapter of SGE. Typical is the following: ". . . our present western world shows, I repeat, not two cultures but one. The very conception of 'a culture' means that it is one and indivisible. If it shows a mixture of interests and tendencies, that fact merely defines a large and well-developed type of culture." (SGE, pp. 16-17)

The fact is, of course, that "culture" no more implies unity and indivisibility than "house" or "horse." The article "a" entirely carries the "conception" Barzun attributes to "a culture." A house divided against itself is still grammatically a single house; a horse split in seven sections, if a horse at all, is (not are) a single horse. And so with "a culture." The expression, taken outside any scheme of theory, is entirely too imprecise to yield any firm implication of unity or multiplicity. It only appears to in the trivial, tautological sense that "a ——" means "one ——," i.e., is singular in ordinary English.

The same fallacy appears in historical as well as in linguistic contexts. About midway in the book, for example, one finds the following very peculiar footnote:

> *In the quadrivium, or upper course, three of the four subjects were arithmetic, geometry, and astronomy. Over the gate of Plato's Grove of Academe were the words: "Let no one enter who is without geometry." This science requirement was new with him and his elder, Socrates. One generation earlier, Aristophanes could still make the Athenians laugh at the idea of teaching astronomy and other unpractical subjects. *Clouds*, p. 220 ff.

How often one wishes Barzun would resist classical allusions! The fact is that a rather thoroughly developed curriculum based on mathematics had been standard with the Pythagorians long before Plato or Socrates. The fact is that Socrates, in contrast to the so-called "natural philosophers" who preceded him, gave very little attention to mathematical reasoning, putting his emphasis instead on the dialectic of moral discourse. The fact is that Barzun's quaint little inference from Aristophanes is simply atrocious scholarship, and totally irrelevant to the point from which it digresses. If one finds, however, this much imprecision in a footnote, how is one to take the genuine point at issue, i.e., that science fought its way into the higher schools of the nineteenth century as an " 'antidote to logic,' as a corrective to the 'monotony of reason' " more exactly, to redress the balance of the curriculum by giving due weight to the direct observation and manipulation of natural objects. Now this is an interesting question in the history of education. Did the theoretical ideal of a balanced curriculum, combined with the Germanic notion that learning should proceed from the concrete to the abstract, bring science into the curriculum? Or were the really influential considerations in the nineteenth century those arising from the presumed practical, utilitarian value of science? Barzun gives major weight to the former, the arguments from educational principles. But just as one declined to accept his comments on Greek education, so does one refuse his conclusions with respect to nineteenth-century intellectual history, the field of study in which his expertise is unquestioned. Scattered quotations prove nothing: to distinguish the influential from the inconsequential, the causally significant from the casually interesting, requires either the intuitive insight of the brilliant critic or else careful judgment in applying theoretical principles to particular cases.

Barzun's competence is criticism; his task in SGE lies in the realm of theory. As he vacillates between the two, the Fallacy of Misplaced Imprecision doubly does him in.

The multiplication of instances, however, can never establish the point I wish to make: that Barzun commits the Fallacy of Misplaced Imprecision not only in repeated details, many of them trivial in themselves, but also and irreparably in the major thesis of his book. I offer the instances to lend plausibility to the major claim which I cannot prove quickly. Let me merely outline how the major argument ought to proceed:

(i) Barzun's main thesis would have to be stated, a thesis easily grasped in personalistic terms: The present cultural malaise of Western man derives from his intellectual subservience to scientific thought and his material dependence on "techne," i.e., "the mixture of machine and soul at the basis of our scientific culture." (SGE, p. 36) Can the thesis be stated in quite literal, non-metaphorical terms? Can it be made entirely clear what is intended by all the operative words in the rough statement above? For example, if Barzun means that scientific modes of argument are used on matters to which they do not rightly pertain, is this to be taken as cause or symptom of cultural malaise? Etc.

(ii) Barzun's attempt to define "science" and to use current thinking in the philosophy of science to justify his case would have to be followed in detail. Requisite precision in a definition is always relative to purpose. For some purposes, Barzun's definition would be entirely satisfactory:

> I understand by modern science the body of rules, instruments, theorems, observations, and conceptions with the aid of which man manipulates physical nature in order to grasp its workings. Taken together, these ideas, symbols, and apparatus form the subject and method of the so-called sciences.

But to make the case that scientific modes of thought have been illicitly exported to realms when their use is pernicious, Barzun must show us *exactly* how "the body of rules, instruments, theorems, observations, and conceptions" which constitute *science* differ from their counterparts in law, policy, art, literary criticism, interpersonal relations, and all the other realms which are (he says) viciously affected by excessive dependence on science. So far, he has not done it.

Nor does Barzun seem to realize that the philosophy of science is just as dialectically dynamic as is science itself. He will take a passage from Whitehead's *Science and the Modern World* (1925) when it supports his case, lay it alongside another from Margenau's *Open Vistas* (1961) as if they were beams from the same structure. The really difficult theoretical questions of the contemporary philosophy of science are, of course, totally ignored by Barzun. Less

forgivable is his apparently deliberate ignorance of an easily discerned shift in this discipline: a score of years ago, philosophers of
science were preoccupied with the presumed basic, ineluctable
differences between scientific and non-scientific uses of intellect
and language. Today the emphasis is clearly on continuity. The
ultimately corrigible nature of *all* statements, for example, is a
principle which unites scientific and commonsense uses of language. One reviewer of SGE put it this way: "Scientific thinking
is simply damned good thinking and nothing more." [16] If not true,
this statement is at least closer to the spirit of the *avant garde*
philosophy of science than is Barzun's reading of it.

(iii) The difficulties arising from (i) and (ii) would have to be
followed to their logical conclusions. The fact that Barzun is far too
imprecise at (i) and inclined to debate rather than argue at (ii)
does not prove that his thesis is false. On the contrary, it is very
likely true, and the task of the critic is to salvage the truth from
Barzun's perversities. Then and only then would we return to the
original question: What place do (or could) scientific modes of
thought have in policy argument? We cannot answer that question
precisely until we have eliminated imprecision from the key ideas.[17]

On the other hand, imprecision does not inhibit our understanding of what Barzun believes to be the rightful limits on the use of
scientific reasoning in matters of policy.

> "In other words, men singly and in groups have notions and wills
> and make demands on life. These wills resist coercion just as these
> ideas resist complete congruence with others. Both will and mind
> must somehow be got round or caught napping before they will
> yield to the self-interest or imposed purpose of another. Accord-
> ingly, leaving aside simple persuasion, which needs no help, what a
> science of man must do to 'solve problems' is to discover means to
> manipulate wills and minds." (SGE, 186). From this it follows
> that "any social scientist in the grip of factuality—that is, who
> thinks that findings dictate choices—is potentially a manipulator."
> (SGE, 187)

If "notions and wills" were things that men have *simpliciter*,
as men have boots and boils, Barzun's case could be unassailable.
But the if-clause is false. Beliefs and desires belong in the category
of subjects, not objects; it is closer to the truth to say that a man *is*

his beliefs and desires than to say that he *has* them; if the latter means that *he* is one thing, his notions and will other things.

But that is not the crucial objection to Barzun's case. What a man believes and desires cannot be described by simple enumeration: we cannot portray the mental life of a person just by adding together statements such as: He believes that circles are round. He desires an opportunity to serve mankind. It is his notion that America ought to stop bombing North Vietnam. Etc. His mental life would be revealed by such statements only if we could discern some pattern, some general drift, continuity, in his thoughts and wishes. And that consistency in mental action is dynamic and corrigible. It reflects, in the unreflective man, bits and pieces of outworn theories. In the reflective mind, these theories are constantly being discarded, revised, and outgrown. Thus persuasion is *never* a simple affair. A man becomes persuaded of the truth of a novel idea or the value of a proposed course of action only by bringing the new into some consistent relation with the basic pattern of thought and action which he *is*. The more articulate and explicit a man is in respect to his beliefs and desires, the more likely he is to follow a consciously theoretical discipline of thought when he persuades or is persuaded.

When one asks in more detail what a "science of man" must do to "solve problems," the answer requires an inversion of terms, i.e., an exposition of how a man of science must consciously, explicitly, ingeniously put his theoretical conceptions into contact and possible conflict with the data of a given situation. And (to this extent Barzun is quite correct) his notions and will *are* subject to external control; the most effective "means to manipulate wills and minds" ought to be superior arguments, based on more encompassing theories and well-established facts.

Barzun or one of his supporters might object that using the terms "scientific" and "theoretical" as synonyms is unjustified. The objection is invalid at one level, quite valid at another. On Barzun's definition of "science" quoted above, the equivalence of "scientific" and "theoretical" is certainly allowable, though his *definition* restricts science to knowledge of the "physical world." Barzun wants to make the question at issue whether the *same kind* of rules, instruments, theorems, etc., which have proved their worth in dealing with physical nature work equally well when applied to human beings considered as such. That question, note, can be treated within the form of cultural criticism, and Barzun's case for the negative is convincing as well as amusing.[18] But remember that the question he raises and does not—indeed, within the limits of cultural criticism, cannot—answer is whether in principle the theoretical mode of thought can be or ought to be used in policy arguments. Physical science provides a paradigm case of the theoretical mode of thought, but it is the use of theory, not the mis-use of physical science models, which is of greatest concern; and Barzun has not produced any argument on *that* question.

He did produce a very strange opinion in regard to what he calls the intellectualist dogma, "the dogma that social improvement is a relatively simple thing requiring a complicated theory behind it, whereas it is in fact a terribly complicated thing which requires a relatively simple theory behind it." (SGE, p. 178) Whereas in fact it is a terribly complicated thing requiring a terribly complicated theory in front of it. The difficulties in applied communism prove, Barzun notwithstanding, not that Marxism is too complex but that it is far too simple. His opinion here is strange, but it does show that Barzun also uses "scientific" and "theoretical" as virtual synonyms.

V. WHERE MAY AN INTELLECTUAL TURN?

Barzun discloses indirectly his views on the nature of theory in education. He speaks of "maxims which go back to Rabelais and Montaigne through the amplification of Rousseau and John Dewey." (HofI, p. 100) Having attempted to distinguish between correct and incorrect interpretations of these maxims, he concludes the section with a curt "So much for theory." (HofI, p. 106) But "theory" in Frankel's sense designates something quite different from a set of maxims. Bertrand Russell has noted this "dislike of all generalizations and all systems. Montaigne illustrates this tendency . . . He has no desire to make his opinions systematic and coherent. Rabelais also . . . is as averse from [sic] intellectual as from other fetters." [19] In this very significant sense, Rabelais, Montaigne, and Barzun are the anti-intellectuals. "A central and basic theme of anti-intellectualism . . . is this: a distrust and dislike of those who approach problems and policies on the basis of science and reasoning rather than tradition and 'common sense.' " [20] Stan Sargents' definition could take Jacques Barzun as its paradigm case.

Barzun's way of being anti-intellectual is typically to commit the Pragmatic Fallacy, an expression we may take to mean the confusion of ethics and logic. A representative example of this fallacy is the following: "Political democracy relies on debate for sifting rival versions of the truth and so does, ultimately, every form of learning, including science. Throughout, public scrutiny and the ethics of controversy must govern." (SGE, pp. 220-221) A debate is defined by the rules of etiquette which govern it. But truth in science, in politics, in law, in education—truth anywhere—is not determined by etiquette at all. Truth is established by logical reasoning and the confrontation of theory and fact. Conditions of freedom and open communication (i.e., ethical considerations) are necessary to the pursuit of truth, but they are that, i.e., necessary conditions, not the actual "sifting" (i.e., logical process) itself. To mistake the two is a clear case of the Pragmatic Fallacy.

Is it merely coincidence that the political consequences of the Pragmatic Fallacy are strongly conservative? Any really radical policy in education—a policy to change the system in fundamental ways—can make its way in the world only if closely, logically tied to a revolutionary theory. Conservative policies can be defended by appeal to tradition and "common sense," i.e., as purely ethical concerns. Within the System one can, for example, proclaim the obligation to teach everyone to read or, at a higher level, to protect the rigor and vitality of the English language. But it takes an effort of speculative theory to propose an effort of scientific research to demonstrate a causal connection between the growth of the System on one hand and the increase of cant on the other. About such a theory we would have one and only one basic question: Is it true? No answer to that question can "dictate" (whatever that means) our choice of what to do. But lacking a fundamental theoretical understanding of the institutional arrangements in which we work, we make choices only within the System.

A conservative like James Bryant Conant is terribly obvious. It is much more subtle to maintain a posture of iconoclasm and at the same time exemplify and defend a form of discourse which assumes the continuity of existing institutional arrangements. But it was, indeed, within the System that Jacques Barzun performed his genuine and serious work of scholarship; it is a certain sub-group within the same system who (for reason having little to do with his serious work) have bestowed their warmest accolades on Barzun, that "foremost defender of Intellect." It would be hard to imagine Barzun seriously concerned to achieve a theoretical understanding of that same System, the practical value of which is so apparent.[21]

In sum, Intellect cannot avoid the hard labor of theoretical, scientific study. Lacking that basis, arguments on educational policy are constrained within the limitations of the System. It is possible within those limitations to pursue the moral and intellectual virtue which Barzun extols and, at his best, exemplifies. But to transcend them, we need a wider use of reason and imagination than Barzun's thought can comprehend.

There is a final twist which is, as you will, amusing, ironic, or pathetic. Barzun likes the contrast between "finesse and geometry" (SGE, Chapter 12); he prefers William James to John Dewey, uncorrupted Art to Science or to Art corrupted by Science. Insofar as his preferences are personal tastes, they are unexceptionable. But he also holds that there is pragmatic justification for his preferences: finesse, James, and Art awaken men to action, they yield "words to rouse the torpid." (SGE, p. 303) Is that claim true historically? In the past, what mode of thought has proved energizing culturally? Where today are we to find sufficient intellectual power to resolve the existential contradictions within the System? Consider the question which opened this chapter: Can any system of mass schooling yield education in the full and honorific sense of the term "education"? Can one now imagine a serious answer to that question which does not include, at the minimum, a scientific theory of institutional behavior? The policy question is, obviously, moral and practical. But uninformed by theory, moral and practical reasoning scarcely deserves the name. Barzun sounds plaintive when he writes: ". . . until Western man reasserts his right to be, as far as he can, a natural and moral philosopher, he will feel like an exile in his own place." (SGE, p. 305) True enough. But the only way, here and now, that one can assert that right effectively is by participating actively in the theoretical mode of thought. This Barzun cannot, will not, do. It is always a bit sad to encounter an exile.

(N.B. Since this was written, Columbia University has announced a major internal reorganization in which Barzun appears to have relinquished all active administrative duties, retaining, of course, his status as professor and advisor to students, faculty, and administration. The word goes about that Barzun, critic by profession, was less interested and effective than he might have been as a seeker of money in Columbia's current fund-raising campaign. One can only hope that among his enormously varied interests and talents Barzun will continue to find time for reflection on American education, perhaps with a philosophical detachment he could not afford while Provost.)

Notes

JACQUES BARZUN

Works of Barzun referred to in the text. (Arranged chronologically by date of original publication.)

(OHF)   *Of Human Freedom* (Second Edition, Philadelphia, 1964)

(DMW)   *Darwin, Marx, Wagner* (Second Revised Edition, Garden City, 1958)

(CRM)   *Classic, Romantic, and Modern* (Garden City, 1961)

(TinA)   *Teacher in America* (Garden City, 1954)

(Berlioz I, II) *Berlioz and the Romantic Century* 2 volumes (Boston, 1950)

(GCM)   *God's Country and Mine* (New York, 1959)

(MinAL)   *Music in American Life* (Garden City, 1956)

(EofA)   *Energies of Art* (New York, 1956)

(1st, 2nd,   "Graduate Study at Columbia" Reports of the Dean of
3rd Report) Graduate Faculties, 1956, 1957, 1958

(TMR)   *The Modern Researcher*, Henry F. Graff, Co-author (New York, 1957)

(HofI)   *The House of Intellect* (New York, 1959)

(SGE)   *Science: The Glorious Entertainment* (New York, 1963)

1 Alan Pryce-Jones (ed.): *The American Imagination* (New York, 1960). Reprinted from the (London) *Times Literary Supplement* (1959). While Barzun appears both as a witty, acid critic and as

an entrpreneur in a disgustingly advertised book club, Mr. Barzun's extensive, scholarly analyses of American life and letters are ignored altogether. That sort of thing must be discomforting.

2   Herbert von Borch: America, *The Unfinished Society* (New York, 1962) p. 111.

3   Virginia C. Simmons, "Why Waste Our Five-Year-Olds?" *Harper's Magazine*, April, 1960, p. 71.

4   N. B. "as a doctrine." The term "classicist" is also used in the academic world to designate an occupation: the study and teaching of Latin and Greek. Despite the nice things he sometimes says about those studies (TinA, Chap. 11) Barzun obviously does not practice that occupation.

5   Babbitt also wrote directly to the issues of educational policies of his own time; see his *Literature and the American College: Essays in Defense of the Humanities* (Boston, 1908). See also: Bernard J. James, "Romanticism and the Ivory Tower," *School and Society* March 28, 1959. Also R. P. Oliver, "The Decay of the Academy," *Modern Age*, Fall, 1959.

6   For Barzun's own treatment of this side of his career, see his Preface to the second (1961) edition of *Romanticism and the Modern Ego*, retitled inexplicably *Classic, Romantic and Modern*.

7   *Educational Wastelands* (Urbana, 1953) *Restoration of Learning* (New York, 1955).

8   I picked up this phrase in conversation with Mr. Bestor. It is very apt, and I must apologize for not remembering the source he cited for it.

9   Bestor: "Education and Its Relationship to Society" *Daedelus*, Winter 1959. pp. 79-89.

10   Charles Frankel: *The Case for Modern Man* (New York, 1955) Chap. VIII. Barzun can appeal to that same tri-partite distinction with a clear recognition that *all* the faculties are necessary for the understanding of any complex phenomenon, "a task for the man who is at once critic, historian, and philosopher." Barzun's "Foreword" to Stephen Taulmin: *Foresight and Understanding* (Bloomington, 1961) (But cf. *infra.* note 21.)

11   This judgment was almost unanimous among the reviewers of *The House of Intellect*. I found no serious, analytical criticism of the book. Even the most scholarly reviewers were reduced to quoting and applauding. For a better than average example, see Edmund Fuller's review in *The American Scholar*, Winter 1960, pp. 118-120.

12   I don't think Mr. Barzun is as alert to this danger as he ought to

be. He writes of having to remind himself that advertising claims are false, (GCM, p. 268) without noticing that most people don't need this caution: a non-selective inattention shields them from the meaning of all written words. Such inattention, with all its dreadful consequences, is necessary to survival; as Dostoyevski said in *Notes From a Dead House* "Man is the being who can get used to anything." For Barzun's diagnosis of this disease, see HofI, p. 99.

13 But not for the reasons Barzun brings out. Compare Chapter 6 and 7 of Barzun's DMW with, say, Joseph Schumpeter's *Capitalism, Socialism, and Democracy* (London, 1954) Chap. III.

14 This story is told in outline in Stephen C. Pepper: "A Brief History of General Theory of Value" in Vergilius Ferm (ed.) *A History of Philosophical Systems* (New York, 1950), pp. 493-504.

15 Max Black: "The Sciences and the Arts: Harmony or Discord?" in *The Growth of Knowledge: The New Threat to Education?* (Ithaca, 1958).

16 John A. Osmundsen: "Is This Thing Called Science Mis-Shaping Our World?" *New York Times* (Book Review Section) April 5, 1964, p. 3.

17 The program I've outlined here for serious study of SGE is still only a program. None of the critics who reviewed Barzun's work seemed to have the foggiest idea what to do with it except quote the always eminently quotable Barzunisms. The most sensible I read was Jeremy Bernstein in *The New Yorker*, November 21, 1964, pp. 236-296. Cf. William E. Boggs in *The New Republic*, 18 April, 1964, pp. 19-21. Edmund Fuller was less full of praise for SGE than for HofI in *The Wall Street Journal*, May 17, 1964.

18 The fact that SGE is disappointing overall does not mean that it *altogether* lacks the verve and depth we expect from Barzun. As always he is at his best when attacking befoulers of the English language. Note especially pp. 210-214.

19 Bertrand Russell: *The Scientific Outlook* (New York, 1931) p. 19.

20 S. Stanfield Sargent, "Edition's Introduction," *Journal of Social Issues* XI (1955) p. 3.

21 It is obvious that Barzun knows exactly what he is up to in rejecting theory: "Unfortunately, it could be shown that it is this passion for philosophizing that has postponed the needful gradual change and brought us to our present pass. . . . For the real philosophy of education is to be found in what is done and not done; it is but distantly affected by . . . the detailed analysis of social

situations and ideals. The present social situation is plain . . . This defines the task of graduate instruction." (2nd Report, p. 10) Barzun may well be right on part of this claim, *viz.* that the passion to achieve a theoretical understanding of the System as a whole and its relations to other institutions may detract attention from those "needful" small changes which would help the System to work just a bit better. Barzun is quite wrong, however, if he takes that truth as implying that "the present situation is plain." To those who are genuinely concerned to know how and why the System functions, the "particular go of it" as Clerk Maxwell would say, it is not plain at all. To those with a theoretical (philosophical) bent, Barzun's concentration on "needful gradual change" *within* the System represents the stance of the reactionary.

5

B. F. Skinner's Philosophy of Human Nature: A Sympathetic Criticism*

I. THE NATURE OF HUMAN NATURE

A myth is unfortunately taught as historical truth in introductory psychology courses. The story goes that since the time of Plato and Aristotle, philosophers have sat in their armchairs and speculated about man and his nature, particularly about the nature of his soul or psyche. Following Greek customs, such speculation was called psychology, and it figured as one of the major branches of philosophy along with ethics, epistemology, and metaphysics. But with the appearance of natural science, some men began to wonder whether it might not be more productive to study mankind with the same techniques that had achieved such spectacular success in the study of nature. John Locke, Alexander Pope, and Jean Jacques Rousseau may be mentioned among those who saw the promised

*This chapter appeared in *Studies in Philosophy and Education,* Spring 1966. Reprinted with the gracious permission of the President of Studies in Philosophy and Education, Inc.

land of a truly scientific study of man, although they themselves never entered it. Thus it remained for the Germans—particularly Wilhelm Wundt—to construct laboratories and to make of psychology an experimental science. Since then there have been many temptations to revert to prescientific practices, but the high priests have maintained the pure faith, and following in the footsteps of Pavlov, Thorndike, Watson, Hull, and Tolman, you too . . . can learn the great secrets of human nature as revealed by the laboratory psychologists.

Those who have come to accept that myth as literal truth will find the title of this chapter passing strange, for B. F. Skinner, by word and by deed, has achieved renown as the foremost champion of scientific psychology against all threatened encroachments of reactionary armchair philosophers. But in point of fact, the case of Skinner may be regarded as an exception which proves the official myth, proves it on closer examination to be totally inaccurate. Let us start all over and say it correctly. Plato and Aristotle speculated on the nature of man's psyche. True. But the proper question to ask is not what they sat on while speculating, but rather whence their right or license so to speculate. In Plato's case it was his own experience in the dramatic days of Post-Periclean Athens, supplemented by a devoted study of Hellenic drama and epic poetry. No wonder that his speculations were cast in the literary form of dramatic dialogues, for therein one can see the play of ideas, in both senses of "play." [1] Aristotle's studies embraced the whole of human knowledge; from them he derived a philosophy of human nature uniquely combining a structural-organismic conception of man's nature with a legal-moral conception. [2]

Now for any student of human nature, we may ask not where he happened to sit or stand while formulating his claims but rather how he *earned the right* to say anything at all about human nature. For, after all, just what do we mean when we speak of some trait or property as pertaining to human nature? Whether in common sense or in the tradition of philosophical psychology, the answer is the same: we appeal to human nature in order to close off further questions. Let us consider a hypothetical dialogue:

A. Why did Johnny steal the candy?

B. Because he was hungry.
A. But why did he *steal?*
B. Because biological necessities will tend to overpower social convention whenever deprivation becomes serious enough.
A. But why do biological necessities overpower social conventions?
B. Because it's human nature, that's all.

Logically, B's last statement adds nothing to his explanation. He had accounted for the particular instance of behavior by showing it to be part of a general tendency in organisms of this sort. His explanation of Johnny's act is as adequate or inadequate, as complete or incomplete, as it would ever be at that point. But when A asked him to account for that general tendency in human organisms, he was faced with a choice. He might either attempt to provide such an account or he might decline to do so. He chose to decline further attempts at explanation and signified his choice by saying "it's human nature."

I want to generalize and say: Whenever a common man, a philosopher, or a psychologist says that a particular trait is a part of human nature, the statement signifies a decision to regard that trait as requiring no further explanation, interpretation, or account. Thus there is a fundamental logical difference between a statement that all human beings have a particular trait T and a statement that T is part of human nature. To say that all human beings have T is to convey information. To say that T is part of human nature adds no information about the human species; it simply signifies the speaker's decision not to entertain further questions about the origin or explanation of T.

One historical example may help to clarify this point. You recall the somewhat truncated account of a social contract to explain the origin of the state in Plato's *Republic*. You recall the absence of such an account in Aristotle's *Politics*. In its place, Aristotle provided the famous "Man is *by nature* a political animal." [3] One can approve or disapprove that decision to abstain from fanciful historical explanations for the origin of society, but one cannot in the literal sense regard Aristotle's dictum as either true or false. It is true, let us agree, that human beings are found almost universally in more or less organized societies. But to say that that fact does not require explanation is not to assert a further fact; it is to register a decision.

My account of what is meant by "human nature" is, however, yet incomplete. We would find it quite strange if someone should say that bipedality is part of human nature. This strangeness is partly accounted for in the fact that today the only serious context in which one could ask for an explanation of man's bipedality is the historical, evolutionary context, and in that context an appeal to human nature is pure tartufferie. But even without the theory of evolution to provide an alternative, we should consider the statement odd. For to regard a trait as part of human nature is to dignify it, and two-leggedness in and of itself is simply not that sort of a trait. It is amusing to recall that medieval theologians accounted for man's being two-legged by his natural tendency to search for God, a search that is no doubt aided by upright posture and upturned eyes. But what is thus dignified is Man-the-upright-God-seeking creature, and we appeal to *that* to account for his (in itself undignified) two-leggedness. Today, of course, we dignify man as being the most complex and perfected product of the natural process of evolution; thus we account for both his bipedality and his tendency to invent sky-dwelling gods by his dignified position on the evolutionary ladder.

Note that we may dignify evil as well as good. When the common man accounts for actions by appeal to such traits as laziness or greed as aspects of human nature, he dignifies the principle of evil in the world just as does the theologian when he says that man is by nature a sinful creature. The Manichean heresy was to overly dignify the principle of evil by making it equal to the principle of good, but neither in common sense nor theology is it heretical to dignify evil—at least to the extent of making it fundamental, basic, in sum, an aspect of human nature.

With that somewhat banal remark, we may conclude the introduction to this chapter, which has shown only one thing: in the history of Western thought and among the plain men of our civilization, the expression "human nature" functions in those speech acts in which decisions are rendered. In saying that a given trait belongs to human nature, one is ordinarily declining to pursue explanations of human behavior.

II. SKINNER'S THREE DOCTRINES

Some people are not content to register their decisions in merely personal acts of explaining, blaming, and absolving. No, they insist on writing or speaking about human nature as if it were an objective feature of the world. Suppose we use the expression "philosophy of human nature" to mean any attempt to be explicit, concise, and consistent in deciding what general traits of mankind are to be regarded as aspects of human nature. A philosophy of human nature, then, is not so much a personal decision as a corporate claim. The courtroom spectator may decide for himself whether the accused is guilty, but the judge's decision has a different status altogether.

By a peculiar twist of historical accident, B. F. Skinner has become a figure in American education whose views are more than those of a private spectator. Skinner has been a pioneer in the use of programed instruction in schools and colleges. His own work with James Holland in producing the first linear program for teaching introductory psychology at Harvard is justly praised, as is the ingenious little machine he engineered to make the program almost cheat-proof. One simply cannot talk about automated education for long without mentioning some of the specific programs and devices rightly regarded as the personal contribution of B. F. Skinner.

But to say all that is merely to make Skinner one among many, and so to miss the unique place he occupies as fundamental theorist for the larger social movement known as programed instruction. Indeed, men like Norman Crowder and O. K. Moore, who have constructed programs quite different in form from Skinner's psychology program, claim with considerable merit that their alternative techniques are actually closer to the Skinnerian view of learning than is Skinner's own. This much is clear: there is an immense difference betwen the interest shown in programed instruction today and that shown nearly forty years ago, when Sidney Pressey produced rather similar instruments. This difference in large part is to be accounted for by Skinner's intellectual achievement in producing a philosophy of human nature appropriate to these new techniques of instruction. I am also convinced that some of the fundamental strengths and weaknesses of these new techniques may be discovered in a systematic examination of that philosophy of human nature.

To question whether any given program or automated device actually teaches, of course, is to ask for experimental evidence. My reading of the evidence convinces me that in some instances these techniques teach extraordinarily well—efficiently, humanely, and durably. In other instances, i.e., under different conditions and with different objectives, the techniques of programed instruction are of less value. Still and all, the fact that teaching techniques are relatively successful does not prove that Skinner's decision to view the human race in a particular way was justified, any more than the occasional successes of psychoanalysis proves Freud to have been correct, or the cures at Lourdes prove Jesus Christ to be a savior. We must look at it in the way I indicated above: the success of programed instruction is not even evidence, much less proof, for Skinner's view. It is rather the purity and elegance of his laboratory research, indicating intense dedication and discipline; it is his breadth of acquaintance with all sorts of literature; it is the originality in style found in everything he touches—these provide Skinner with a warrant or license to declaim on human nature and command our attention, though not necessarily our agreement.

The Skinnerian philosophy of human nature may be stated as three fundamental doctrines, two of them positive and one negative, as follow:

A. Man is by nature an active organism.
B. Man is by nature an organism that learns from interaction with its environment.
C. Man is not by nature anything else.[4]

I shall argue that the first of these is a revolutionary doctrine, and that much of what seems so strange in Skinner is really the consequence of this revolutionary insight. The second, I shall argue, is a corollary of the first but important in its own right, especially for a philosophy of education. The third is the most difficult to swallow; it creates the major source of conflict between Skinner and the humanists. It is in respect to what Skinner denies that the issues of consciousness, freedom, and the *distinctively* human aspects of human nature arise. I suggest toward the end of this chapter the beginnings of an analysis in which these issues may be a bit more clearly understood than they usually are.

A. In a beautifully precise way, Skinner's insistence that man is by nature an active organism constitutes the Newtonian revolution in the science of behavior. Newton's first law of motion, that all objects tend to remain in constant velocity unless disturbed by outside force, represented his decision to abandon once and for all Aristotle's search for the *cause* of motion itself. To give up Aristotle's search meant to abandon all efforts to find God or Love or First Cause of all kinds, and Newton's resolute "Hypotheses non fingo" was a recognition of exactly what he had abjured with his law of motion. As a scientist he now restricted himself to explaining *changes* in motion, which is a far cry from trying to account for motion as such.

This way of putting the distinction between Aristotle and Newton is inexact, of course, but to make it entirely precise would take a higher level of scholarship than I possess. Just to begin, Aristotle's ideas about motion are all intermingled with his general theories of change. (E.g. Physics, 201a.) Movement, i.e. change of place, is merely one, and for Aristotle rather the least interesting, form of change. Generation and corruption, becoming and perishing, are to a biologist more important concerns, hence Aristotle's tendency to regard *mere* locomotion as accidental and unworthy of sustained philosophical attention. Of course if change of place is itself a *natural* motion (as, for example, the upward motion of fire is something which occurs by nature), then it becomes of considerable theoretical interest; on the other hand, deviations from the natural (the disordered and constrained) are mere accidents again and thus outside philosophical attention. (De Caelo 300b–301a)

The truly distinctive consequence of Aristotle's taking change of essential quality as the paradigm case for understanding motion is this: Aristotle could not even recognize the existence of acceleration, hence he could not conceive of change in *rate* of motion as central phenomenon to be handled by a theory of mechanics. (Physics 225b–226a) Partly his problem was the same as that inherent in Zeno's paradoxes: without a mathematical theory of limits, change in rate of change leads to infinite regress. In contrast Newton's so-called "method of infinitessimals" gave him a technique to handle the conceptually confusing notions of "acceleration of acceleration" and "velocity at a point"; which means that the absence of velocity or of acceleration is simply a special case of velocity or acceleration. Thus the change from zero velocity to a finite velocity presents no more *philosophical* challenge than the change from one finite velocity to another. Hence the problem of explaining motion as such has been bypassed.

Likewise, with the doctrine that man is by nature an active organism Skinner abandons the search for the causes of behavior as such and thus frees himself for scientific attention to the causes for *changes* in behavior. This may appear a matter of little concern, but its consequences are serious. I shall indicate only two of the more important.

1. In abandoning the search for the cause of behavior as such, Skinner can forget all about the very confused notions of motives, drives, needs, desires, will, and entelechy which have variously been used to explain human behavior. Given the intellectual preference for simplicity, people have sought always for the single-motive explanation: that behavior is caused by a push from behind or a pull from ahead. The push from behind is best exemplified in the idea of behavior's being caused by tissue needs, neurological arcs, or endocrine ejections. Now Skinner does not deny, of course, that certain reflex actions occur from these or like causes. But he does reject, and quite properly, the notion that what people *do* can be accounted for in this way.[5] The doctor taps your knee and asks: "Did your leg jump or did you kick it out?" The distinction is quite clear, even though in a particular instance we may not know how to answer. We might say, "Do it again and let me see." Asked over the telephone, "What are you doing right now?" none of us would say "I'm dilating the capillaries in the skin of my face," even though at the moment that might be the most prominent physiological response occurring in the organism.

From the beginning, when psychology was a branch of philosophy, psychologists have been trying to explain why human beings act or behave or, simply, move. One may say, in general terms, that so-called prescientific psychologists tried to account for human action by some teleological principle, i.e., by affirming some goal outside the organism which inexorably pulled or lured it into motion. Scientific psychologists, on the other hand, attempted to account for human action on the basis of physiological reflexes, and when these proved inadequate as explanations for behavior, the scientific psychologists hypothesized the existence of some general cause of action within the organism, in the light of which stimulus-reflex explanations for behavior could be made.

This is what makes it possible to understand why Skinner's doctrine that organisms are by nature *active* may be regarded as equivalent to the Newtonian revolution in physics. Just as philosophers of nature from Aristotle through Kepler have been concerned, and in some instances obsessed, with the question of why objects move, it was Newton's decision to abstain from hypotheses on that question and to seek instead explanations for *changes* in velocity in physical objects. Who first noticed that progress in philosophical thought is less a matter of answering questions than it is a matter of just getting over them? It remains to be seen, of course, whether Skinner's formulations of the functional relations within the data will have the role in advancing science that Newton's did. But in the negative respect, they stand together: *Hypotheses non fingo* could well be Skinner's motto.

Now in effect, not to formulate hypotheses on the ultimate springs of action is to deny the relevance, if not the truth, of all other formulations. The hostility of certain philosophers and psychologists to Skinner can be explained only on that basis. The hedonist who says that man is by nature a self-serving animals may argue violently with the idealist who claims that man's basic motive is self-transcendence. But Skinner moves them into the same well-armed camp from which they launch joint attacks on the apparently innocent doctrine that man is by nature just an active organism. "Active toward what end?" "Whence the source of his activity?" "But so are monkeys and dogs and cockroaches active. How is man distinctive?" We will return to deal with these questions later.

2. The second revolutionary consequence of the activity doctrine is that Skinner does not have to treat consciousness as a cause of behavior but must instead, regard consciousness and, indeed, all mental actions as behavior-to-be-explained. It would be a rather enjoyable bit of intellectual history to show the various forms and vicissitudes of the belief that *thought causes action*. Atomists and idealists, materialists, rationalists, and empiricists have all agreed on two things: (a) that thoughts cause actions and; (b) that it is difficult to explain how this occurs, since it is clear that thoughts do not cause action in the same way or same sense that some

events cause other events in the ordinary physical environment. There is sound reason for this universality of agreement, namely the linguistic fact that if someone asks you, say, "What caused you to vote for Barry Goldwater?" you would reply with some reference to a mental phenomenon, e.g., "I thought he was the less objectionable candidate."

This question and answer sequence has identical *grammatical* form with such sequences as "What caused you to fall?" "I stepped on a banana peel." Now it has been one of the major tasks of twentieth century philosophy to show that this grammatical identity is not equivalent to *logical* identity. The efforts of psychologists have been, in the main, to show that the former explanatory sequence can be reduced to something like the latter.

I do not know if and how much Skinner's ideas have been influenced by contemporary behaviorism in philosophy, e.g., by the later works of Ludwig Wittgenstein, and by that of Gilbert Ryle.[6] But in one important respect, Skinner more resembles the British philosophers than the American psychologists. For the latter have accepted the really sticky assumption, namely, that in the voting example there are two distinct events, one named "Thinking that Goldwater is the less objectionable candidate" and the second named "Voting for Goldwater." The problem is to show that the first causes the second within the same sense of causation that is used when one says that event named "stepping on banana peel" causes event named "falling down stairs." When this proves very difficult, the psychologist is likely to say that mental causes are not the real causes, a conceptual move which merely enhances his difficulty: now he has to invent a metaphysics to separate real causes from mental causes.

But Skinner, perhaps because he does not have any general theory of causation, has never taken this approach to the so-called "problem of consciousness." For Skinner, like the philosophers, has in general just denied that there are two events, insisting that there is only *one*, event, namely voting for Goldwater under a particular set of internal and external stimulus conditions.

It is perhaps just at this point that Skinner's particular way of putting things has caused more controversy and confusion than the position really warrants. A certain Joseph Wood Krutch, literary critic and nature lover, has accused Skinner of wishing to abolish reason from an active place in controlling man's action and destiny. The charge, of course, is absurd, but one must recognize certain poetic justice in its being made. For Krutch derived *his* views from that perennially favorite utopian novel, *Walden II*. And in that book, Skinner used a very deceptive literary device, one which deceived even such an old hand as Krutch. One rather disgusting character in the novel is a philosopher named Castle, who raises all the usual questions one puts to any utopian. "What are you going to do about freedom?" "How can you be sure that people who think freely will choose to continue this ideal life?" Now Skinner does not allow his protagonist, Frazier, to deal with these questions on the so-called philosophical level. To all such questions, Frazier has one stock response "Just look around you and see!" It is the same response Skinner himself gave when pressed by such questions as "Are you sure that pigeons can be taught to guide missiles?" [7] It is, let us admit quickly, a very effective literary trick. It adds verisimilitude to the tale, so much so that Krutch writes as if Walden II really existed within the borders of Hecate County. But, of course, there isn't any Walden II, and even if there were, that wouldn't answer the questions. This matter of mental causation is a problem in conceptual analysis: Skinner seems to say that all problems which cannot be answered by laboratory evidence are pseudo problems anyway. We are not surprised that this raises some stir among those who have a vested interest in exactly those problems Skinner is trying to dismiss from serious attention.

May we summarize at this point? The decision to regard human beings as by nature active organisms means that Skinner does not have to hypothesize about the apparently peculiar causal relationship between internal mental events and external, behavioral events. But his way of talking about his decision seemed to indicate *either* that there were no such things as mental events—a direct negative answer, as it were, to William James's famous question "Does Consciousness Exist?" [8]—*or else* that it would be *better*, socially and morally, if reasoning and thought did not have any causal efficacy in human affairs. Both those positions are patently absurd. Neither of them is a *necessary* consequence of Skinner's more fundamental insights. But since this presumed causal efficacy of thought had so long been regarded as a *distinctive* trait of human nature, it is not surprising that Skinner became the major target of the aroused humanists and humanistic psychologists.

B. To say that man is by nature an organism which learns from its environment is not to say very much positively; the intent is interesting only in the negative sense of denying the need for any theory of learning, if we mean by a theory of learning some basic system of hypotheses to explain why learning is possible. There is, of course, another sense of the expression "theory of learning," meaning just the statements of functional relations among the variables which seem to have most significance in affecting changes in behavior. Thus Skinner's decision to concentrate on rate of responding in his experimental animals may be said to follow from a *theory* (to that point untested) that rate of responding was functionally dependent on such variables as mode of reinforcement, constancy of stimulus conditions, and the like. In that latter sense, everyone who tries to influence any organism's behavior may be said to have a theory of learning. But this is quite different from the elaborate conceptual schemes—the models, the black boxes, the mediating responses, the hypothetical constructs and intervening variables—which figure as recognized theories of learning.

In the final analysis, only history will provide a dependable judgment whether Skinner's rejection of learning theory is justified. But from the standpoint of being useful to educators, there is much to recommend Skinner's way of thinking. If variables intervene between the teacher's action and the learning of the student, and if the state of these variables is both uncontrollable and unknowable, then it follows that neither learning nor failing to learn can be accounted for adequately by reference to the teacher's actions. What happened must be explained always by the interaction between the teacher's impact and the prior internal state of the organism. Thus we can never be *sure* that any pattern of discriminative stimuli and reinforcement was the cause of learning or failure to learn. It may well be that with a different state of the unseen variables, a different result would have followed. It's no peculiarity of teachers and curriculum specialists to desire such an escape hatch in the face of failure even if it logically requires also a show of humility in the face of success. (The contrast between Skinner and most teachers is easily visible just at that point: Skinner has neither excuses nor humility.)

Apparently, the only logical alternative to regarding the internal state of the organism as a variable is to regard it as a constant. On its surface the latter is absurd. Any given organism varies within wide ranges in a number of different dimensions. Likewise, the range and dimensions of variation vary among the individuals of a given species, among species, and, over time, within a given organism. For every means we possess of measuring the psychological and physiological states of organisms, the rule is variation. It is patently false to hold that states are constant.

The answer is not merely to affirm that internal states are variables but to try to be more explicit about how they intervene between organism and environment. A hungry pigeon is more active than a full one, but it's the activity level, not the hunger, which is significant in determining rate of learning. Likewise, it is easier to establish a conditioned reinforcer in a hungry pigeon than in a full one, but it's the effect of the reinforcer, not the state of the organism when it was established, that causes learning to occur. These principles apply directly to classrooms: Don't worry about the youngster's motivation, just get him active. Establish *some* secondary or conditioned reinforcers which are actually effective in shaping behavior. The active organism, selectively reinforced, will learn (whatever the variation in its internal states) even though unseen variables may determine its activity level and also effect what objects will serve as reinforcers. The only theory of learning at all useful to educators is one that formulates functional relations among these external variables. That at least is the impact of the second principle in Skinner's philosophy of human nature, and I tend to believe him.

III. STATEMENTS ABOUT HUMAN NATURE ARE DECISIONS

But is there nothing else? Are men to be regarded simply as active and malleable organisms standing at the same level as their four-footed, or eight-legged, scaly or feathered friends? Is the behavior emitted in writing this sentence merely a conditioned response, differing only in complexity from a planarian's mindless passage through a ceramic maze? Such questions give us pleasant little shudders, a mild sort of conceptual itch, but they present no basis for conceptual clarity. Is there any way to formulate the conflict between Skinner and the humanist so that even if the conflict cannot be resolved its bases can be made precise and visible? Is it possible to draw that line, which is deeply engraved in human thought, the "line between man as a conscious, reflective being and man as a part of physical nature, conditioned by and acted upon by his environment?" [9]

Let us approach this topic with all the tentativeness and indirection it deserves. A psychologist recently asked a philosopher for a definition of the expression "learning a rule." The psychologist wanted a definition which would apply equally well to a planarian's learning the rule that all turns are to the right and a philosopher's learning the rule that all definitions must be contextual. But the philosopher wisely refused to give an answer, recognizing that there is something peculiarly relevant to the line between man-the-conscious-agent and man-the-conditioned-animal in this notion of learning a rule. Let us see how and where the line might be drawn *within* the notion of learning a rule.

The pigeon pecks the disk steadily and rapidly while the blue light is on; when the light turns yellow, the pigeon pecks rapidly until reinforced, then waits nearly a full minute before resuming its activity. It's a well-adapted pigeon. Providing that the pigeon's total environment remains reasonably placid, this pattern of behavior can be maintained for a number of years.

Now what do we want to say about this behavior? From the experimenter's point of view, the whole affair may be described as conditioning on two schedules of reinforcement with effective discriminative stimuli. But what has the pigeon learned? If we ask it that way, we must answer in one of two ways, each ultimately reducible to the other. We may say either (i) that the pigeon has *learned* to maximize gain under the blue light and to minimize energy expenditure under the yellow light; or (ii) that the pigeon has *learned the rule* that a blue light is a signal for variable ratio reinforcement and a yellow light is for constant interval reinforcement.

Now it may not be immediately obvious that (i) and (ii) are mutually reducible. But try putting them together by asserting (i) *and* (ii), then asking whether there is redundancy. To one who knows the appropriate generalizations about behavior under these two different schedules of reinforcement, the assertion of both (i) and (ii) *is* a redundancy. Or assert (i) and deny (ii). Assert (ii) and deny (i). In either case one ends up saying nothing. This is what I mean by saying "reducible to." Equally well, I might have said "mutually implicative." The point is the same: if one attempts to make clear what *in this instance* is meant by "learning to," one refers to the rule, to make clear what is meant by "learning the rule" one refers to what the pigeon has learned to do.

The standard moves to distinguish dispositional language from direct behavioral language can be used here. "The pigeon has learned the rule that X" does not reduce to nor imply "The pigeon is now X-ing." We may say truly of a pigeon fast asleep, head under wing, "*That* pigeon has learned the rule that X" while it is patently false that the pigeon is now X-ing.

Let us call this instance Paradigm Case I (PCI). Assuming that the pigeon stands somewhere between man and planaria on the evolutionary scale, we may expect that cases analogous to PCI may be found at each of the extremes. It is easy to find them. The planarian learns to turn right at each fork in a maze, learns the rule that only a right turn will bring it to food. An office worker, whom we will call Alfredo, learns to sort out all the contents of his in-basket before working on any one item, learns the rule that the in-basket must be checked in its entirety before working on any one item, etc.

PCI is not an empirical generalization about the behavior of a particular pigeon, planarian, or employee. For one can very well say: "This pigeon has learned the rule that X, but he didn't X this morning." One cannot say: "This pigeon always X-es, but he didn't X this morning." One can say: "I don't know whether he's learned to X or not; sometimes he does X, sometimes he doesn't." One cannot say: "I don't know whether he always X-es or not; sometimes he does X, sometimes he doesn't." If we mean by an empirical generalization a complex statement of the form, under certain conditions C, if event A, then always event B, it is clear that PCI and all analogues are not empirical generalizations.

Is PCI a probability statement? We can well imagine a scientist declaiming: "I'll say that the pigeon has learned the rule that X, if and only if in at least 75 per cent of the proper circumstances he X-es." Now what are we going to say to the scientist? When the scientist is talking about the pigeon, we should feel very foolishly quibbling if we should respond: "I'll admit that the pigeon X-ed 75 per cent of the time over fifty trials, but I'm not convinced that he's learned the rule that X." Would 85 per cent of the time convince us? 93 per cent of 63 trials? If he behaves in accordance with a rule in a reasonable proportion of the suitable circumstances, we must agree that he's learned the rule. We may argue whether a given proportion of the instances out of what size sample constitutes a *reasonable* proportion, but having agreed that the organism has learned to behave in the specific way, we cannot then deny that the organism has learned the rule.

But this conclusion, N.B., tells us nothing about the concept of *learning.* It does not establish that the organism has learned to X merely to show that in fact the organism X-es some *n* per cent of the time. My point here is a different one: in PCI and analogous contexts in which an organism has learned to X, we can always formulate some rule, X', such that to say that the organism has learned to X implies that the organism has learned the rule X', and vice versa. This is one sense of the expression "learning a rule." [10]

But let us look again at Alfredo, the office worker. Isn't it clear that if we're told that 75 per cent of the time he checks all his in-basket before working on any one item, we may still ask: Yes, but has he learned the rule that governs this kind of action? He may be simply curious: he may simply have a habit which operates most of the time but not all the time. Or again he may behave quite randomly, and our observation of 75 per cent consistency may represent nothing but poor sampling techniques. In the latter case, of course, we deny our original hypothesis that he behaves (has learned the behavior) as posulated. But even when we admit that he does behave as postulated, it is an *open question* whether he does so because of the rule.[11] The general conclusion is this: only when we wish to say that he acts as he does because of the rule, would we wish to say also that he has *learned the rule.* (There are, of course, degenerate cases to which this general conclusion doesn't apply.)

Now is this conclusion significantly different from that reached in regard to PCI? There, you will recall, we decided that if the pigeon has learned to make the discriminations in behavior, he has learned the rule. In specific cases we may be in doubt whether he has indeed learned to behave in the specified way, but if he has, then he's learned the rule. In respect to Alfredo and his in-basket (let us now call this Paradigm Case IA) we add a further qualification, viz., that he act in the specified way because of the rule.

But are PCI and PCIA really so very different? In one interesting detail, yes. For notice: suppose that after describing the behavior of the pigeon under the two different colored lights, the experimenter is cross-examined: All right, he behaves as you say, but did he learn to make those discriminations? What could the experimenter take the question to mean? That a pigeon is born with that behavior? That's absurd, and so is the question. But it's not absurd when asked about Alfredo. It makes sense to say of even a refined piece of behavior like checking all the contents of an in-basket, that the agent didn't *learn to do* it, that he does it unconsciously, or from idle imitation, or from curiosity, or from habit. We may in the last instance, ask how or where he acquired the habit, but there is a difference between doing something because one has *learned to do* it and doing something from habit. And so we're back to the original qualification: if Alfredo the office worker has learned to do X, then it follows that he has learned the rule that X. But in neither instance are we to grant that this has occurred merely because Alfredo X-es, but only if we can believe that he X-es *because* of the rule that X. The line of questioning would be meaningless in regard to the pigeon in PCI.

This linguistic difference, of course, may or may not signify anything important beyond itself. The psychological neologism—"The organism has learned the behavior"—covers that distinction, and we must get underneath it to see that while the neologism applies both to the pigeon and to Alfredo, we can ask questions about the latter which would be meaningless asked about the former. And the difference is not at all in the behavior as such. PCI actually involves a much more complex task and delicate refinement in action than does PCIA. Thus there is an initial presumption that if the linguistic difference amounts to anything, it amounts to a basis for distinguishing Alfredo from a pigeon, that Alfredo's nature is different from the pigeon's.

But so far that difference is mere presumption unless we can explicate what this linguistic difference might point to. Mr.

Thomas Green has recently published a paper which labels the distinction we're talking about as that between conforming to a rule and obeying a rule.[12] The former, he says, is behavior, presumably subject to analysis as operant conditioning; the latter is the area of human action. Since the goal of all education, according to Green, is to expand the range and freedom of action, thus narrowing the area of mere behavior, and if, as Green implies, operant conditioning applies only to changing behavior, not to freeing action, it follows that the behaviorism of operant conditioning—taken either as a *method* of teaching or as a *language* for analyzing whatever occurs—is inapplicable at those points where education is doing its most significant task. This charge, I believe, is the most serious one to be leveled by the humanists against B. F. Skinner's philosophy of human nature as the foundation for educational policy. I now wish to translate this charge into the terms of the just preceding analysis and, I hope, at the end of this chapter to mitigate some of its force.

The first of Green's expressions—rule-conforming behavior—seems to me an excellent label for PCI. All the conclusions we reached about the use of the term "learned" in connection with PCI apply here. If the pigeon has learned to conform to the rule, then it has learned to make the relevant discriminations, etc. If not, it has not. But the label is not an explication. We don't know what it is that makes PCI distinctive as a kind of learning just by calling it "rule-conforming behavior."

The expression "rule-obeying action" seems less appropriate as a label which we might want to apply to any paradigmatic instance. It is somewhat contrary to common idiom: one obeys a command or a commander, one follows a rule or ruler, one keeps the law, and if one does so, one generally has no need to keep a lawyer. When a poster admonishes the young to obey the law, it usually portrays a man in blue who comes to stand for the "Law." An instance of rule-obeying action that strictly followed idiom would be a case in which one were commanded to do X against a rule which forbade X and one then obeyed the rule rather than the command. Apart from a situation in which commands are present, obedience seems to be an idle concept.

Thus, I prefer to stay with the more awkward expression "doing something because of a rule" as a way of designating what we're after when we ask whether Alfredo has really learned the rule governing action toward the contents of an in-basket. But even though Green's label does not help us much, perhaps his analysis of the concept may.

Green distinguishes three senses in which one may be said to have learned a rule—active, verbal, and critical. A speaker of a language may have learned the rules governing agreement in numbers between subject and verb without being able to state it; he has learned activity only. A man who's lost his arms may learn, indeed may teach, the rules governing efficient swimming or skating without being able to follow them. His learning and teaching are verbal. But, says Green, the critical sense can never appear by itself, nor, more importantly, can either of the other senses appear apart from the critical sense. His point here seems to be very well taken. Consider a man whose grammar was generally unexceptionable but who never seemed aware when he or those around him spoke in ways that violated the usual rules. This would be an out-of-the-ordinary case, of course; but if it did occur, I think we should want to say that the individual had learned certain linguistic habits, as Southerners learn to pronounce the long "a" as a triphthong, rather than say that the individual has learned a rule. If we apply our open-question argument here, we get the same result: we admit that in a reasonable proportion of the instances our out-of-the-ordinary individual's behavior is in accordance with the rules, but we still question whether he's learned the rule, in the sense that he does what he does *because* of the rule. If we discover no evidence whatever of a critical response when he or those around him violate the rule, we should then deny that he acts as he does because of the rule.

Likewise, a person who uttered verbal formulae that sounded like rules but who never made critical judgments on behavior which failed to measure up (or measured up in some superlative degree) would not be asserting rules. I may learn to say: A man ought never look his mother-in-law in the eye. In learning to say that I'm not learning a rule. If a blind Navaho learns that, he has learned a rule, albeit unfortunately for him not an active one. Yet in the critical sense it may function as a rule. The blind Navaho hears that Johnny One Horse brazenly stared at his mother-in-law; he mutters disapprovingly. He has learned the rule.

Now we come to a rather difficult turn in the argument. Green and the humanists generally want to say that if the agent acts because of a rule, his action can neither be taught by operant conditioning nor accounted for in the language of behaviorism. Or, in our previous mode of discourse, a philosophy of human nature which regards man as just another active, malleable organism fails against that most distinctive instance: a man acting in a certain way because of a rule. Yet in a paradoxical way, *if* Green's analysis is correct, behaviorism emerges triumphant. For Green makes criticizing the mark of having learned a rule, and I can surely both describe criticizing in behavioral terms and teach it by operant conditioning. I can condition a grammatical discrimination and also condition a wince reaction when the rule is violated. (I say "I can . . ." It is understood to mean: "Those who know how to do such things can in principle . . .") I can teach a youngster the following verbal formula: "In swimming the breast stroke arm recovery is done under water and as close to the body as possible." I can teach him to applaud proper recovery and to boo and hiss when a breast stroke swimmer allows his arms to break water. Furthermore, and most importantly, I can explain the how and why of my teaching in terms that make no appeal to man's being anything other than an active and malleable organism. Have I taught the youngster a rule? Suppose he doesn't understand a single word of English.

Something is terribly wrong here. Perhaps we may find a clue to the difficulty in reconsidering the question of someone's learning or teaching a rule which he either cannot follow or cannot express verbally. One may both learn and teach grammar without being able to state the rules of grammar; to deny this would be to deny that grammar was taught and learned by most of mankind. One can learn and teach the rules of swimming without being able to swim. Fair enough. But these cases are derivative. Can we find a case in which one could neither X without having learned the rules for X-ing nor learn the rules for X-ing without X-ing? Although one can learn to speak without learning rules for speaking, explicitly, one cannot learn the rules for speaking without speaking. (Oh, a mute person can learn the rules for speaking by reading and writing, but then for that mute person, reading and writing may be said to be his [only] way of speaking.) So we are getting on the right track. I propose that one cannot learn to *reason* without learning the rules for reasoning, nor learn the rules for reasoning without reasoning. Again the second case should be obvious; if a person has learned the rules for reasoning he has reasoned, else we would not call what he learned rules for reasoning. But the first case may not be quite so clear. We might think that a person could learn to reason correctly without hearing of *modus ponens* or the rule of detachment. Yet this is to misconstrue what constitutes a rule of reasoning. If a youngster learns to distinguish between a valid and an invalid argument at any level, that distinction has *as such* the quality of a *rule*. The child of six recognizes that it's a sufficiently strong argument against the statement that it rained hard last night to point out that the ground is quite dry this morning. The rule is: Don't believe that it rained hard last night if the ground is quite dry this morning. This rule is not nearly so general as the rule

$$((p \supset q) \cdot \sim q) \supset \sim p$$

but it's no less a rule for all that. Aristotle's logic is not nearly so general as modern formal logic, but no less rule-like in quality.

The rule underlying the argument above is this: if we want to get at the heart of what's meant by "doing X because of a rule," we must find that paradigm case in which one could *not* do Y without *ipso facto* doing Y *because of a rule governing the doing of Y*, and then showing in respect of X, that the case either reduces to or is analogous to Y. If Y is reasoning, we are apparently on the right track. It's ordinarily circular to say that a man is reasoning correctly because he's following the rules of reasoning. The clear circularity is indicated when we ask which rules of reasoning, and the answer comes back, as it must, "those which apply in this case." "Because he's following the rules of reasoning" only helps us communicate the same meaning which might sound too bald if merely stated as "He is reasoning correctly." (The most sense we can make of a noncircular interpretation is to imagine a very long and difficult chain of arguments such that one can stay on course only by frequent explicit appeals to formalized rules.)

Let us now look back at Alfredo. Is he going through his in-basket because of a rule, or isn't he? I submit that the answer is not to be found in his expressing (evincing, showing, reacting to, etc.) approval or disapproval of his own or another's behavior, but rather in what he would say if asked: "Why do you usually go through your in-basket before working on any one item?" If he says "Habit," or "Curiosity," or "Do I?" then he's not doing it because of a rule. Suppose, on the other hand, that he argues that there is no necessary relation between the spatial order of these items in the basket and their urgency. But, as he also informs us, urgent matters ought to be handled before less urgent ones. Therefore he must make the discrimination between urgent and non-urgent matters before taking care of any one of them. Then we want to say that Alfredo acts as he does because of a rule. Let us call the action of the very rational Alfredo Paradigm Case II.

Let us acknowledge the righteous indignation of those who claim that rules may be invented to justify any action, that Alfredo is being a hypocrite, indulging his curiosity instead of buckling down to work—then invoking a high-sounding rationalization to justify his laziness. It may in some instances be difficult to tell from what Alfredo says whether he is really PCII or not. Alfredo may find difficulty himself in telling the truth about why he acts as he does. It may be that in most instances PCIA partakes of elements from both PCI and PCII. But that doesn't keep the paradigm cases from being distinct. Reason has often been used to make the worse appear the better cause; but again it is only by reasoning that we ever realize that causes may be classified as better and worse.

But do these actually explain the distinction? There is only this much to be said in favor of the present analysis: it puts "doing something because of a rule" in the context of justification, not the context of behavior. It isn't that Alfredo's learning *process* as such is different from the pigeon's; it is rather that Alfredo can learn to do something which the pigeon cannot do, viz., to justify (or as the case may be, to rationalize) his action. And this explains why we can ask of Alfredo: "Has he learned the rule?" We are asking not simply about what he does but whether he does it in a certain way, to wit, whether when he acts as he does, he is also able to explain and justify his action as according to the rule. There is usually no way to determine whether he's prepared to justify his actions just by looking at his action: usually we have to ask him. And we cannot ask the pigeon.

Honesty commands me to make an admission: I may have misinterpreted Green in order to make a point. When Green claims that the critical sense of rule-obeying action is a necessary condition for either the verbal or active sense, he probably means what I mean when I say that the context of justification, not the context of behavior itself, determines whether an agent is acting because of a rule. I interpreted Green's "criticism" to mean *behavior* of winning or applauding, of shouting "Boo" or "Hurrah" on certain stimuli. Now Green may have meant this: nothing that he says specifically denies that interpretation, but in all likelihood he meant by "criticism" the making of critical judgments, supported by reasoning. But it is necessary to stretch things in order to make it doubly clear that Green's distinction between behavior and action is *not* a distinction between two kinds of human doing but between doing on one hand and justifying on the other. Green made that distinction, but he didn't make it clear that *that* was the distinction he made.[13]

The convinced behaviorist must have his opportunity for reply before we ask whether emendations are necessary in Skinner's philosophy of human nature. Behaviorist: What do you mean by a "context of justification"? If you mean simply that Alfredo under one set of stimuli emits the motor behavior of emptying his in-basket and under a different set of stimuli emits the behavior of *talking* about his action—then "context of justification" simply refers to a particular sort of behavior under particular stimulus conditions. And *that* behavior, i.e., talking about emptying in-baskets, is taught and learned by the same principles of operant conditioning as is emptying in-baskets. So all your analysis of "learning the rule" amounts to is this: in PCI, we say the pigeon has learned the rule if he emits the pecking behavior at the proper rate under the suitable stimulus conditions; while in PCII we say that Alfredo has learned the rule if he emits the proper motor-scanning behavior under one set of conditions *and* the proper verbal behavior under a second set of stimulus conditions. This may be interesting to those who are interested in that sort of thing, but it imposes no demands for basic explanatory principles beyond those given in what you've called Skinner's "philosophy of human nature."

What are we to do with Behaviorist? We feel embarrassed by his charge because we not only cannot answer it, we know that in principle it cannot be answered in a way that will satisfy his canons for an answer. He will recognize all and only those differences in behavior we can point to, but here we're asking him to recognize the difference between behavior and something else. Only if we can give a behavioral analysis of the phenomenon of reasoning will he acknowledge its existence; and if we give a behavioral analysis, how can we expect him to call it anything other than behavior? And if we cannot provide a behavioral analysis, how do we know what we are talking about? Is the phenomenon merely an introspective datum? We're embarrassed then because we ourselves tend to accept those canons which would rule out in advance all answers that might be made to Behaviorist's original charge.

Now if we can find some phenomenon which is indusputably an objective feature of human life and if we can show that *this* phenomenon resists behavioral analysis, we may be close to breaking the circle which Behaviorist has drawn to protect himself. Reasoning (justifying, interpreting, accounting for, etc.) will not do as this phenomenon because they break down all too easily into public and personal phenomena. The public phenomenon looks as if it were just verbal behavior, while the personal or private aspect—after all if I'm justifying my action, I'm performing a deliberate act—becomes an inner business of intent, purpose or motive which we've already ruled out of discussion.

No, the attack has to be on verbal behavior itself. Skinner saw, of course, that his whole case for reductionism rested on showing that using language could be accounted for in the same terms as any other sort of behavior. He wrote a book entitled *Verbal Behavior* which has with some justice been called "impressive." [14] But just about all students of language now regard it as completely inadequate.[15] The details of that argument are quite awesome technically, but the gist of one crucial element reduces to something very simple: one cannot account for the commonplace phenomenon of distinguishing between sentences and groups of words which are nonsentences by reference just to stimulus conditions, reinforcement conditions, and linear discrimination and generalization. A child of five can easily distinguish sentences from nonsentences in combinations he has never heard before, even nonsentences which are actually more probable statistically than combinations which he recognizes correctly as sentences. More briefly, language is a matter of form, not frequency. And no generalization or discrimination among frequencies can ever account for learning this form. Such, at least, is the conclusion reached by students of language who differ widely among themselves on other matters. (It is instructive, perhaps, that Skinner, like Freud, makes a much better case in explaining lapses from normal language usage than in explaining the learning of language itself.)

In sum, Behaviorist must acknowledge that learning and using language is behavior, and he must admit that *so far* no adequate analysis of this behavior has been given within the limits of Skinner's philosophy of human nature. This situation does not force Behaviorist to give up his denial of any traits distinctive to human nature, i.e., qualitatively different from the traits found in other animal species; for Behaviorist can always continue research in the hope that his denial will be substantiated by a demonstration of language-learning adequately described in terms of operant conditioning. Such a demonstration, in turn, might make it possible for Behaviorist to account for PCII (Alfredo's rational justification for sorting his in-basket) in precisely the same terms as those employed in PCI (the pigeon conditioned on two schedules of reinforcement).

Or Behaviorist might simply succumb and add a third premise to his philosophy of human nature, e.g., that Man has a Rational Soul, the activities of which are not adequately accounted for by those principles of behavior applicable to man as just another biological species. Or Behaviorist might say that all animals are machines, i.e., complex systems describable mathematically in terms of inputs, transformations, and outputs; on this track the first two premises of Skinner's philosophy of human nature can be rewritten ("Man is a machine which . . .") and the third formulated as a statement of the difference *in degree* of complexity between man and other organisms. And there are many other options open to Behaviorist.

Which of these options is closest to the truth of man's nature? The question is absurd. For statements about human nature are neither true nor false. Instead they are *decisions* about the limits within which other more specific questions are to be pursued. Decisions strictly speaking may be wise or foolish, justified or unjustified, even consistent or inconsistent, but not true or false. We have to judge a decision relative to the purpose for which it is made.

Now we may view the purpose of a philosophy of human nature as follows: In principle any line of questioning and research on man's thought and action can extend indefinitely. In practice, one has to stop somewhere. A consistent set of decisions on where and when to stop questions on human behavior is of great value in furthering research and practical action, especially in education.

It should be clear from the argument in Part III of this chapter that the decision *not* to seek for some distinctive characteristic in human action that sets it apart from pigeon behavior is probably unwise. But it is less unwise, all things considered, than the decision to regard that distinctive characteristic as already known. ("Man is *animalis symbolicum*," etc.) From the point of view of educational research and practice, the best strategy is to pursue to the limit the search for explanations of human learning in precisely the same terms we would use in describing pigeons' learning. It is not *true* that PCI and PCII are identical, but we are better advised to formulate our statements of school aims and methods as if they were identical than to act as if we knew precisely how they differ.

EPILOGUE

Professor George L. Newsome of the University of Georgia wrote a most gracious response to the original version of this chapter; his response appeared in *Studies in Philosophy and Education*, Winter, 1966. Dr. Newsome's treatment of this chapter showed that I did not succeed in getting across my main points. Let me recapitulate them briefly.

(i) It might be thought that a policy argument should begin with a philosophy of human nature. Indeed, this sounds like a good idea. But if we look more carefully, we find that the expression "human nature" does not refer to some *thing* about which we can know the truth. On the contrary, it registers a *decision* to cease explaining or justifying. Thus if we appeal to human nature in arguing educational policy, we have come to the point where we no longer find it possible or practical to pursue the search for reasons. "It's just human nature" is not the ultimate reason in educational policy, for it's no reason at all. We *do* have to stop giving reasons. The only question is when and where. This chapter has not answered that question; but it has showed that *that* is the question raised by the expression "human nature."

(ii) It might be thought that the language and techniques of behavioristic psychology, if they were made central to any educational policy, would result in a diminution of Man's estate, a denial of his rational being, or something. An education based on pure behaviorism would be indistinguishable from brainwashing, it might be thought. Further analysis, however, has showed that those thoughts are rather idle. The central issues of educational policy are not going to be answered either by adopting or by rejecting the language and techniques of Skinnerian behaviorism. An educational program can promote freedom or slavery whether or not cast in Skinnerian language, whether or not it uses automated reinforcing devices. Policies can be just or unjust, wise or foolish, full of faith or lacking it—all without regard to whether these policies involve Skinnerian language and techniques.

Thus we can neither solve nor forget the policy issues that face us simply by adopting (or rejecting) Skinnerian psychology. I believe Skinner would agree with this last statement, though he sometimes seems to argue that the language of behaviorism is a kind of automatic solvent for educational ills. I believe that we would do well to keep to the language of behaviorism as much as possible in policy arguments. It is clean talk—astringent and forceful. Using that language we may not be so all-fired eager to get inside "the hearts and minds of children," which is a good thing. We ought to start our policy argument, not with a philosophy of human nature, but with a premise that the hearts and minds of children constitute sacred territory from which we ought to be rigorously excluded. Using language and techniques of behaviorism should help to keep us on our own side of the fence.

Notes

B. F. SKINNER

1   Practically all of the Platonic dialogues may be considered treatises on human nature, individual or collective.

2   Aristotle's *De Anima, Ethics,* and *Politics* are more or less explicit formulations of theories of human nature. But references to human nature appear "naturally" throughout his writings; thus "[Human beings] are necessarily either good men or bad—the diversities of human character being nearly always derivative from this primary distinction, since the line between virtue and vice is one dividing the whole of mankind." (*Poetics,* 1448a) This is a clear case of using the idea of human nature to exclude further questions; in this instance the question "Why are some men good and others bad?" has been forestalled.

3   *Politics,* 1253a.

4   These are my statements, of course, not Skinner's. But I should defend their congruence with what Skinner *does* say in *Science and Human Behavior* (New York, 1953).

Statement A is simply a summary of the position stated in Chapter 3, "Why Organisms Behave."

Statement B follows from Section II, "The Analysis of Behavior," which gives the details of *how* all organisms, including men, learn from interaction with their environment.

Statement C is a logical consequence of Section III in which Skinner attempts to show how anything *sensible* one would want to say about private mental events can be said in the language of behavior.

5 *Ibid.*, Chapter 4, "Reflexes and Conditioned Reflexes."
6 Gilbert Ryle, *The Concept of Mind* (London, 1949). Ludwig
   Wittgenstein, *Philosophical Investigations* (Oxford, 1953). Skinner comments on philosophical behaviorism in "Concept-Forma-
   tion in Philosophy and Psychology," Sidney Hook (ed.), *Dimensions of Mind* (New York, 1960), pp. 226-30.
7 B. F. Skinner; "Pigeons in a Pelican," reprinted in the enlarged
   edition of *Cumulative Record* (New York, 1961) pp. 426.01 ff.
   Krutch's treatment of Skinner is found in his *The Measure of Man*
   (New York, 1954), Chapter 3.
8 William James, "Does Consciousness Exist" in *Essays in Radical
   Empiricism* (New York, 1912).
9 D. F. Pears, *Freedom and the Will* (London, 1963), p. 12.
10 There are many controversial matters just on the periphery of the
   simple point in this paragraph.

   (i) The distinction between X-ing n per cent of the time and
   learning to X was suggested by H. B. English, "Learning—There
   Ain't No such Animal," *Journal of Educational Psychology*,
   XLIII (Oct., 1952) 321-30, and further developed in certain un-
   published papers by Komisar and Colin Campbell. Even if all we
   know about A is that he has learned to X, we can still formulate
   some rule X^1, however trivial, such that "A has learned to X"
   implies "A has learned the rule that X^1." But to say "A X-es n
   per cent of the time" does not imply *any* "A has learned the rule
   that X^1." This fact, easily demonstrated by substituting descriptions of various (more and less complicated) behaviors, proves the
   connection between "A X-es n per cent of the time" and "A has
   learned to X" in a matter of *decision*, not implication. For implication is transitive: if it held between "A X-es n per cent of the
   time," and "A has learned to X," it would also hold between the
   former and "A has learned the rule that X^1" at least for some
   (possibly trivial) X^1.

   (ii) When X becomes some skill such that to say "A has
   learned to X" is scarcely distinguishable from "A has learned *how*
   to X" (e.g., X = play golf, swim, etc.), then the implication
   works only one way—*from* "A has learned to X" *to* "A has
   learned the rule that X^1"—and not the reverse. I believe, however,
   that even in those issues it is possible to discover a "pure" sense of
   "learned to X," i.e., a sense from which the skill element has been
   eliminated, such that the implication is again reciprocal. Take the
   following case: A boy went to camp and is asked "Did you learn
   to swim?" If he says "Yes," we can formulate *some* rule, e.g., he

learned the rule that one must move certain of one's extremities in order to progress through the water, so that if the boy's claim is true, the statement that he learned the rule is true also, however trivial. But the statement that he learned the rule does not imply that he learned to swim.

Suppose, however, that the boy says "I learned *how* to swim, but I also learned to hate it, so much so that only to save a life, my own or another's, would I ever swim again." In that case, what he has learned *to do*, i.e., to avoid swimming whenever possible, can equally well be expressed by the *rule* he has learned. In most instances, rules and skills are mixed in discourse, but they *can* be separated.

11 The analogy is to G. E. Moore's "open question" argument against naturalism in ethics. The general utility of the open question argument is shown by C. D. Hardie, *Truth and Fallacy in Educational Theory* (New York, 1962), pp. 17-23.

12 Thomas F. Green, "Teaching, Acting, and Behaving," *Harvard Educational Review*, XXXIV (Fall, 1964), 507-24.

13 For a more careful analysis of Green's argument on its own merits see Thomas F. Green, *et al.*, "Discussion," *Harvard Educational Review* XXXV (Spring, 1965), 191-209.

14 Mary Jane Aschner, "The Language of Teaching," in B. O. Smith and R. E. Ennis, eds., *Language and Concepts in Education* (Chicago, 1961), p. 118. Cf. Mrs. Aschner's more extensive and commendatory treatment of Skinner in "The Planned Man," Chapter 15 of *The Educated Man: Studies in the History of Educational Thought*, Paul Nash, A. M. Kazamias, and Henry Perkinson, eds. (New York, 1965).

15 See Noam Chomsky's review of *Verbal Behavior* in *Language*, XXXV (1959), 26-58.

6

Paul Goodman: A Systematic Thinker Fights The System

Does the System irresistibly consume its effective critics? Will the Establishment make any hostile outsider a member by the simple expedient of acknowledging the truth and justice of his attacks against it? This tendency has often been observed in American education and usually deplored. It has been said that John Dewey's ideas were admitted into the public schools, there to be emasculated, if not turned diametrically against their original intent. Language meant to castigate gets transformed into a system of slogans used to justify. There are many ways to disarm a critic.

Whether one regards this tendency to encapsulate criticism as deplorable or otherwise, one cannot evade the fact that it is the mark of any institution which proves capable of sustaining itself historically. For the critic, however compromised when ingested, usually succeeds in making the institution change—just a little, perhaps, but enough to prevent "paralysis of the body social," that disease which attacks and eventually destroys any society seeking protection in unchanging stability.[1] The American public school, as an institution, is not likely to succumb to that ailment: it encapsulates, disarms, and distorts all critics who appear even mildly dangerous; but it also alters itself in the process. It would appear to have a long life ahead of it, like the Roman Catholic Church, which in so many strange and wonderful ways it resembles.

The test will be what happens to Paul Goodman. The challenge presented by Goodman to public education is a deeply serious, metaphysical one. The sheer existence of the System is undeniable, of course. But its reality is deniable, and the forces of argument typically used by Goodman constitute a denial that the System is "really real," to use Whitehead's expression for metaphysical being. Of all the writers I discuss Goodman is the only one who could offer this fundamental, metaphysical affront to the System. His academic background includes a doctorate in philosophy at the University of Chicago, where he arrived only shortly after Brameld had left. Goodman's doctoral dissertation (written with the classicist Richard McKeon) *used* Aristotle's *Poetics* to analyze and explain a corpus of literary works (*The Structure of Literature*, as it was finally published), while Brameld's dissertation (written with the pragmatist T. V. Smith) *expounded* Marx's thought to those presumed ignorant of it. One can glimpse intriguing parallels between Goodman's metaphysics and Aristotle's, intersecting at right angles Brameld's and Marx's.

We will not explore these relations of intellectual geometry, for Goodman is not Aristotle, nor, somewhat more of a pity, is Brameld Marx. The point is that Goodman received the training of a metaphysician; if one looks closely and reads carefully, one can see that Goodman practices metaphysics in his thinking, as other men might practice psychoanalysis or Christianity or linguistic analysis. He asks whether what appears to be really is; he makes explicit the criteria by which reality and illusion may be distinguished; he asserts the moral obligations which reality places on human action and refutes the false claims that arise from illusion.

Goodman can make his metaphysical attack against the System only because he is not part of it. It belongs to his future biographer to explain all the ins and outs of Goodman and the System. One can taste a certain bitterness in Goodman's treatise on the "academic man"; and the academic world has its compensating gossip about Goodman's behavior while he was briefly on the staff of X college or Y university. But feelings and tales are largely irrelevant: many men, who are far more bitter toward academic life than

Goodman is capable of being toward anything, have maintained their "tenure" and will continue to do so until their TIAA checks start coming in. Furthermore, the stories told about Goodman can always be topped by others about men (and women) who are the very models of academic success. The objective fact is what counts, namely that Goodman has been outside the System for nearly all his adult life.

This is not merely a matter of money. He says, "for more than a generation I worked for less than I needed to support myself and family, and now I am paid more than I need. But it makes little difference either way." [2] Goodman is right; the money is not the difference. From actual deprivation to relative affluence has been the career of many of Goodman's contemporaries *in* the academic world and in other parts of the System. But it does make a difference that Goodman's career has been on the outside. The System is not a *closed* system—in the full logical sense that, from the point of view of those inside it, no questions other than internal questions can be asked. But the System is psychologically a pre-potent stimulus; i.e., from the point of view of those inside it, all questions about education are almost automatically translated into questions about the System: Is it working well or poorly? Would this or that change improve it? And once one begins treating these questions as the serious questions about education, one comes to sound like Conant or Brameld.

Now Goodman, like Barzun, could just ignore the System; he could appeal to Will as a sufficient guide for educational effort. He could do so, but only at the price of irrelevance. For the System, even if only as backdrop for the stage of educational effort, dominates and qualifies all present educational thought and action. Goodman alone could see stage, backdrop, and actors from a vantage point off-stage. He could distinguish between natural scenery and stage setting, between speeches and serious speech. From causes that are mostly personal to Goodman (and therefore irrelevant to this work), he found himself increasingly compelled to announce those differences, to act in the political, not the theatrical, sense. But having entered the political realm, Goodman becomes a source of arguments that are noteworthy for their form, their force, and their consequences.

I want to explain the basic form of Goodman's argument, to show how this form is peculiarly appropriate to Goodman's poetic as well as philosophical talent, to criticize the extension of his form of argument beyond its inherent limits, and finally to return to the original question whether the System can successfully ingest him—and the consequences either way.

I. GOODMAN'S DIALECTIC: FIRST STAGE

As might well be expected, the basic argument is dialectical, not deductively logical. It begins with a value judgment: What is, is wrong. It then asks: Why is it? What causes these objectively intolerable conditions to exist? Who is responsible? Various attempts to answer these questions are listened to—usually with increasing impatience—then all are rejected. Is there no reason for these conditions?

Is no one responsible, when the facts themselves bespeak irresponsibility? All this last is crescendo. This is followed by a pause, a drawing of breath to permit hearing the inevitable question: Then what are we going to do about it? The answers are of two kinds. One is very straightforward and commonsensical: those things could be done right this very day, if only . . . But there's the rub. If only men and women were the fully serious, active, and responsible creatures they *might* be, the world would not be in the chaotic situation it is. So the second kind of answer begins to emerge. To be saved, we must build for ourselves a bigger, free world, one of more reality and less illusion. But building a world, whether done by God or man, is a work of art, not politics. So the second kind of answer takes us beyond the scope of this book on educational policy, and I shall say little about Goodman the artist.

Just for mnemonic purposes, let us diagram that dialectical movement as follows. It is, remember, an interchange between You and Goodman, "You" representing the world of convention in general, the System in particular.

YOU	GOODMAN
A. I. Mutely present your world to Goodman.	2. articulately and discriminatingly: "Your world diminishes the human estate."

B. I. "Perhaps it does, at least it seems so when you describe it. But why does it diminish the human estate? Does it only diminish the human estate?"

2. Only the serious is real. Your world is unserious, unreal. That's why on balance your world diminishes the human estate."

C. I. "Then what am I to do?"

2. I propose $P_1, P_2 \ldots P_n$."

D. I. "I doubt that I can do $P_1, P_2 \ldots P_n$."

2. "No, You probably can't. You must build a world in which you can. Come join me in the task of world building."

The Capacity for Personal Affront

I mentioned above how Goodman came to possess the training and the detachment necessary to regard the System as metaphysically dubious. But prior to asking questions, even metaphysical questions, about a major social phenomenon like the System, Goodman takes a somewhat unusual attitude toward it: Goodman approaches institutions the way most of us approach other persons. (I have very little to go on, but from my own experience I believe that Goodman approaches other persons the way most of us would like to but don't for lack of skill or courage.) From our experience in schools, in the army, in jobs, in banks, in police stations, and so on, most of us learn to approach institutions as we would physical or intellectual structures. One can be curious about a structure, but one cannot care about a structure in the sense one cares about persons. Structures can hurt a person, but they cannot insult a person, again except in an obviously metaphorical sense of the term "insult." One can love a structure, e.g., geometry or General Motors, but *that* kind of love can be neither requited nor unrequited, whereas one's love for another person is always either one or the other. Some kinds of interpersonal relations are possible only within a system of impersonal structural relations: one can be civil or uncivil toward another only within a set of rules which define civility. One can make, keep, and break promises only within the institution of promising. But one cannot be civil or uncivil *to* the rules of civility themselves, nor make a promise to the institution of promising.

One can take those interpersonal, albeit institutionalized, actions only toward other persons.

But the institutions themselves are conditioned by the pervasive fact of non-institutional relations—sexual, visceral, and perceptual.[3] In this way, as well as in others, social structures differ from purely physical or intelectual structures. Thus if we approach General Motors exactly as we approach a Buick or a problem in geometry, we miss something of great importance about General Motors, namely that it is composed of human animals who move, eat, see, love, and die, who can be led or shoved, fed or starved, seen or ignored, made love to, or killed.

Now what attitude—What range of emotional response? What physical response? What set of linguistic conventions?—is appropriate to a social structure? The history of social thought shows an increasing preoccupation with just those questions, and a full explanation of the deceptively simple answer given by Goodman would require relating his response to that whole history. But this much can be said simply: Goodman *begins* by looking at a social institution as an aggregation of human animals. To begin here and then to go on to say a lot of other things is to transcend the reductionist tendencies in both Marx and Freud. It is different from saying that *after all* or *in the end* or *at bottom* social institutions are nothing but devices for feeding and sheltering the human animal in a hostile physical environment or for regulating his erotic, reproductive behavior.

Before Goodman begins, he looks at institutional relations as a direct confrontation with other human animals. Other people with great effort have learned to confront works of art in this way—directly, immediately. But of all the persons writing on educational policy, Goodman is unique in having this highly cultivated capacity for directly confronting his fellow human beings.

But confrontation implies openness to affront. The analogy to works of art holds. For most adults the ability to be personally affronted by even a highly shocking work of art has to be acquired through training. Otherwise we become vaguely uncomfortable; we allow our attention to wander; we become diffusely peevish. But we cannot muster the directed anger of personal affront unless we have been trained to do so; this applies as well to social institutions as to works of art. It is for some future biographer to show how

Goodman's academic training, his practical experience in psycho-therapy, and his unusual style of life from childhood have combined to give him this highly tutored talent; but the fact is that he has it to an extraordinary degree.

The Direct Value Judgment

Fortunately, the era has passed in which ill-trained pedants cry "That's a value judgment!" as though they had caught a hapless victim *in flagrante delicto*. Philosophers are still very interested in value judgments; their efforts, however, are no longer directed toward striking value judgments from rational discourse but rather in classifying the many different kinds of statements which can be fitted (sometimes with difficulty) under the rubric "value judgments," explicating the criteria appropriate to each kind, and analyzing the function of each in various sorts of arguments.

In a policy argument, we seek a conclusion ("Therefore we ought to do so-and-so") which has the force of compelling assent from all rational creatures. We may never achieve this aim entirely, but that is our goal nonetheless. Now Goodman begins the statement of his typical argument with the following kinds of assertions:

(a) I confront human beings living their institutional lives.

(b) I find them engaged in actions which stunt and stultify their full human growth.

(c) This condition is insulting to me and to the entire human race.

Just as it is essential that a good drama critic confront a play as drama, not as a business enterprise nor as an ineffable exhalation of Pure Spirit; that an art critic confront a painting as painting, not some other thing; and that the poetry critic confront a poem as just what it is, so it is essential that a social critic confront a social institution as the setting for human action. To be a good critic it is not sufficient that one be able to confront that thing as the thing it is and not some other thing, for the critic may lack the wit and articulateness to *say* anything interesting about what he confronts. But it is an essential talent. Goodman possesses it in unique degree among contemporary social critics, but even so he has lapses, as we shall see.

It is in respect to judgments like (b) that the orthodox logical positivist insisted that the "value element" be rigorously separated from the "question of fact." In Goodman's writing, this (b) will sound like this: "It was obvious . . . that the children were muffled. They sat in a dejected posture and they could not, physically could not throw out their voices." (*Compulsory Mis-Education,* p. 45.) [4] "In a milieu of resignation, where the young men think of society as a closed room in which there are no values but the rejected rat race or what they can produce out of their own guts, it is extremely hard to aim at objective truth or world culture. One's own products are likely to be personal or parochial." (*Growing Up Absurd,* p. 179, hereafter abbreviated as GUA.)

I have chosen these two quotations to illustrate several features of the (b) judgment. An obvious question one might ask about it is this: Is it objective or subjective? Consider the first quotation: one might be tempted to analyze it into two quite different sorts of statements, one objective—what the situation really is—and the other subjective—Goodman's personal reaction to what is. So analyzed, the first quotation might read:

"The children sat quietly at their desks until they were called on. The teacher had difficulty hearing answers given by the children. And I do not like this kind of classroom." The difference between objective and subjective is clear: any person possessed of normal perceptions, a reasonable command of the English language, and an opportunity to observe that particular classroom must agree to the first two sentences in our translation. Hence, they are objective statements. But the last sentence will be true for some "I's" and false for others. It is true for "I, Paul Goodman," and false, let us say, for "I, Viscount Montgomery." [5] Since its truth depends on variations in personal feeling, it is subjective.

This method of analyzing statements like our first quotation is quite usual and quite useful for certain purposes, e.g., for training prospective teachers to distinguish between their descriptions of student behavior and their reactions to that behavior. But I shall attempt to prove that this analysis *does not* and *cannot* yield an accurate translation of Goodman's statement.

I want, first, to show that the *claim* that children are muffled and dejected is not the same as the two claims that they are sitting quietly *and* that I, the speaker, do not like their sitting quietly. Why did we analyze the original into its two components? We did so, notice, because it *may* be the case that Goodman was wrong, that the children are *not* muffled and dejected but merely quiet. It may be Goodman's error to confuse muffled dejection with mere quietness because Goodman, for some reason, does not like quietness in children. But then the fact that "The children sat quietly . . . and I [Goodman] do not like [it]" can be *true* while ". . . the children were muffled . . . dejected . . ." is *false* proves that the former is not an adequate translation of the latter. (It is obviously a criterion for adequate translations that true sentences are true and false sentences are false in the new expression.)

Consider next this matter of "physically could not throw out their voices." This is a much more complex judgment than is "the teacher had difficulty hearing. . . ." To say that children *could* not make themselves heard means, in this context, that they were trying to but not succeeding; that their intentions were *not* to discommode the teacher for their collective enjoyment, *not* to conceal inability to answer correctly for ignorance or lack of skill in English, *not* to avoid the peer group odium which attaches to teacher's pets, etc. Rather, the children consistently failed to make themselves heard and understood because in this situation the muscles used to make the voice heard at some distance simply did not respond adequately to the children's intentions.

Thus Goodman's original statement can be proved false if we discover later that the children were deliberately speaking too softly, e.g., just to annoy the teacher. But notice that this evidence would not falsify the statement that the teacher had difficulty hearing. And surely it is a corollary of the criterion for adequate translations that evidence which will falsify the original statement must also falsify the translation. Therefore, the translation is not adequate.

Perhaps my proof destroys only a straw man; perhaps my analysis of Goodman's statement into its objective and subjective components is just faulty analysis, while a good one would yield a translation adequate on the criteria given. I cannot *prove* that any translation would fail, but there is a reason which seems sufficient for believing that no such attempt would be successful.

The translation would have to be couched in terms which are neutral with respect to the logical distinction between behavioral and dispositional predicates, a distinction easily recognized if one considers the ambiguity in a term like "quiet." This term is ambiguous in the sense that it can be used with equal facility as a description of particular instances of behavior *and* as a description of general tendencies or dispositions in behavior. In the first sense, we may say: "Amazing! Arnold has been quiet for five whole minutes." In the second sense: "Arnold is a quiet child, has been since he was a baby." This ambiguity in the term "quiet" could scarcely ever cause any confusion in speech, for context would always make clear which sense is meant.

To see that these two senses are distinct, though not unrelated, of course, one can try a simple test. Imagine an observer who possesses the talents mentioned earlier as requisites for an "objective" judgment, i.e., normal capacities for physical perception and command of the English language. Such an observer of a primary school classroom could report: "Arnold was quiet for time interval T_1-T_2." But then the observer might ask for an explanation of Arnold's behavior: "Why was he quiet?" If we say, "Because he is a quiet child," we are not uttering a mere tautology. So far as it goes, this is a perfectly valid explanation. Whether it goes as far as it should depends on our original purpose in asking for an explanation. For certain pedagogical purposes, "Because he is a quiet child" is all the explanation we need. It tells us that if we want him to emit a large quantity of verbal behavior we will have to provide rather unusual stimulus conditions, etc. For purposes of more profound therapy, the explanation may be of no use whatsoever.[6] But the point is: it *is* an explanation, not a tautology. Hence "quiet" is being used in two senses.

(Note that we can give a dispositional sense to just about any behavioral description: "During interval T_1-T_2, Arnold was waving his arms violently." "Why did Arnold wave his arms violently?" "Because he is a waving-his-arms-violently-type boy." It is not hard to understand why we have a single predicate for both senses of "quiet" and why we have to construct the dispositional predicate for many other behavior descriptions. If the behavior of waving one's arms violently were something we had frequent reason to single out, comment on, and moralize over—then we should likely have had a special word to designate that behavior. Perhaps that special word would have been "bractive"; if so, "bractive" would have both a behavioral and a dispositional sense.)

The terms in which Goodman describes human beings are dispositional, not behavioral. Logically, they *have* to be dispositional. His indictment of the System, as we have sketched it, is for what it does to the people in it, not what people in it do. Therefore, he has to describe in dispositional terms what he sees in the System. But our normally endowed observers who give us an "objective" description can tell us only of the overt behavior that goes on. Therefore, no set of behavioral statements as required by the narrow sense in which we are using the term "objective" here can be an adequate translation of Goodman's dispositional language.

In a precisely analogous manner, one can distinguish between behavioral descriptions and language which describes intentions, i.e., what people are doing or trying to do. Again, the "objective" statements can be only behavioral descriptions. But Goodman indicts the System because it causes intentions to fail; it makes it impossible for people to communicate, to "throw out" their voices, to "aim at objective truth or world culture," and to reach many other distinctively human goals. Thus Goodman has to describe human action by its intentions, while the "objective" observer could never see nor say anything about intentions. Therefore no translation of Goodman's appraisals into purely "objective" description could possibly be an adequate rendition of the original.

I should not have gone on so about this matter if I had not heard and read so often that the trouble with Goodman is that he makes value judgments or that he is so subjective. What I have demonstrated is that, even if one takes Goodman's very simple and obvious descriptions of classroom behavior, one *cannot* formulate them in purely "objective," behavioral terms. However, there are two quite different conclusions one could draw from that argument: One could conclude, therefore, that the type of description–cum–appraisal found so typically in Goodman's writing is to be abolished, since it cannot be made "objective" and only "objective" judgments have a legitimate place in educational argument. On the other hand, one could conclude that the distinction between "objective" and "subjective" judgments, however valuable it might be in some contexts, is simply inapplicable in this one. Goodman's descriptions–cum–appraisals may be true or false, right or wrong, valid or invalid *in substance*, but they cannot be eliminated from intelligible argument just because *in form* they do not fit a particular canon of objectivity. Needless to add, I draw the second conclusion, not only for Goodman but also in general. One cannot legislate in advance what form of statement is appropriate in an educational argument; one has to look at arguments which compel rational assent and note the form and function of the statements which comprise them.

Thus if Goodman is to tell us what he sees when he confronts the System, he must be allowed to speak of dispositions and intentions. He sees not only a bent posture, but dejection and despair; not only drunken and ill-controlled posturing but a general loss of connection with a dependable world. Where another might see only an adolescent gulping a piece of pie à la mode, Goodman perceives a general inability to take on solid food, hard ideas, and tough responsibilities.

If these reports are to be accorded any status in serious argument, they must be corrigible. If Goodman only "sees" these phenomena, in quotation marks, then their report is poetry, or myth, or idle chatter. But he says that he *sees* dejection, despair, and infantilism, so his report must be corrigible by evidence of *some* sort. What sort of evidence can be adduced to confirm or, more importantly, to disprove this kind of report? I wish that I could give a clear, firm answer; all I can actually supply is a refutation of one initially attractive answer.

After a brief training period, a student of biology can look into a properly functioning microscope and see protozoa. An untrained person who looks into the same microscope will see a shaking, spotted liquid surface. A mildly enthusiastic bird watcher of an afternoon will see three purple grackles, two goldfinches, a nuthatch, and several unidentified birds. The last category will not be seen by the really avid enthusiast nor the first categories by a person who notices only a bunch of birds. Because it frequently becomes important in testing the weight of evidence, e.g., in law courts, the distinction between seeing something directly and other sorts of inference–recognition is ready to hand in ordinary language.

Baxter, a witness with good eyesight, swears that he saw Clayton, a suspect, standing all alone in broad daylight only ten feet from where he, Baxter, was watching. Baxter and Clayton have worked in the same small office for ten years and have been the closest of companions in their off-work hours. The defense attorney, attempting to shake the story, asks Baxter by what distinguishing marks he was able to recognize Clayton. The attorney's ruse may or may not succeed, but if Baxter follows the logic of the English language, he will simply reject the question: he did not recognize him *by* any distinguishing marks, he just *saw* his long time acquaintance standing there. His report is corrigible, of course. He may have been lying; he may have been mistaken in what he saw. If there is overwhelming evidence that Clayton was in Bermuda and a skilled actor had impersonated him, Baxter might have to admit "I thought I saw him, but it seems I didn't." His mistake was in the logical category of seeing, not of inferring, or diagnosing, or recognizing from distinctive features, or something of that sort.

Now it might be claimed that Goodman stands to dejection, despair, and infantilism as a biologist to amoebae, a bird watcher to a tohee, or Baxter to Clayton. There is much to be said for this view. It takes account of Goodman's extraordinary experience as teacher, therapist, novelist, and poet. With his heightened sensitivity, he should be able to look at human beings and there see (not just "see") feeling-states invisible to less acute observers. On this view, his reports have to be given credence unless we have other compelling reasons to believe that he is lying or mistaken. And that is the initially attractive answer to the question of how Goodman's statements that he sees feeling-states can be significant and corrigible.

However, the analogy breaks down when we come to *say* precisely what it is that Goodman sees and the rest of us do not. Above I used the nice-sounding but essentially meaningless term "feeling-states." But this will not do for serious discourse. For the terms we used to describe some kinds of emotions change when Goodman uses them. Suppose we walk into a classroom with Goodman. He says: "The children are dejected." We say: "They don't appear so to us. Inattentive and withdrawn perhaps, but not dejected." He says: "Look more closely. See that backbone bent over. Hear that weak voice." We say: "Oh yes, now we see the dejection." We have not, in this case, changed the meaning of the term "dejection." We have merely learned to look at more subtle cues for its presence.

But now we go with Goodman into other classrooms. He says: "These children are full of rage, grief, shame, despair and sexual desire." We say: "They do not appear so to us. A little tense and clumsy, perhaps, not well coordinated, and rightly uninterested in these silly lessons. But they are not in the throes of the violent emotions you named." Goodman says: "Oh yes, these violent emotions are there all right. It's just that they are retroflected and you can't see them."

But we reply, "No, when we say a child is enraged, we *mean* that he is acting with noticeable violence and hostility toward the people or things around him. For an older child and an adult we will allow that anger, or even rage, may be controlled, but in that case we *mean* that his face is red, his fist clenched, his eyes narrowed, breath short, and so on. We don't see *those* things in the behavior of the children you ask us to observe, though we agree that what we do see is not the free and graceful action we should like to see in children."

Thus we have to distinguish between rage and "rage," grief and "grief," despair and "despair," etc. We have to admit, I think, that Goodman really sees what he claims that he sees, and that he can see (not just "see" in a metaphorical sense) attributes of human action which are invisible to most of us. But how is he to *label* what he sees? When he uses terms like rage, grief, despair, etc., he is liable to the retort that the normal observer can recognize rage, grief, despair, etc., when he sees them, but simply *does not* see them in the typical classroom where Goodman sees them. I want to say: Goodman sees "rage," "grief," "despair," etc., but these terms for feeling-states being used in an unusual sense.

From the standpoint of policy argument, this distinction between the standard uses of terms like rage, despair, etc., and Goodman's special use, which I designate by quotation marks, is of central importance. In the standard senses of these terms, if a normal observer announces that a large proportion of the children in a certain school are constantly in a state of rage, grief, despair, etc., then that fact takes precedence over many other considerations in the demand for action. Suppose a newspaper columnist reports that most of the children at Silas Lapham Junior High School are always in a state of rage or grief or despair or all three. Suppose he has pictures showing the tears, the flailing fists, and the facial contortions of these violent emotions. Suppose the local television studio broadcasts motion pictures with the full sound effects of enraged, grief-stricken, and desperate children. Then the existing machinery for political pressure can be used to effect some immediate change in Silas Lapham. The causes for that sort of reaction from the children would be relatively easy to discover and correct: a sadistic teaching staff, physically dangerous surroundings, extreme deprivation of food and drink, etc. The remedying of these conditions would take precedence over many other demands for change, e.g., over the demand to reduce the rate of drop-outs, over the need to improve the school's average on standard tests in mathematics, etc. The only other consideration which would take priority over correcting such violent emotional reactions from the children would be a very high rate of death or hospitalization of the same or other children. Even that is not clear, for any conditions which produce a high incidence of rage, grief, despair, etc., would be likely to produce a high casualty rate at the same time.

But normal observers like newspaper reporters do not see these violent emotions in the classrooms Goodman visits. Nor do they see the vicious cruelty, danger, and extreme deprivation which could be expected to bring out these extreme emotions. When instances of violence do occur, they have to be called unmotivated or explained by reference to the general malaise of the times or low morale or equivalently non-explanatory concepts. Policy responses to these unmotivated acts of violence in schools are equivalent to those made out of school: police protection is kept at hand to act as a deterrent or to make retribution swift and certain if the deterrent fails; violators are segregated or punished.[7]

These two common sense uses of the terms rage, grief, etc., give us clues to what Goodman means by "rage," "grief," etc.; but they provide *only* clues. We still do not know exactly, and in that failure of exactness lies the need for Goodman's further arguments. The two ordinary uses of the terms are to *describe* very emotional behavior and to explain *extreme* acts of various sorts, particularly though not exclusively, acts of violence. One way of understanding Goodman is to hold that his uses are exactly analogous, except that he has increased the degree of emotional intensity. What the ordinary observer would describe as apathy, withdrawal, at most, dejection, Goodman would describe in much more intense terms. The sporadic acts of overt violence and the much more frequent acts of escape (physical *and* mental) that children engage in would then be put together and explained as caused by "rage," "grief," "despair," etc. There would seem to be an obvious strategy to this move by Goodman. He wants us to regard a situation which produces "rage," "grief," "despair," etc., with the same abhorrence, the same immediate political pressure we would show if a school caused rage, grief, despair, etc., in children.

Toward the acts of violence and the acts of escape found among school children and other dependent people, Goodman would have us feel concern and compassion, as we do toward people who act out of rage, grief, despair, etc.—replacing the attitude of un-comprehending counter-hostility we have toward people whose un-motivated acts of violence threaten persons or institutions.

I think this first interpretation of Goodman's use of these terms is indeed the only logically tenable one, but in this interpretation there is one very obvious defect in Goodman's position: it does not provide any reason for changing anything we are now doing in schools. *If* schools produce rage, grief, despair, etc., in children, *that is* an immediate and sufficient reason for changing conditions; but if schools produce only "rage," "grief," etc., *that is* a reason for change only commensurate with many other reasons for doing many other things through the limited channels of political action. It has no commanding priority. It is true that Goodman wishes us to give commanding priority to the relief of "rage," "grief," etc., but his wishes have no more commanding power than do his words used in unusual senses. Goodman leaves it open for his critic to say, "Yes, we agree that things are not quite well in schools, but it would take a *great* deal of political effort to put them right, and in the meantime things are not quite well in a lot of other places, too. We have a war to fight in Vietnam, another against poverty in vari-ous spots around the country, a lagging rate of economic growth. The problems of children and youth will have to take their turn. Unless you can show a better reason than an unusual way of using ordinary words, school reform of any fundamental sort stands rather far down on the list of political priorities."

I believe that Goodman has to accept this counter-move and go on to provide a better reason, which I think he can provide. But sometimes he seems to reject it, and to argue (this is the second interpretation of his use of the terms "rage," etc., which we've been discussing) that "rage" is really rage, "grief" really grief, and so forth. These are really the same states, only in the first case they are "retroflected" or "repressed" or "inward," which makes them positively worse, so that the full moral force which would be aroused by a high incidence of rage and grief ought to be mobilized to even higher pitch to alleviate "rage" and "grief." This, I take it, is an ultimately untenable argument. There may be reason and utility in this shift of meaning in terms for purposes of psychotherapy ("Your constant sleepiness is really an expression of anger against being a woman."); but one cannot read those new meanings *directly* into the language of politics. They will simply be disregarded, or if caught up and used, then their use will inevitably be an irresponsible one.

There is a third interpretation of Goodman's use, which I think true and compatible with either of the two above. We are in the midst of a revolution of extended sensibility which has been going on for about a century and a half. In this struggle, the major revolutionists are literary artists, which is not to say that the revolutionists are major artists. Some are, e.g., Jane Austen and Charles Dickens; but neither Harriet Beecher Stowe's *Uncle Tom's Cabin* nor Anna Sewall's *Black Beauty* can be considered a major literary masterpiece, though each was of major effect in extending our sensibilities to the sufferings of chattels and animals. Whatever other labels may be attached to him, Goodman must surely be called a fighter, perhaps a guerrilla fighter, in this revolution of extended sensibility. We have already become sensible to suffering in children caused by physical pain and deprivation and by the more obvious forms of mental cruelty, but Goodman pushes us to take a more advanced position on that same front, i.e., to recognize suffering in children and other dependent human beings as inherent in life itself. And then another advance: in the kind of mechanical society that we have allowed to be erected around us, nearly everybody is a dependent, suffering the rage, grief, and despair which are inseparable from dependency itself. This is a long way from the battle Mrs. Stowe fought to make us sensitive to the physical and spiritual sufferings of slaves who have brutal masters. We next had to become sensible of the suffering which is inherent in slavery itself, and then we had to widen our notion of slavery so that we could become sensitive to the spiritual degradation of any man who is subject to the autocratic, dictatorial control of another. Then somewhere between *All Quiet on the Western Front* and

Catch-22 we were extended once more. Having accepted that meaningless death, pain, fear, and deprivation diminished man to the status of slavery, we now had to become sensible of the diminution of man by his captivity in meaningless nonsense itself.[8] Finally Goodman wants to extend this last sensibility to children and young men and women who are captives of the System, which to Goodman is rather a paradigm case of what is meant by meaningless nonsense.

Sometimes Goodman uses the conventional weapon for this kind of warfare: a work of literature which stimulates our imagination and allows new sensibilities to enter. This is true of his novels and short stories, some of which are discussed below in connection with the concept of "building a world." In addition, many of the essays in *Growing Up Absurd* are essentially literary in the same sense: just the simple metaphor of the rat race in a closed room is a literary device ("literary" used in a non-pejorative sense) which opens our imagination at least a little. But his way of talking about rage, grief, despair, etc., in *Mis-Education* may be likened to guerrilla tactics. The front of sensibility has not actually been extended far enough for us to feel that children and youth suffer such torments merely because they are forced to do stupid things for senseless reasons. But Goodman bluffs: he writes as if he held that position; he demands the political leverage that goes with the victory. If he is challenged too sharply, a bomb may explode anywhere, e.g., in Newark, or New Haven, or Detroit, or in your own home town. So the "front" disappears, there is no longer a clear line separating those deprivations and indignities which we will not allow children and youth to suffer from those which are tolerable in the context the larger society. Thus Goodman can move in educational circles like a fish in the sea.

This book, however, is not intended to be a handbook for insurgents or counter-insurgents. One may be or become a committed warrior on either side, but that is not relevant to the question: What is the logical status of the argument for those who do not believe that Goodman's "rage" is rage, "grief," grief, etc.? I take it that those who believe those terms equivalent would be logically committed to the propositions that schools as presently constituted are intolerable places and that their dissolution should be among the very top priority items of political concern in this country today. For others, the answer would be more equivocal. We should not deny that Goodman sees what he says he sees. Nor should we refuse to acknowledge that the activities and emotions he reports are indeed diminutions of the full human estate. But from the point of view of serious argument on educational policy, it does not justify any change at all in the System to say that its operation diminishes the full human estate, not even a specific change which will enhance the values presently being sacrificed. For even if we grant that some particular values now lost could be saved and enhanced by a particular change, we still have to ask: "Yes, but at what other cost? What values presently being achieved by the System will be lost by the change? What is the *economy* of your proposed changes?"

II. GOODMAN'S DIALECTIC: SECOND STAGE

We have to re-phrase our questions because the System is a functioning reality. It does achieve certain values, as we shall see below, which would be almost inconceivable apart from the System. Its costs are heavy also: Goodman has pointed to some of them very clearly. But the costs are not *so* high, as actual rage and despair would be, that they do not have to be balanced against the goods produced by the System. Therefore, we have to turn to the next phase in our dialectical argument:

Why is it so? (You)

Because of the unreality of your world. (Goodman)

As was demonstrated in detail in Chapter 3, Brameld wrote a great deal about what he called "ontology" but not once presented an argument to show that things we ordinarily take to be real are not or vice versa. Goodman talks very little *about* metaphysics or ontology, but many of his arguments can be analyzed as one or the other of the two basic forms of metaphysical discourse: either that something is (or is not) real because it meets (or fails to meet) certain criteria of reality, or else that some course of action is right (or wrong) because it accords with (or fails to accord with) the demands of reality.

Note that I said that Goodman's arguments *can* be analyzed as fitting these classical forms. They are not written in the way philosophers (of the sort Brameld treats) write metaphysics. I believe that Goodman self-consciously constructs his arguments with very carefully developed and highly sophisticated metaphysical categories. However, he does not write philosophy as do academic scholars; he writes, in his terms, classical literature: "the concrete blending of observation, memory, criticism, reasoning, imagination, and reconstruction in order to find-and-give human meaning." (CofA, p. 89) [8] It would be untrue to Goodman, and probably impossible, to rewrite his metaphysics in the academic formulas he so dislikes. But I think that it is within the same concept of literature Goodman upholds to attempt at least a blending of criticism and reconstruction to find-and-give a meaning to his sense of "metaphysical crisis." (GUA, p. 172)

This expression itself may be of some help in explaining the difference between Goodman's enterprise and that of the academic philosophers Goodman reads and admires, i.e., the modest linguistic analysts. The latter write treatises on descriptive metaphysics, defined by one of its leading practitioners as being "content to describe the actual structure of our thought about the world." It is contrasted with "revisionary metaphysics," which is "concerned to produce a better structure." [9] Now neither descriptive metaphysics nor revisionary metaphysics, as Strawson defines them, could produce a crisis. Problems, yes; puzzles, yes—with all the excitement and commitment that intellectual problems and puzzles produce for some people. But what could we possibly mean by "crisis" prefixed by "metaphysical"? Just nothing at all?

It is relevant (and I am convinced that it is by Goodman's intent) that the expression "metaphysical crisis" occurs in that rather large section of *Growing Up Absurd* which Goodman devotes to the language used by various types of young men who stay outside the System. Strawson, in describing the methods of metaphysics, notes that "reliance upon a close examination of the actual use of words is the best, and indeed the only sure, way in philosophy." [10] Goodman, following that way exactly, encounters a crisis. How does it occur? His close examination of the actual use of words reveals *little structure* of thought and almost no world, in the sense of ordered cosmos. Goodman really does try to find some reality he can describe with contentment, but there just is not any. That is certainly a metaphysical crisis.

But there Goodman was talking specifically about the Beats. It is their use of a very special and ever-changing jargon that reveals the absence of a structure and a world. When we see why their language has this effect, Goodman believes that we can also see the same crisis—sometimes at a lower, sometimes at a higher, level of intensity—throughout the various groupings that comprise our society.

The Beats, then, have a special significance as a mirror of the larger society, and they cannot distinguish between reality and illusion. They can recognize the obvious illusion, the phantasms without substance, in the rat race in a closed room, Goodman's expression for the endless and inescapable pursuit of the mostly worthless. The Beats can recognize these illusions and withdraw from them, but they cannot recognize them *as* illusions, for that would require contrasting illusion with solid reality. The latter is not only a concept absent from their language but also an experience absent from their lives.

Then what is reality? If we had to choose one word from the Goodman lexicon to equate with "reality," that word would be "seriousness." If it is real, "for real" Goodman would more likely put it, then it is serious, and vice versa. But finding word-for-word equivalence will not help us much. We still have to ask: What is it to be serious? To answer that we must use some of the idiom of academic philosophy.

Recall Strawson's distinction between descriptive and revisionary metaphysics. Which is the better kind of metaphysics? It all depends on what you want it *for.* If you are looking just for a structure, it is unimportant. It is a matter of temperament whether you prefer the cautious analysis of the actual structure of—for example, scientific thought as given by Kant—or the imaginative construction of a possible world as given by Hegel. But if that structure has to perform another function, specifically if it has to provide a basis for *action,* then its choice no longer can be simply a matter of aesthetic preference. For one cannot seriously assert Pope's "Whatever is, is right," nor Hegel's *Das Weltgeschichte ist das Weltgericht.* If a person really wants to act in accordance with the moral demands of his world—and that is the prayer of every religious person who consciously *means* "Thy will be done"—then he must build a world to include a morality. Non-religious persons are under no such logical obligation. They are morally obligated to do the right, but it is not necessary to believe that the right is demanded by the structure of the world. In purely logical terms, the world may be morally neutral or even fundamentally hostile to human morality, but man does not live by logic alone. It is probably more natural to take a religious attitude, which involves accepting the belief that human action ought to be regulated by the most basic structure of the world, than to take the heroic stand that one must act rightly *against* the basic structure of reality. From the former belief, which is central to the religious position, it follows that a metaphysics, i.e., an explicit formulation of what features of the world are *really* real, must include a substantive morality as one of its basic constituents.

In this sense, Goodman is a religious philosopher. The real world, the serious world, for him is not just any possible or even actual structure; it has to be one which exerts genuine moral demands on a person's conduct. Therefore, Goodman is not and cannot be a monist of either the materialist or idealist variety. It is possible, of course, to build a logically consistent structure of propositions asserting the existence of only material objects or of only mental objects, ideas. But the genuine demands on conduct arise from both sources. (Some idealist philosophers have denied that genuine demands on conduct do arise from purely material sources, but that is not to be taken seriously after we have learned to think of the human being as a psychosomatic entity.) Thus the real world has to include both material and ideal elements.

Suppose we just look around us. Where do we find a model for the fusion of matter and thought? Different philosophers have answered in different ways: The hylomorphism (matter-organized-in-forms-ism) of the Aristotelian-Thomistic school provides one possible answer. John Dewey's method of empirical naturalism provides another.[11] Goodman's "Gestalt-Communitas" is in this same philosophical tradition.

For an individual, *being serious requires a Gestalt, a fusion-in-form, of thought, feeling, and physical action.* So far Goodman and Dewey march together. But Dewey never really saw much beyond the inventor's laboratory or the painter's canvas as the model of this Gestalt. Goodman certainly does not deny that Dewey's are relevant and valuable models, but why make them exclusive? They fit relatively few people and situations; they do not fit, for example, the deep joy of sexual intercourse, the growth of self-awareness through suffering, nor even a full belly-laugh at bawdy humor, which are likewise relevant and valuable models of what it means to be serious. But being serious, that is, bringing one's feelings, thoughts, and body into full contact with the external world, means that one can be hurt. If the reader will excuse a modish way of speaking, we may call this an existential paradox in the human condition: what a man must do to be saved, i.e., to live a fully human life in a real world, can be a source of such pain as to make it impossible for him even to try for salvation. It's the task of therapy to help remove the more debilitating consequences of the too-painful intercourse between a human being and his world.

But that side of Goodman's thought is outside our purview here.[12] It is not irrelevant, however, to note that Goodman's world is suffused with faith. "Therapy" for him is less far removed from "education" than it is for most people. Obviously the concept of therapy implies a belief in the recuperative, regenerative powers of the organism; it is conceptually quite distinct from the idea of repairing a purely physical object. Goodman's *theory* of man-in-society likewise includes a deep sense of helpful powers that may be called on to assist the recovery and renewal of men and their institutions. It is not pessimistic but rather exactly the contrary when Goodman asserts that education makes therapy necessary: the converse is that therapy, with what that implies of God's Grace to man, makes education possible.

Goodman's theory of reality requires a concrete interpenetration of idea, feeling, and physical action. Now the Idea of Mankind, has no limits; but not so the reality of men-in-society. The human scale stretches so far *and no further*. Its limit defines a community. To provide a material base for a community is the sole but very broad function of architecture. The only way that the civic virtues, justice and freedom, can achieve reality is by their incorporation in communities and in the concrete relations of communities to each other. If productivity is to be measured in real or serious units, these must be related to the activities of men-in-communities. Economic abstractions such as Gross National Product are not merely abstract; they are totally unreal. Men can and do play with these unrealities to conceal their boredom or loneliness and despair at being cut off from anything serious.

Since reality is such a scarce commodity, we should not be surprised by the brisk trade for ersatz. But we shouldn't be fooled by it either. In the notable absence of *community* in the modern corporate world, *no* human activity can be considered fully serious. Thus *everyone* is in the same condition as the Beatnik who cannot separate reality and illusion. If no human activity is fully serious, if there is nowhere a full unity of thought, feeling, and action, then all human endeavor is merely a shading of illusion. There simply is no real world in which we can find clearcut moral demands on our action, for what purports to be the real world lacks this essential criterion of seriousness. The physical action of an apprentice mechanic has no organic unity with his feelings for things and people nor with his beliefs about himself and those he is supposed to serve. The declarations of a state's governor on juvenile delinquency have no connection with the actions and feelings of the youth nor with those of the adults who live and suffer with them. The tender, carefully cultivated feelings of middle-class boys do not provide impetus for nor receive stimulation from action in a larger, conceptually articulated world; instead life and literature become merely attenuated stimuli for more feeling.

These are the facts of the world to which Goodman points. His technical problem philosophically is now patent: since he stands within the tradition which holds that the morality of action must be rooted in the basic structure of a real world (the religious attitude discussed above) and since the world we actually live in is one of formless illusion, not structured seriousness, how is a man to know *what* he ought to do? He cannot, with Dewey, point to the seriousness of an experimental scientist or artist and say: Go ye and do likewise. In fact, after having made his point that the failure of the System is a metaphysical failure, there is little more that can be said. If we are rooted in unreality, if our thought-feeling-action is disjointed and unserious, it is not surprising that our System diminishes man and his estate. It is not surprising that children show "rage" and "grief" and "despair": to lose a real world and be forced to live in ersatz could crush even the most heroic adult spirit. But that is how things stand.

Here is the low point in Goodman's dialectic. If it were not for the faith which suffuses his therapeutic view of things, arriving at this point would lead to suicide. But with his faith in therapy,

Goodman can acknowledge the metaphysical crisis without casting himself into nothingness. The biological processes continue even in spiritual crisis. In individuals, cells do their work, and hunger and sex keep men moving. In society, goods get produced and distributed—albeit blindly, heedlessly, and permeated with destruction. Since the fundamental processes of nature which produced us in the first place are still working in us and through us, the dialectic does not stop at its nadir. You, the other, the world of conventional wisdom, can always open your eyes to what is around, can always say: "Yes, this is awful. What are we to do?"

III. GOODMAN'S DIALECTIC: THIRD STAGE

And now a rebirth is possible. With a serious cry of anguish, the first step toward salvation has been taken. But a therapist is not like Billy Graham. A blind man cannot make a "decision" to see; a hopeless cripple cannot "decide" to walk. The faith of the therapist, unlike the faith of the evangelist, is not in miracles but in the slow, often painful and drudging processes of growth.

So when first the eye is raised to Heaven, when first the serious question is asked "What are we to do?", the battle is only begun. The therapist must have a small second step ready—one that can be made within the very limited powers of the new patient. Thus Goodman has prepared a rather long list of things people can do *right now* to get started. We can substitute eurhythmics for calisthenics in elementary schools. We can make school attendance a matter of choice for certain children whose homes and neighborhoods have more educative value than the ordinary school. We can stop all this hysterical emphasis on reading as the cure-all for problems of adolescence. We can abolish grading in high schools and colleges. We can require a couple of years of serious work as a condition for admission to some of our most prestigious undergraduate colleges. We can encourage small groups of students and scholars to form self-contained communities, using the necessary resources of large universities while maintaining independence from the university administration.

Some of these proposals, e.g., the last one mentioned above, are described in some detail by Goodman, with at least a show of attention to the logistics of implementation. (CofS, pp. 168-175)

Others, like that of eurhythmics, are merely thrown into a discussion of something else, the assumption being made apparently that those whose curiosity is piqued will trouble themselves to find out at least what "eurhythmics" means. However well thought through in detail, the argument for every one of these proposals is exactly the same: Here is some artificial restriction on a human being, some extrinsic limitation on the growth-promoting forces which are always around us. Then let us remove this restriction; let us *stop* doing whatever it is we are doing now. Often just stopping is enough; at other times it will be necessary or at least helpful to replace present practices with others more attune to life and growth.

Such simplicity is startling; it is also deceptive. Let us follow one example. Grading is degrading, so let us stop it. This is certainly straightforward enough, and it calls out an equally straightforward objection. We cannot teach well or even study well unless we know how much we have taught and learned. We simply must have periodic examinations of students' progress.

Fine, says Goodman. Test whenever it is necessary. It even does students good to cram for tests; it helps them organize and synthesize their learning. But those values of *testing* do not require the impositions of *grading*, as that institution flourishes in American schools and colleges. There are many quite specific evils which come from the institution of grading. It is not at all necessary to the enterprise of teaching and learning, so why do we not simply abandon it?

Apparently, the first step toward correcting the situation on Goodman's terms is the serious consideration of a possibility like abandoning the practice of frequent and invidious grading of students. But it is not easy to consider seriously such a change. Goodman can overcome the objection that grading is necessary because testing is necessary. But imagine the reaction of a really sophisticated and unillusioned upholder of the System, one who has been well-trained in the techniques of latent function analysis, i.e., the way of looking at an institution to see how it *really* works in relation to other institutions, which often turns out to be directly in opposition to how it says it works. Such a defender of the System might reply in words something like these: "Your school System

is not just an enterprise for teaching and learning academic subject matter. It is also a social institution serving the larger society
in many ways, some of them open and obvious, others subtle and
complex. Our teaching of certain knowledge and skills is easily
understood, but it takes more acuity to see some of the other functions we perform. The structure of our new society is not a simple
matter of two or three social classes; it is a pattern of finely differentiated colors and textures. You cannot teach youngsters *to live*
in such a system just by teaching them *that it exists*. No, they
have to learn to live in that sort of world by living in a simplified
version of it, which is what the System provides. They have to
learn to live with the contradiction between actual practices and
traditional, ideal profession; the System teaches them by constant
example. The larger society demands a strict discipline of personal
tastes and commitments by a vast apparatus of external and impersonal rewards and punishments, which we could, but here will
not, specify in detail.

"Once you begin to think about all the subtle and complex ways
in which your System, from kindergarten through graduate school,
serves to mold personality and develop habits of social cooperation
necessary to the operation of the larger society, you will have to
agree that constant and unremitting grading is essential. We cannot seriously consider abandoning grading any more than we can
seriously consider abandonment of our corporate system of economic production or our elitist system of politics.

"So it is well to say every now and then that grading ought to be
abandoned. It keeps the System from settling into complacency.
For example, teachers in the System must constantly be on the
alert against the tendency to grade on personal whim or taste, and
they must make sure that grades maintain at least the semblance
of impersonal justice, for only so can grading perform well its invidious and anxiety-producing functions. It is good also to carve
out little enclaves within the System like the honors programs in
very prestigious secondary schools and colleges—where grading
does not hold—for thus we can dangle the carrot of release from
pressure of grades before those who, since nursery school, have
been threatened by the stick of failure. We must resist those professional testers who would make evaluation altogether standard

across the nation; for such standard tests, while necessary for crucial screening procedures like college admission, do not have the constant motivating force that comes from a teacher's eye on the pupil and pencil on the grade book.

"Thus we need you reformers from left and right. You help us to keep flexible in our constant adjustment to ever shifting demands from the larger society. But, please, do not think that we can consider your proposals seriously, in your sense of 'serious,' i.e., with a view toward unifying thought, feeling, and action."

Our problem here is to find some basis for rational argument which can compel the minds of both Goodman and the defender of the System. The usual comment when this point is reached is to say that the opponents have reached an impasse in values or a basic metaphysical conflict or something of the sort. These things are said usually to indicate that the possibility of rational debate has disappeared; the issue is to be resolved by force—of arms, money, or personality as the case may be. But perhaps those who throw in the words "impasse in values" or "metaphysical conflict" are giving up too soon; perhaps the limits of rationality have not been reached.

I deliberately phrased the words of the defender of grading so as to indicate that he is not particularly enamored of either the System or the larger society it serves. So it is useless to argue that the System is not entirely just or that it produces unnecessary sufferings in children. This is not the issue. The attack of the hypothetical defender of the System may be put briefly as follows: Goodman cannot be taken seriously when he proposes that grading be abandoned within the System, for the purposes of the larger society served by the System require the institution of grading. To talk seriously of abandoning grading would require not only a drastic reconstruction of the System but also a prior revolution of the entire social order. Now serious talk about revolution must be couched in political terms. Unless or until Goodman is willing to take responsibility for the political measures necessary to make it possible to abandon grading, his proposal is mere air.

The defender of the System is not upholding its justice or kindness to children; he is only protesting that the System exists, that it is real. His criterion of reality is that of social coherence: any sub-system (e.g., the System) of any society (e.g., contemporary America) is real if the functions of that sub-system support, and are supported by, the functions of the other sub-systems of the society. Policy discussion is serious to the extent that it articulates the actual, real, structural features of the society. Goodman's talk, on this criterion, is not serious.

Note that this way of attacking Goodman can come from any point on the political spectrum. Conservatives and revolutionaries, the polar extremes, tend to regard a society more as a monolith; they demand that it be maintained or destroyed as a whole. Liberals of various shades tend to regard the structural-functional connections that constitute a society as limited in extent; political action taken to solve a particular problem must take account of the structural-functional connections that constitute *that* problem, but beyond certain limits the effects of a particular action can be ignored in the process of "piecemeal" social engineering. Still all— liberal, revolutionary, or conservative—agree that serious policy discussion requires careful attention to the details of political power necessary to effect or prevent change, general or specific. In Goodman's failure to provide such political analysis, they would say, is found a sufficient proof of his lack of seriousness. Goodman cannot be the therapist to lead the metaphysically ill back to the world of sanity, for Goodman himself is either unable or unwilling to recognize the real world around him.

We will not recognize that the possibility for rational argument has passed merely because two sides of a quarrel seem to have disagreed on what to regard as real. To keep the disputants from evading the issue, we can force a confrontation by simplifying and diagramming the disagreement.

Level I

GOODMAN

A human being can separate reality from illusion only when he can unify his actions, beliefs, and feelings. (Act so that what he does expresses his feelings and beliefs

DEFENDER OF THE SYSTEM

Quite apart from whether it enables individuals to act rationally or feel wholesomely, the System (and the larger society of which it is a part) is real, must be believed about what he is acting *on* or toward. Feel that his actions are his own, i.e., express his beliefs and his intentions. Believe that what he does and how he feels about what he does are genuine, rational responses to an ordered world outside of him.)

in, analyzed, and rationally understood. The question whether the System also calls out unified (active and emotive) responses is a normative, not a metaphysical question, a matter of what ought to be, not what is.

I think we can conclude that the disagreement between Goodman and the System is two-fold: partly it is a difference in use of the expression "real world," and partly it is a difference in the meaning of seriousness which follows. The first disagreement is rather easily resolved. Goodman wants to restrict the expression "real world" to that portion of existence which exercises a moral authority over our conduct. There is adequate sanction in common sense language. (The father tells his adolescent son: "I don't care whether you like your new boss or not. Out in the real world you have to learn to take orders!"). Goodman's usage also has sanction in our traditions of theology. ("God exists necessarily." and "One ought to do the will of God." together mean that the most real aspect of the world exerts a moral force on human conduct.) But there is no necessity in following that usage. The word "real" also has other uses in common sense. (The son above may say "Yes, but he's a *real* bastard," as a way of denying that any moral obligation exists to obey his boss.) And theology is not without its heretical branches in which the reality of the Devil is metaphysically equivalent to the reality of God. So when the System's man says that, whether good or bad, the social order is *real*, he is not exactly talking nonsense.

So this level of the argument is fairly easily resolved. We distinguish the expression "real world$_g$" from the "real world$_s$." The System is part of the real world$_s$, but it is not included in the real world$_g$. This last proposition should be agreed to by Goodman and by any System's man, e.g., Conant, or Brameld, or any other.

But the agreement is quite limited, being merely a mutual recognition that the expression "real world" can be used in different senses. But what about seriousness? Let us follow the argument:

Level II

<table>
<tr><th>GOODMAN</th><th>DEFENDER OF THE SYSTEM</th></tr>
<tr><td>To be serious is to be actively engaged in a real world$_g$. The world of contemporary American society is not a real world$_g$. Therefore one cannot be serious in contemporary American society. But not to be serious is to be less than a full human being.

Therefore, to be a full human being one must escape the System and the society of which is it a part.</td><td>To be serious is to be actively engaged in the real world$_s$. In contemporary American society the real world$_s$ is in need of total change (revolutionary, Right or Left) or continuing structural-functional revisions (Liberal).

Therefore to be serious is to be actively engaged in doing what needs to be done *for* and *with* the System.</td></tr>
</table>

How is this divergence to be handled? Here are two radically conflicting moral demands offered to men and women and to boys and girls who wish to lead serious and responsible lives and to shape their world toward higher ends and purposes than it now serves. The conflict is not new. Plato's Socrates was condemned for corrupting youth, that is, for calling them to give their allegiance the city laid up in heaven, perhaps another way of saying the real world$_g$. The Christian Church has never succeeded in finding a final resolution between the demands *civitatis dei* and *civitatis terrae*; each generation has had to find a new compromise.

Because the conflict is a very ancient one, we ought to know something about it. We ought to have learned to say something helpful instead of merely moaning "impasse" or "basic disagreement in attitude." What we ought to have learned is this: the burden of freedom is on the defender of the System; the burden of integrity is on Goodman. In the present situation, Goodman seems to be bearing his burden better than the System's man bears his.

To recapitulate, let us imagine an educational "workshop" or "conference" devoted to the problems of adolescence. Let us imagine Goodman confronting Superintendent X of the Metropolitan School System. X is a good man and a clever man. His word is respected by all, and he cares deeply for the often troubled young men and women who come under his institution's jurisdiction. Goodman charges that many of these troubles might disappear if only grading were abolished. Superintendent X acknowledges that this is probably true, but one cannot seriously consider abolishing grading unless or until major social changes are made, changes which require more political power than X and all his fellows (including Goodman) can muster. Goodman says that since X is unwilling to abolish grading, X is not serious. X says that since Goodman will not face the problem of political power, Goodman is not serious. After this, Goodman treats X's pleas for more money (for counseling and guidance, psychological services, diversified curriculum, and attitude building) with scorn or condescension. X treats Goodman's pleas for autonomy and freedom in the same spirit.

In practice, the confrontation usually ends right there. But in principle it is possible to carry the argument further. Superintendent X has agreed, let us say, that grading produces bad consequences *for certain individuals.* He proposes to remedy those evils by specific help (guidance, changed curriculum, etc.) for those presently being injured. He can go further; he can point to school programs which operate without grades—"opportunity classes" for the academically inept, non-graded "honors" courses for those whose talent has already been amply proved, or special programs for "majors" in art or music. In every case of this sort, there is a specific, relevant reason why this child should be either exempted from the pressure of grading or provided specific help when this pressure becomes overly painful. It is politically possible to mitigate the worst evils of grading, but against the pressure of employers, parents, college admissions officers, and moralists-in-general, it is not politically possible to abolish the institution of grading completely. When Goodman charges X that these exemptions and remedial services are not as general nor effective as they should be, X can respond quite correctly that that is not the System's fault but rather the fault of the larger society to provide adequate money and human talent to run the System at maximum effectiveness.

Furthermore, Superintendent X, if he is *very* clever and thoroughly understands the logic of the System, and without violating that logic in any way, can challenge Goodman to come into his high school, select a dozen boys who are being badly hurt by the institution of grading, and teach them however he wishes without giving them any grades. One can easily hear X's peroration: "Paul, you want educational freedom? Come into my school and you will find it in abundance."

Now Goodman cannot accept this kind offer, for what he demands of the System is far more radical. Superintendent X can easily accommodate Goodman in the System. His will be Opportunity Class XIc, and belonging to it will be duly noted on the students' records. In fact, acceptance of Goodman's class would soon make "Goodman" irrelevant. It is a fundamental premise in the System that any educational program good for one youngster is good for all who share his educational attributes. Let us define a certain syndrome of reactions to the institution of grading as "grade-induced neurosis." Having grade-induced neurosis is an educational attribute. But being selected by Goodman for a special program is purely happenstance. Hence, in the logic of the System, if Goodman's work with the boys he selected seems to go well, Superintendent X will simply add to the System a program of reduced pressure for youngsters suffering grade-induced neurosis. It will not take long for teaching in this program to become a recognized subdivision of Special Education, with appropriate certification standards and training classes in the larger colleges of education. Goodman's name will be enshrined in the first chapter of the textbook entitled *Administering the Remedial Program for Grade-Induced Neurosis in Your School*, but Paul Goodman, the man who wanted to help adolescents, will have become irrelevant. The example is facetious, the moral is not. Inherent in the idea of the System is the irrelevance of any individual. If education within the System depended entirely on the particularities of individual teachers and therapists, not only would there be no system of education, there would be obvious injustice for those youngsters whose teachers or therapists happened to be poor ones. If Goodman were to enter the System, any success he achieved would strengthen Superintendent X. In proposing a different logical model for argument, Goodman must stay aloof. He must resist any attempt to be an "influence" within or through the System.

If we can think of the System as a huge circle and Goodman as a very small one just outside it, we can view Superintendent X's offer as one of ingesting Goodman. Since the System is quite permeable and internally flexible, it might become significantly different by virtue of taking in Goodman and his ideas. But it would still be a System. What Goodman is asking is that the System allow those who want to to withdraw from the huge circle and attach themselves to any little satellites that happen to be around. The emphasis is to be put on "those who *want* to." The System already has avenues of egress for those who have the relevant educational attributes. But what about those who, for a greater or longer period, simply opt to get out?

Here is another of those continental divides in educational thought. If we take the System's point of view, the idea is absurd. If we take Goodman's point of view, the idea is the most obvious good sense. Let us try another confrontation.

Level III

GOODMAN	DEFENDER OF THE SYSTEM
Some youths who are forced to attend school against their wishes do not learn much academically and they are damaged in very important ways.	All youths are entitled to receive the best education society can provide and they can absorb.
Therefore, those youths who are being penalized more than helped by the System should be allowed to withdraw from it.	Neither a particular boy or girl nor their parents can make the most intelligent judgment on what education is best—best in general or best for the particular boy or girl. Therefore, to receive their educational rights all children must be compelled to attend schools where qualified leaders chose their educational program.

Immediately you can see that while these arguments issue in contradictory conclusions, they are not (as were Levels I and II) genuine confrontations. Goodman and the System are now talking past one another despite our best efforts to pull them together. There is apparently no way rationally to compel either to accede to the argument of the other. The System's man cannot take Goodman seriously except when Goodman is advocating policies which, in principle, can be generalized and applied to everyone in the System who possesses the educationally relevant attributes. Goodman cannot take the System seriously except when the individual teacher or therapist within the System is willing to do whatever is most immediately valuable for the particular youngster, regardless of whether the action taken can be generalized and regardless of whether the action taken can be justified by its long-range consequences for the youngster's future success *or* for the perpetuation of our present social system. The System's argument cannot be accommodated in the formal scheme used by Goodman, while the latter explicitly rejects the logic of the System.

But even if there is no logical reconciliation between Goodman and the System, surely, you will want to say, we can find some way of effecting an institutional compromise. The System can simply allow Goodman to conduct his school or non-school on different principles. But the fact is, of course, that the System cannot do this; at least it cannot happen formally and explicitly. There are too many legal, economic, and social barriers to overcome. If Goodman and his boys are to be protected rather than harassed by the police, they must be recognized as a school; that is, all sorts of safety and sanitary regulations must be acknowledged and obeyed. They must support themselves in an economy which makes it almost impossible to be decently poor. If they are to receive money from philanthropic foundations, they must be legally incorporated as a private, non-profit corporation, withholding income taxes and unemployment insurance payments for employees, reporting on W-2 forms annually, etc., etc. On the other hand, there is no community which can provide genuine social support for their learning outside the System. A middle-aged man and a dozen boys wandering the waterfront of New York could expect, at the very best, to be casually ignored. The boys might be gaining independence, self-insight and self-control, language skills, and refined tastes for thought and objects; but nobody would notice or care. Or they might be degenerating into self-indulgence and learning to exploit the compassion of others. No one would care about that either. It is only through the System that the larger society notices the youngster and his education. And what it notices most are the grades he makes.

So all the simple, practical steps advocated by Goodman are simply not practical at all. They would be practical in the real world$_g$, but the real world$_s$ is quite a different matter. Goodman, as therapist, has enticed his patient to open his eyes, to see the dreariness around, and to ask what may be done to relieve it. But when Goodman begins pointing out simple, practical steps that may be taken along the path to health and sanity, the System intervenes and the path disappears.

No matter how patiently and rationally we follow the disagreement between Goodman and the System, it ends in an irreconcilable conflict. The conflict is not in "values," whatever that might mean. Nor is it in politics, for the System is amenable to challenge from Left, Right, and Center. The conflict is irreconcilable because it is in logic, i.e., in the criteria which one holds as applicable to a policy argument. By Goodman's criteria, the System's arguments are not serious, and vice versa.

Thus Goodman-the-angry-prophet, who sees "rage" and "grief" and "despair," has given way to Goodman-the-therapist, who tries to help his patient to be serious, i.e., to unify his scattered feelings, beliefs, and actions. But that proves impossible in the System's world, so Goodman-the-artist emerges.

It takes us outside scope of this book and beyond my competence as a critic to consider Goodman's place in contemporary American literature, but it is important for the present argument to note that Goodman means it quite literally when he talks of a work of literature as building a world. This is very unfashionable talk, of course, in a generation which regards serious literature as necessarily evincing the alienation of the artist from the world.

It is equally unfashionable among left-wing groups which see the work of the artist as explaining, justifying, or criticizing a world which, as world, exists quite independently of the artist. But among men of letters (his preferred self-designation) Goodman is distinctive exactly as he is distinctive among proponents of educational policy. He is consciously (sometimes distractingly, *self*-consciously) engaged in metaphysics even while he is writing a polemical blast against the System or a love scene. Indeed the love scene may *be* a polemical blast against the System and also a philosophical treatise on the Aristotelian distinction between "making" (as in "making out" or "making the scene") and "doing" (as in "Whatcha think yer doin"?). This makes it hard for his critics to know what to do with his literary prose, for he has to write in a form and style quite different from the alienated novel or the *New Yorker* short story. (I do not speak of his poems, for most of them, the best anyway, seem to me directly expressive of the intense, personal lyricism which surrounds the man like an aura. I do not speak of his "classical" short stories, like "Our First Visit to Niagara," which show how perfectly Goodman *can* write in traditional forms—when those forms are, to him, fresh and functional. I speak only of the protracted, surrealist non-novel *Empire City*, the contrasting super-realist non-novel *Making Do*, and certain short stories and "protest" poems which, like the non-novel, do not celebrate so much as cerebrate Goodman's mostly unhappy encounters with contemporary American society. This way of dividing up his literary work would be vandalism if the concern were aesthetic criticism. But these prose works do show the scope and limits of the world Goodman asks us to join in building; that is our interest here.)

Some men could write social criticism in the morning and novels in the afternoon, and the two forms would share only a common author. But Goodman is an uncommon author, and his novels and criticism—literary as well as social—are equally aspects of Goodman-in-the-world. For Goodman is a product of (among other things) that most distinctive movement in all really contemporary philosophy, from European existentialism through British linguistic analysis to American pragmatism: the movement which blurs if it does not completely obliterate the distinction between saying and doing. J. F. Austin tells us *How to Do Things with Words;* Jean-Paul Sartre entitles his autobiography, the story of his action in the world, *The Words.* John Dewey says that "symbols as such must be finally understood in terms of the function which symbolization serves. . . . A universe of experience is the precondition of a universe of discourse." The common point in all of them is this: If you want to know what a man means when he says something, try to find out what he is doing in or by saying it. It is in just this way that we have tried to show the meaning of Goodman's educational writing. But how shall we describe what he is doing in or by writing his novels?

Goodman's formula, that he is building a world, is perhaps true, but it is a highly metaphorical way of speaking. I should like to offer a gloss on that formula. It is clear that building a world is not, nor is it like, describing a world. This is not to say that Goodman does not on occasion write photographically accurate description. The point is really a technical one. Philosophers generally accept the principle of infinite description: given any finite slice of reality, there is no limit to the number of true statements that might be asserted about it. The kitchen table on which I am now writing can be described in the language of physics, chemistry, biology, economics, aesthetics, cookery, etc. But novels describe kitchen tables only *en passant*; their focus is on human action. And the language of action is that of motive, intention, desire, will, impulse—in short, movement-directed-by-mind.

It is somewhat difficult to explain philosophically but it is simply a fact of life that a camera can record movement-directed-by-mind. Given a clear photograph of human beings in easily recognized action there is a "natural" description of the action, i.e., one which ordinary men would unhesitatingly assign to the photograph. "The boys are playing football." "That man is walking his dog in the park." From the clear and easily recognized cases there is a gradual shading to the completely indeterminate image. But even projective techniques, like the Rorschach test, take their point from the fact that *some* visual stimuli *do* allow "natural" descriptions.

The relation of a "natural" description to the thing described is reciprocal: given a "natural" description of some event—for example, "The Rover Boys are playing football in Fairmount Park right now."—one knows immediately what standpoint the describer has toward the event (in this case that of an external observer), and one knows immediately what further details fit the first description and what do not. For example, "vigorously" fits, even "oleaginously" fits, by badly strained metaphor; but "culturally" doesn't fit at all, unless one redefines "culturally" to mean something else, such as "civilly" or "genteelly" or "as boys of that age and class usually do."

What we mean, then, by a descriptive novel is one which adopts a particular, easily identified standpoint toward the world *and* builds consistent, fitting details around "natural" descriptions of events. Goodman's novels do now one, now the other, but never ("Well, hardly ever.") both together. In the *Empire City*, especially in its earlier and more imaginative sections, Goodman writes from a peculiar standpoint, as though hovering about 4'8½" above each of his many characters when describing their thought, feeling, and action. This slight elevation gives him a little more perspective than his characters but not enough so that he does not have to move overall his point of view when shifting from one actor to another. Each particular description has a strained and subtle plausibility; they do fit together, not to form a "natural" description of the world but to build a pattern or configuration in which the strained plausibility of the isolated perspective becomes a "natural" part of the whole.

Perhaps in the *Empire City* Goodman's technique of building a world (as opposed to describing one) originated in the same Gestalt-ish, phenomenological metaphysics that one finds in his *Gestalt Therapy*. The qualified "perhaps" is important: surely the compassion, the humor, and the vitality of the novel cannot have come from any metaphysical doctrine but only from life itself. And the same may be true of the novel's form: Goodman may have *lived* a phenomenological life, one in which he no more accepted the "natural" Gestalt of a fixed cultural milieu than his youthful hero accepted school as a place for education. In any event, the origin does not matter; the technique of building a world in *The Empire City* is a recognizable literary technique.

But building a world is something other than literary technique in *Making Do*. The very title itself must be seen as a denial of the basic Aristotelian distinction between making and doing. The work of the artist is making; the highest art of all, beyond the painter, poet, or philosopher, is making communal life itself a work of art. That is the art of political leadership.

Before making life beautiful, man must do many things just to live. The work of the world must be done before the work of art can be made. But today a man cannot *simply* do what must be done and then go on to make his work of art. Instead his entire creative talent must go into first making do, just escaping from engulfment in a senseless, inhuman society. The Cold War is its most pronounced symptom, but sickness pervades the system. To make do is to survive with a selfhood more or less intact. After that, there is no time nor imagination left over to make anything else. Even making out is problematical.

Making Do is Goodman's way of making do, not making art. It does not describe a man coming across, it *is* a man coming across. The criteria applicable are those of action not art, i.e., moral not aesthetic. This fact caused some reviewers of the book difficulty because they simply did not have the categories in which to say anything interesting. To say that the writing is bad, as did the reviewer for the *New Yorker*, is like saying that the dust jacket is purple and white—true but not particularly revealing. It is not as art but as action that it is to be judged.

What is the act? Just that of presenting (not representing) a man and his friends, people who manage to make do. If the reader now wants to build a world, he knows some of the architectural problems. The pose of the artist who has a special role in world-building has been given up altogether. We see, rather, just a man: a crotchety man who can do the right thing if he has time and energy to figure out what is the right thing to do. His mind is molded by clichés, partly Populist politics, partly Freudian psychology, partly humanist ethics; but he sometimes escapes the mold and thinks a clear and loving thought about the world around him. He has no final answers, but he has sound and sensible ideas that outsiders applaud and then seem to forget.

The act of revelation is also an act of invitation. You do not have to be Superman to engage in world-building. All that is required is that you run the risks without too much complaining. You do not have to be reborn; one birth is enough for any person to have to go through. But you do have to be serious in the details of living with other people. When your thoughts and feelings and actions cannot flow harmoniously together, you must suffer. When they can, you will enjoy life, you may even achieve ecstasy.

The only prohibition in this striving-to-become-a-world is against reliance on existing institutions: you do not need schools in order to have culture and education; you do not need police in order to have personal safety; you do not need churches to have faith; you do not need marriage for love. If you have the values, or even if you are serious about seeking them, it is possible to build institutions to protect the values—small, home-grown, open-ended institutions rather like those built by the Founding Fathers, who were quite serious about *their* values. The Establishment today neither possesses nor seeks the values which its institutions putatively (as in the Spanish, *puta*) preserve; the best the System can do is not make it entirely impossible for serious people to get on with their lives.

In *Making Do* a man and his friends try to be serious and fail, although not completely, in their attempt. The book is neither a call to arms nor an argument. Nothing is proved in it nor by it. So what is its place in policy argument? I would suggest that this little novel, really a bad novel, is the non-existence proof for an alternative to the System. An existence proof is a standard form of argument in formal logic and mathematics; e.g., you prove that a set, S, is not empty by showing that there exists at least one element, E, such that E is a member of S. Analogously in other sciences, one cannot prove a generalization from the existence of one confirming instance; but if we prove that there exists some (usually quite complex) set of conditions under which a phenomenon P occurs, we can subsequently attempt to analyze those conditions and find the *precise* cause of P. Thus an existence proof (in principle) terminates the inquiry in mathematics, while it serves as the starting point for much empirical research.

In policy argument its function is different still. The System really does not need existence proofs. The ordinary mode of argument is to point to certain practices as being superior (only occasionally with reasons provided for *why* these particular practices are better than others) and then to urge that these practices become more widespread. It is an evolutionary process: the major forces are random variation and artificial dissemination.

But Goodman, proposing a truly radical departure from the System, must first establish the *possible* existence of what he proposes. We do not have, as once we had or like to think we had, a large range of alternative schemes of education in a large number of experimental schools. No, we have only minor variations within the System, and, as our "communications" improve, those variations will become miniscule. There are no *actual* educational enterprises to which Goodman can point to prove, *a fortiori*, the *possible* existence of radical options.

So he must invent the option. If he were a Utopian writer, as he is in a very clear sense a Utopian *thinker,* he could portray an imagined world as both desirable and credible. B. F. Skinner, who is not a Utopian thinker at all, did take this path to make his case for the possible existence of *his* radical option. But *Making Do* is neither Utopian nor anti-Utopian. If it says anything about whether men and women can build a world in love and freedom,

it seems to say that right now the system will not permit it. Making
do is the best you can do. Perhaps when the system loses its last
breaths of inherited vitality, something else will be possible. Till
then, hang on, get tired and angry, and hang on some more.

Goodman's moral, if there is one, concerns neither the making
of an artist nor the doing of a political moralist. It concerns a
third basic category—being. Thus we come full circle to the religious attitude. Faith and despair are the exclusive and exhaustive
alternatives: if the world of man and nature seems right now to
enforce absolute despair, there are yet deeper currents of being.
These flow not only around us but within us as well. To counsel
faith is to be intellectually dishonest, but to *be* faithful is to be
true to natural self. Just because the world we would build does
not exist is no sufficient reason to deny that it is real.

EPILOGUE

But, you say, this still does not tie the threads together. Goodman had some very practical proposals, but we cannot put them
into operation until the System is loosened up at the seams. We
do not have the power to do that loosening; indeed the only way
we might achieve it is to build a counter-System which would have
most of the vices of the present System. Now Goodman admits all
this, but when we ask him what to do, he says, "build a world,"
and when we ask what that means, all we get is *Making Do*. That
leaves us little better off than we were, when it comes to making
fundamental decisions for schooling. When the questions get
tough enough, you say, Goodman cops out.

You are right, of course, but it isn't clear how right You are nor
how long You will be right. Goodman's advocacy of anarchy comes
down to one little proposition: The demands which others put
upon a person are always limited by that person's legitimate drive
to unify his own thoughts, feelings, and actions. Community occurs
when persons discover or create harmony in their actions, thoughts,
and feelings. Let's hold that in mind for a moment.

The Spanish Civil War proved what one would have predicted:
that anarchists don't make very effective soldiers. But, from the
definition above, one would judge that the anarchical community
is the ideal educational environment. That is to say: the anarchist

has reason to claim that his non-System will achieve those genuinely educative values to which even the System is, in principle,
dedicated. Thus Goodman, when he is true to his most profound
theory, does not advocate warfare against the System nor even poli-
ical pressure within the existing polity. He invites us to transcend
the polity within which education is necessarily subservient to non-
educational values and to create a *community*, in his sense of the
term, the only legitimate educational polity.

At times Goodman will *argue* that only in a new polity can the
contradictions of the System be resolved: Thus the System, not
education itself, creates an irreconcilable conflict between the educational needs of the individual and the educational needs of society. Thus the System creates the contradiction between intellectual
standards and the justice of educational equality. Etc. But the
System seems to survive these contradictions.

But can individuals whose thoughts, feeling, and actions are fragmented survive contact with those who are serious? Can a fragmented System survive when *somewhere* there is the lure of genuine
community? If one listens attentively to today's students, if one
notices the emptiness in the offices of the Establishment, if one
strives to help those responsible for preserving the System where it
is most immediately and desperately threatened—well, it isn't quite
so clear how right You are. Perhaps Goodman's dialectic will pre-
vail. Indeed, it is hard to imagine any possible future's being otherwise.

Notes

PAUL GOODMAN

Works of Goodman referred to in the text.

Paul Goodman with Percival Goodman *Communitas: Means of Livelihood and Ways of Life* (Chicago, 1947)

The Structure of Literature (Chicago, 1954)

(GUA)   *Growing Up Absurd* (New York, 1960)

Our Visit to Niagara (New York, 1960)

The Community of Scholars (New York, 1962)

The Lordly Hudson: Collected Poems (New York, 1962)

Making Do (New York, 1963)

(CME)   *Compulsory Mis-Education* (New York, 1964)

People or Personnel: Decentralizing and the Mixed System (New York, 1965)

1 Arnold Toynbee: *A Study of History* (London, 1939-1955) Vol. VIII, p. 529.

2 Goodman's letter in *Commentary* XXXIX, 2 (February, 1965), p. 8.

3 Note that biological relations and functions are conditioned by cultural phenomena in a very obvious fashion. It is not at all ob-vious, however, that a cultural phenomenon like promising is cor-respondingly conditioned by biology. This is not to say that just because the limitations and constraints of biology are not obvious that they don't exist; indeed, it has been one of the genuine

achievements of psychoanalysis to bring to saliency just these un-obvious constraints which biology exercises over culture.

4 "The question regarding the validity of a valuation amounts to asking for a higher acknowledged norm under which the value falls, and this is a question of *fact*. The question of the justifica-tion of the highest norms or the ultimate values is senseless, be-cause there is nothing higher to which these could be referred." Moritz Schlick: "What Is the Aim of Ethics?" reprinted in A. J. Ayer (ed.): *Logical Positivism* (Glencoe, 1959) Schlick's essay appeared first in 1930.

5 Bernard L. Montgomery, First Viscount Alamein Sachs, Memorial Lecture, Teachers College, Columbia University, November, De-cember, 1954.

6 See S. Bromberger: "An Approach to Explanation" in R. J. But-ler (ed.): *Analytic Philosophy*, Second Series (Oxford, 1965) p. 72 ff.

7 Since writing this chapter I have read Jonothan Kozol's *Death At An Early Age: The Destruction of the Hearts and Minds of Negro Children in the Boston Public Schools* (New York, 1967). As did many others, I found the book deeply disturbing. (Cf. Robert Cole's review in *New York Times* "Book Review," Sunday, October 1, 1967.) In relation to the thesis I advance about Good-man's extended senses of "rage," "grief," "despair," etc., Kozol, it seems to me, is making two somewhat different points: (i) There really is a great deal more actual rage, grief, and despair among some children than our ordinary newspapermen are likely to see. But (ii) there ought to be a great deal more rage, grief, and despair among the other children. Only our systematic mis-education of their emotions makes them feel shameful and hum-ble in response to conditions that should make them grievously angry and desperate. In relation to the metaphor (developed just below) of guerrilla warfare in the revolution of extended sensi-bility, perhaps Kozol represents the return to more conventional tactics, i.e., those of the muckraking journalist who, counting on agreement in *values* among his readers, can write vividly flat de-scriptions of conditions which violate those values.

The thesis in the text that the political response to "grief," "rage," and "despair" is different from the response to grief, rage, and despair has been curiously and tragically confirmed in Phila-delphia after rally of Negro high school students before the Board of Education offices on November 17, 1967. According to the

Civil Liberties Record, December 1967, p. 5, (a publication of the Greater Philadelphia ACLU).

"At Police Commissioner Frank Rizzo's order, police waded into the crowd with nightsticks swinging. School children and adults were clubbed to the ground and beaten as they tried to protect themselves. Many persons were injured seriously enough to require hospitalization; bystanders who had nothing to do with the rally were also beaten; clergymen and women, white and Negro, were among those badly hurt."

As television and film records made abundantly evident, these actions created very genuine grief, rage, and despair, evoking massive political and legal efforts to prevent their recurrence. This kind of urgent response unfortunately would not be forthcoming to equally well-documented instances of "grief," "rage," and "despair."

8   Erving Goffman has been a particularly brilliant guerrilla fighter in this revolution. Goffman took the sociologists' techniques of latent function analysis, techniques usually employed to show that apparently useless ideas and institutions actually have some hidden functional value in preserving the system, and turned those techniques right-side-up, i.e., used them to show that apparently functional and sensible ideas and rules, as they are actually used, have the real but concealed effect of creating chaos and degradation. In the metaphorical as well as the literal sense, the guerrilla fighter wrests his weapons from the oppressors. See especially Goffman's *Asylums: Essays on the Social Situation of Mental Patients and Other Inmates* (Chicago, 1962) and *Behavior in Public Places: Notes on the Social Organization of Gatherings* (New York, 1963)

9   P. F. Strawson: *Individuals: An Essay in Descriptive Metaphysics* (London, 1959), p. 9.

10   *Ibid.*

11   John Dewey: *Experience and Nature* (2nd Edition, New York, 1929), p. ii.

12   Perhaps it is a mistake not to undertake a full analysis of Goodman's concept of therapy. The reader is invited to pursue that task for himself, beginning with *Gestalt Therapy* by Goodman, Perls and Hefferline, and continuing through Goodman's self-therapy as recorded in *Five Years* (New York, 1966). The latter contains the aphorisms, the former the theory which makes an aphorism rise above the trite. Thus (from *Five Years,* p. 10) "I undo myself because of a theory that I, alas, believe: that hap-

piness, satisfaction is the necessary ground for the full exercise of power." This is not a mere paean to the power of positive thinking because Goodman *does* have a theory, in the full, honorific sense of *theory*, in which feeling, thought, and action are necessarily related.

Footnote to Epilogue

This chapter really should include a full appreciation of Edgar Friedenberg's contribution to the revolution of extended sensibilities and to the formation of new polities outside the existing System. But I find that that appreciation would require a full treatment of his works, not only his books dealing directly with educational policy, but also and perhaps more significantly his critical essays in *Commentary, The New York Review of Books, The New Republic* and other periodicals. In one sense, Friedenberg is turning Goodman's doctrines of seriousness into a criterion of criticism—and applying it with great skill to human events as well as to treatises on education and related questions. In another sense, Friedenberg's contributions are very different from Goodman's. But exactly how and why they are is a matter that could not be explained in a footnote. Friedenberg's books on education, broadly conceived, include *The Vanishing Adolescent* (Boston, 1959), *Coming of Age in America: Growth and Acquiescence* (New York, 1965), *The Dignity of Youth and Other Atavisms* (Boston, 1965). See McClellan's review in *Teachers College Record* (February, 1967) Volume 68, No. 5, pp. 427-429.

7

Where Is the Polity?

If one determined to prove that things are not what they seem, one could scarcely find more telling examples than the policy-proposals examined here. Theodore Brameld, the radical Reconstructionist of the twentieth century, turns out to be a timid high school teacher of social studies. Paul Goodman, the wildly irresponsible anarchist, turns out to be a systematic metaphysician. B. F. Skinner, the cold psychologist who would transform human education into animal training, becomes the staunch defender of personal freedom and intellectual integrity. And Jacques Barzun, the apostle of intellect, upholds mindlessness in educational policy. Only James Bryant Conant turns out to be just what he appeared: the devoted servant of the System which he helped make and vice versa.

Is there a lesson to be learned from all this? Perhaps it is that educational writings are more complements to than expressions of the writer's personalities—on the surface anyway. But any man who keeps on writing, as have the authors examined here, will eventually leave enough clues that his true intentions may be revealed. In which case, the lesson may be: do not produce an extended corpus of educational writings unless you are quite sure what you want to say. The present book proves how difficult it is to learn that lesson.

But what lessons are there for readers, not writers, of the literature of educational policy? Those whose civic and professional duties connect them to the continuing debates on educational policy must regard this literature as embodying ideas and information that make a difference in what we ought to do in education. If this literature does not, then nothing in our contemporary culture does; and, facing an educational crisis with *no* intellectual resources, we are in desperate straits indeed. This truly might be what one could claim to have learned from this study: the literature is fragmented, sterile, and bogus. We should do well to forget it, trust our untutored intuitions, and do what we feel is best.

But even as that idea is advanced one senses immediately the difference between *simply* acting on intuition and advancing the idea that acting on intuition is the best thing to do under the circumstances. Simple action, if there really is such a thing, invites reaction; an idea advanced becomes an advanced idea, inviting controversy, debate, even progress perhaps. The most radical challenge to the whole thesis of this book would be to hold literally that intellect—as a communal, political and not merely personal affair—has *no* place in the formation of educational policies. The search for a polity would end very quickly if that counter-thesis could be established. Yet it obviously cannot, since it is self-contradictory: if one held that as a matter of policy, educational activities are to be conducted as expressions of will, not common intelligence, then one would have to argue for that policy by appeal to common intelligence. If an individual teacher outside any organized school simply refused to argue, simply refused to explain or justify any of his teaching activities, *we* should have to debate whether, as a matter of policy, we should allow him access to students. His would be simple action inviting our reaction. But if that teacher should himself enter the argument to defend his right to teach as he chooses, he would thereby lose his immunity. He must appeal to common intelligence, common beliefs, common values. Despite Jacques Barzun's flirting in that direction, the appeal to will offers no escape from the hard, patient work of policy argument.

I. IN SCIENCE?

The polity, then, is to be constituted by common intelligence, not will or intuition; but Barzun raises another salient issue. What place does science have in the logic of educational policy? The history of modern thought is littered with dull aphorisms which attempted to separate science logically from value or policy concerns: Science can tell us only what is, not what ought to be. Science merely describes the world; it never really explains it. Science deals exclusively with abstractions; it cannot comprehend the vibrant reality of concrete existence.

We once believed that we could clearly distinguish mere descriptions of the world from evaluations or explanations; we could then assign to science its limited role and to something else—metaphysics, theology, phenomenology—the rest. Such talk is today merely boring. There are many highly complicated and unresolved questions in the philosophical analysis of such concepts as "description," "explanation," and "evaluation." But it is clear that each of these terms can be qualified by "scientific" to produce a meaningful expression. We speak of "scientific evaluation" or "scientific explanation" more often, probably, than "scientific description." The interesting questions are precisely how (if indeed it is precisely that) these mental operations are different when scientific as opposed to literary, historical, or common sensical. For questions like these, the old clichés merely blur the important distinctions.

The same line of thought applies to the notion that science is too abstract to encompass the reality of educational issues. It is quite true that no scientific description of classroom interaction can capture the fullness of the existential event. But it is equally true that neither can any other description, commentary, treatise, videotape, or poetry of the event. The limits of science *in general* are the limits of language *in general*. That is trivial. In particular, science achieves precision in the same manner as does poetry—by selection, refinement, exactness of analogy. The difference is that in science, analogy can be explained by laws and theories, whereas in poetry the analogical relationships must be (or at least usually are) intuited with immediacy and heightened feelings. But that either poetry or science can claim closer connection to the reality of concrete existence is absurd.

Thus the usual stereotyped ways of isolating science from policy argument will not work. But the opposite error must also be combatted, i.e., the attempt to treat science as the paradigm of human intelligence and to force on the logic of policy arguments a model derived (by whatever means) from science. This error in thought is frequently (perhaps justly) associated with the instrumentalism of John Dewey. It has been detected and corrected many times. Here the key point is this: the body of literature we have been studying does not support the view that science is the model for intelligent argument in educational policy. On the contrary, none of the writers considered here argues "scientifically" himself or even argues that one ought to argue scientifically on policy questions.

Just saying it does not make it true. Just what is involved in the claim that educational argument is intelligent only if it is modeled on science? Let us attend, as Conant would have us do, to a certain historical tradition dating from the seventeenth century: that social and literary tradition we unhesitatingly call science. We note that some of those writings (the most clearly central in that tradition) can be rationally reconstructed into the form of *theories*. It is very difficult to say exactly what that form is, but twentieth-century philosophy of science has advanced far toward understanding the "structure of science." [1]

With at least a minimum understanding of what that logical structure is, we may re-formulate one's question thusly: Does our hypothetico-deductive model of scientific theory provide the form to which educational policy argument should *conform*? Note on one hand that any particular discipline in science serves as a model of men in careful, disciplined, effective communication with each other only because the hypothetico-deductive theory has precisely limited the area of common concern. In the literature of educational policy, on the other hand, the major, basic question is: What *is* of primary concern in education? Conant's answer, for example, is noteworthy for its simplicity and consistency: The System and the American society it serves are of first concern. It would be easy enough, but unnecessary here, to present comparable answers from the other authors. More to the point: it would be impossible to provide any meaningful formula which would include the basic concerns of *all* the authors. Within any theory based on scientific discipline, of course, it is quite possible to define the concern of those participating in the discipline. Therefore, scientific theory cannot be the model for educational policy argument.

But then is there no relation? Must we entirely give up the major hope of Anglo-Saxon philosophy in the twentieth century: that science, as the most perfected form of human intelligence, can provide us an ideal and a hope for perfecting our intelligence in dealing with moral and political questions? There is very little reason to believe that this hope was a sensible one; there is no way of reading the literature of educational policy as supporting that hope. Indeed the hope that science (taking a narrow view of the term "science") would save us may have been a positive detriment in the search for rational educational arguments.

All the authors considered in this book have been influenced by the scientific mode of thought, as indeed what twentieth-century American who thinks at all has not? Goodman and Barzun have been influenced from across the fence. Goodman has worked through and out of the materialistic metaphysics of Sigmund Freud. For Goodman science can be a serious affair for human beings. That it usually is not is simply an easily observed fact about contemporary society rather than a psychological or logical necessity. Barzun calls science "the glorious entertainment," trying very hard and quite unsuccessfully to establish that *logically* scientific statements are not related to reality as serious statements are. But for Goodman and Barzun—humanists to the core—the idea that the study of inanimate Nature is the model for all affairs of men is patently absurd. After all *who* studies inanimate Nature? Men and women related to each other and to traditions of action and belief. To understand *that*, the humanists' categories, not the physicists', are appropriate.

Skinner and Conant begin inside the world of science, Conant deep inside and Skinner on its marches. But Conant moved so quickly and easily into the rhetoric of the historian, and indeed moved back into the teaching of science as history, that the direct influence of scientific thought on his educational arguments is hard to establish. Even when he was engaged in educational "research" he never, so far as publications show, conducted a scientific type experiment in education or even paid serious attention to those who did. "Research" was for him the activity of the historian (examining records), the journalist (interviewing significant persons), or the lawyer (holding hearings and inquiries).

Conant's neglect of (if not outright disdain for) a scientific approach in education cannot be explained by his practicality. As someone must have said, theory is pretty practical if you know how to use it: only by means of theory can one translate a practical problem into a technical problem, i.e., one of refining control of desired ends by isolating the really significant independent variables which produce those ends. Conant never once looked on education in that way, and the interesting point is the "never once." As will be argued later, no one *can* think of educational policy generally as a technical problem or series of them. But that the extreme technical competence of an organic chemist never came out in his educational writings is at least an amusing fact.

With Skinner the case is not so clear. His point of origin was surely technical, as defined above. If the main argument of the chapter on Skinner is correct—that the influence of Skinner can be to enlarge the realm of educational freedom by decreasing the number of variables the school must control to produce a required result—his achievement is indeed a technical one of the highest order. But this achievement enters into policy argument only as a possibility, not a social fact. Whether it will be actualized is a policy question, and Skinner has shown little inclination to transform that policy question into a technical problem. There is no inherent reason why it could not be treated technically; there are intellectual models and physical machinery available to make a technical analysis of any set of phenomena, however complex. A consistent tendency in educational administration toward preferring and seeking technical solutions to policy questions has been observed.[2] There is nothing in the use of these models and methods of analysis which logically prevents their being used in policy arguments, i.e., in arguments where ends and values as well as means are at issue. A technical model is obviously easier to use when a single goal has been agreed upon and the problem is *simply* the discovery of what independent variables can be most neatly and cheaply manipulated to achieve that goal. However, sophisticated techniques can work even when this easy condition does not obtain.[3] The point is that Skinner shows no interest in these models. It is quite clear in all his writings that when he is talking about the psychology of learning he uses a technical mode of analysis in a very precise way. When he is involved in a policy argument he does not use it at all.

Brameld is the proving case on the use of science in policy argument. From the beginnnig Brameld has looked on the "social sciences" as a solvent to melt away prejudices and ancient customs so that more liberal ways of thinking could be brought to social problems. However, it is true, and Brameld eventually recognized, that the opposite of liberal thought is illiberal thought, of which ancient and inherited prejudice is only one example. Modern illiberalism can use the social sciences for its purposes quite as easily as can liberalism. Brameld kept searching for an inherently, necessarily liberal social science, one whose ideas would "explode" the cake of custom so that truth and justice would flower.[4]

However, there is no such science. (And if there were it would not be anthropology because that science can be used in policy argument to glorify and preserve ancient customs as easily as to combat them). Brameld's own use of the social sciences, particularly the quasi-anthropological technique to promote social democracy in Puero Rico, is obviously forced. Culture, class, and evolution are no longer theoretical terms in a science of anthropology when Brameld uses them to explode customs. In any event, Brameld has never showed the slightest interest in considering education as a technical concern in which his favorite theoretical concepts are used to isolate significant and manipulable variables to achieve precisely defined ends.

Scientific theory and its derivative, the technical approach to problems, are not used in policy arguments by the authors we have considered. Anyone who claims that we ought to achieve a polity for education on the model of a scientific discipline must answer satisfactorily two quite controversial questions. First, can the incompatibility of ends and concerns in educational policy be accommodated within some theoretical and technical analysis? (It is no good to argue, as above, that there is no logical *im*possibility in such a development. The point requires much more than *that*). Second, is it possible in such a theoretical and technical scheme to utilize intellectual resources such as the writers considered in this book? A scientific approach which cuts itself off from the policy proposals *actually* being brought forth, argued, refined, and superceded would be useless. We have not achieved adequate answers to both those questions even in economic policy, where it should be much easier. The sensible approach to the place of science in educational policy argument, then would be (i) never to cease from the search for adequate theory and the use of technical analysis in solving limited problems, but (ii) *not* to delay serious policy argument while awaiting the emergence of scientific techniques. If the conclusion seems obvious to you, let us hope together that others will find it so.

II. IN A DEMOCRATIC ETHIC?

If only Conant were right! If only it were possible to uncover the hidden ethical argreements that unite Americans as touchstones to test the genuineness of all policy proposals in education! The impossibility of such an outcome is logical, not merely social. Even if there were common visceral responses which unite us as Americans (and I see no reason to believe that there are such), these would not serve to test policy. For policy proposals are statements: they must be tested by principles, not peristalsis. The basic democratic principles to which we might appeal do not (and cannot be forced to) yield unambiguous answers to the important policy questions in education. In fact, questions have importance in policy debate only as they are *not* answered simply by appeal to universally accepted democratic principles. Consider the following: all children and youth have equal rights to an education. Appeal to such a principle might enable us to answer clearly *some* policy questions, e.g., "Should we the nation, as a matter of policy, prohibit all deliberate education other than what can be bought and sold in a freely competitive market?" But that is not an important question, really. Not even such a laissez-faire liberal as Milton Friedman would advocate that education be treated *exactly* as a commodity to be bought and sold for profit.[5]

But if a democratic principle, like that of educational equality, provides clear answers only to unimportant questions of educational equality, it does not follow that there is no connection between policy and principle. In fact, the connection is close, intricate, and indeterminate. It is close because it is almost impossible to say where policy ends and principle begins. The example which contrasted the principle of educational equality against the policy of laissez-faire economics makes the same point, for in that example the close, organic connection has been ruptured, and a logical disparity can then be noted. It should also be noted that this is not the way policy argument proceeds in serious contexts.

Is it intricate? Yes, because principles operate in policy argument not as separate entities appearing in sequence but as complex patterns—interweaving, now reinforcing, now contradicting one another. The principle of educational equality contrasts with the principle of educational freedom: all children and youth have the right to choose for themselves what education they shall receive. In the total pattern of principles applicable to policy debate, the principle of educational freedom is a very minor strand, disappearing entirely at many points and clearly subordinate to others, e.g., to the principle of educational equality, at those points where it does appear. But it *is* an ethical principle in education, and the total pattern would be different if it did not exist. When actual policies are debated, this principle plays its part, however minor. The pattern of principles is modified by time and changing circumstances; the status of the principle of educational freedom in relation to other principles may, hopefully will, be enhanced. But the intricacy of the relations among principles and between principles and policies will undoubtedly remain the most obvious feature in the picture.

These relations are indeterminate as is the priority of the chicken or the egg. The polity is determined by principles, but also vice versa. One who cannot sense the normative force, perhaps even the *relative* normative force, of such principles as educational equality and educational freedom simply cannot participate in the political discourse on education. This fact is discovered not by examining principles in the abstract but by careful attention to just where arguments hinge in actual discourse on educational policies. This is not to say that such principles are ultimate or immutable. It is a profound and continuing philosophical question whether ethical principles, in education or elsewhere, are all derivable from some super-principle like natural law, whether they are prescriptive only, emotive only, evaluative only, or some combination, or other. However, the question of how these principles function in debates on institutional policy cannot be answered by such purely philosophical investigations. The reasoning is simple: philosophically speaking, the principles of educational equality and educational freedom are at a par. If a philosophical theory of the ground and meaning of ethical principles is adequate, that theory must account for both the principles of educational equality and of educational freedom in exactly the same way. (I.e., if one is prescriptive, so is the other, etc.) But in the language of educational policy, they are obviously not on a par. Educational equality, at least in the sense of equality of treatment within educationally relevant categories, is institutionalized in schools.[6] But educational freedom is not institutionalized nor, without quite extensive changes in the total society, could it be. Yet educational freedom does function as a regulative idea in policy arguments, for example, when considering the extension of the elective system into the junior high school.

Thus the indeterminacy in the relation of democratic principles to the polity of education. Not to accept the democratic principles is to exclude oneself from the polity of education, yet the function of these principles in educational discourse is not determined by their status as principles but by the historical accidents which made schooling the System, peculiar institution it is in this country. Since it is the very core of this institution which is at issue in the present political struggle, we cannot appeal to our principles as exclusive guides, anymore than we can do away with these principles altogether.

III. THE PROFESSION OF EDUCATION?

The most important thing to say *for* this idea is to point out how the notion of a profession of education catches up and justifies the omnipresent hostility between teachers and administrators. The teachers, on this view, are the real professionals in education; administrators are professionals in finance, or public relations, or (forgive the phrase!) toilet-seat-management. All power to the teachers' communes! Let administrators serve as representatives to and for teachers! With expertise in the techniques of their craft and a full acceptance of the democratic principles of education, the teaching profession is the ideal locus for full, honest debate on the basic issues of educational policy, the natural point of contact between the politics of the society as a whole and the policies to guide the society's schools.

This view, to repeat, does present an attractive alternative to a polity of System-serving administrators, the latter being an appraisal of the present polity dominant in the consciousness of most teachers. But the appeal of "the profession of teaching" is mostly emotional not rational. (a) The appraisal of the present polity is vastly oversimplified. The complexity of power relations within the System is ignored. The intricate interconnection between the System and other institutions is glossed over with loose talk about "public relations" and the like.

The "professional" literature of the school administrators does not help the situation. Attempting to transform themselves into a genuine profession with practices grounded in theory, school administrators have come to talk about their work in frighteningly mechanical terms. This come from a poor philosophical understanding of science, theory, and action, and from insufficient power and authority to handle the really tough responsibilities they face daily. However it may look to classroom teachers, school administrators do *not* constitute a self-and-System-serving polity.

But (b) even if the diagnosis were right (which it isn't), the proposed cure would be worse than the disease. To make the profession of teaching the basic polity of education is to pre-judge *the* fundamental political question: Shall classroom teaching in organized schools be the dominant, perhaps sole, form of education in our society? Barzun, Goodman, and Skinner—each from a very different perspective and for various reasons—say no. But the profession of teaching would have to identify the good of education and the good of the classroom. This might seem to some a moral gain over the administrator's view that the good of education is the good of the System. The point is moot and irrelevant. Policy debate has already taken us beyond the identification of education's value with *anything* else. We have to find a locus for the polity where the full range of issues can be opened. The profession of education, broadly or narrowly interpreted, will not do.[7]

IV. THE LOCAL COMMUNITY?

This can be either a simple or a profound idea. It is simple if "local community" be taken to mean "local school district." The local education authorities in this country do an admirable job (indeed, when compared with their counterparts in other countries, an amazing job) of mediating between "professionalism" and "democracy" in schooling. Both words have to be in quotation marks in this context; neither is used in its ordinary sense. "Professionalism" means the tendency of the System to operate for the primary benefit of its functionaries, not its clients. "Democracy" means respect for persons, in the sense that God does not respect persons, i.e., that an individual's standing in the System reflects his standing in the community at large. "Professionalism" unrestrained would reduce every client of the System to a number to be manipulated automatically. "Democracy" would give a rich and personal education to children of rich and personable parents, the other kind to others. Local school boards restrain both tendencies without destroying either; the System could not operate (not, at any rate, in this country in this century) without the local school boards.

But the very functioning of the local education authority precludes its serving as a locus for *policy* argument and decision. Only by being non-partisan on the important policy questions can the school board mediate between those who run the schools and those who pay the bill. Leaving aside all the cant about a school administrator's duty as community leader on matters educational, one can still recognize the potential conflict between the professionals and the community power structure. It is the duty of the school board to see that that conflict remain potential. To articulate the basic policy arguments in a context where serious decisions are made would be to unleash disastrous forces. The local education authority *must* take the position that basic policy-decisions have already been made elsewhere—e.g., in the Supreme Court, the State Department of Public Education, the Bureau of Educational Research at a state teachers' college—and that *its* job is to enable us all to live and operate within those policies. To repeat, it does that job admirably; to think of its doing the other job, i.e., serving as the locus for serious policy argument, is simple minded.

There is, on the other hand, a profound idea in the expression "local community." It may be an exaggeration to say that America's most pressing task in the last third of the twentieth century is to discover, or if necessary to invent, a viable form of local community in a corporate world. I tend to believe that it is not an exaggeration, for I cannot see any possible way to eliminate gross social evils such as violence, ugliness, madness, and inequality of economic condition except through the emergence of genuine communities. To mention social goods—peace, beauty, sanity, and brotherhood—is to entail the idea of community. "Without the family, man cannot live; without the πόλις man cannot live well." Perhaps Aristotle's aphorism is an understatement. This century may teach us that without the πόλις, the local community acting as a polity, man cannot live at all.

However, even if this is true, right now there is no local community which *can* undertake to argue and decide fundamental questions of educational policy. How shall *we* induct our youngsters into this fantastically rich and wonderful and impossible culture that is ours? How shall *we* relate our adult disciplines of thought and action to the child's world of fantasy and intuition? How and how far shall *we* respect individuality? Privacy and inwardness? How shall we free *our* youth from subservience to present social norms and yet reveal our society as inviting lifetime commitment? How shall we balance compulsion and attraction wherever *our* community life touches the lives of our children?

Perhaps it is only in a local community that such questions can be asked meaningfully, only there that "we" and "our" can mean anything concrete and authentic. But if that is so, then nowhere does a local community exist with the power and self-consciousness to ask and answer, in action, questions of this sort. In sum, to point to the ideal of local community as the locus for actual political debate and decision is to point to something profound. Indeed it is probably only when people living reasonably contiguous lives undertake to transform themselves into an educational polity concerned with *their* children that they achieve genuine community. Yet *that* transformation is possible only when ideas and arguments that are being advanced and criticized throughout the nation and world flow into the decisions local groups are making about the education of their own children. Thus the institution of genuine local community and the discovery of a worldwide polity of education are correlative achievements.

V. ALL OF THESE—AND MORE

One asks a rhetorical question not to get an answer but to open a line of thought. Since a polity cannot be located in space, the question "Where is the polity?" will obviously go unanswered. Yet our search for an answer may have led to at least one important truth: there is no one intellectual tradition nor one social institution which can claim the pre-eminent role in educational policy making. If the responsibility is given to the federal government, education becomes simply an instrument of national policy, ancillary to reprehensible economic and military purposes. On the other hand, not to raise basic questions of educational policy in all branches of the federal government is to deny militants of the revolution of rising sensibilities any direct access the most important decision points in our society. But if revolutionists do not have a base in other institutions, they are soon swallowed up in Washington.

Militants will not find a natural home in the System or subSystem, but they should find it possible to survive in many alien locales: among those who pursue a science of education, among those who practice democracy and the larger number who preach it. They will be in the professional organizations and scattered amongst parents and community leaders. They will penetrate Jesuit seminaries and state teachers colleges. They will found experimental schools and colleges; they will confound the placid and unconcerned.

But above all they will *talk*. They will shout, whisper, gesticulate; speak in prose, poetry, proof and prayer; demonstrate, remonstrate; doubt, affirm, deny, contest, avow; strike poses and propose strikes. The question is: will they listen to each other and to the nagging of obdurate social reality? Will they argue? Will they engage in discourse or in speech making? It is, of course, difficult to maintain the militant stance while engaged in political, i.e., at least minimally polite, argument; but is it impossible? If so, there are few chances for educational reform, and none for educational revolution.

Hence it is essential to transcend propaganda and achieve a literature of educational policy. A literature is the intersection of creativity and criticism, the joint domain of passion and reason. Militancy is rightly disciplined only by rational disagreement and appeal to common intelligence. The stuffiness of professionalism is to be relieved not by breaking school windows but by letting the wind out of the windbags.

Psychologically we, as a nation, are ready for an educational revolution. Politically, we are unready. The issues are unarticulated, the forum not made ready. It is by participating, however remotely, in a literature of educational policy that the American people can overcome political illiteracy on educational matters. The writers treated in this book have made a start toward that end.

Notes

WHERE IS THE POLITY?

1 For this point of congruence and difference between science and other forms of rational understanding, see Ernest Nagel: *The Structure of Science* (New York, 1961), especially the Introduction and Chapters 11 and 12. For beautifully detailed, exact, and easily compared philosophical views on the nature of scientific arguments, see Israel Scheffler: *The Anatomy of Inquiry* (New York, 1963).

2 James E. McClellan: "Theory in Educational Administration," *The School Review* Vol. 68, (Summer, 1960), pp. 210-227.

3 R. Duncan Luce and Howard Raiffa: *Games and Decisions: Introduction and Critical Survey* (New York, 1957).

4 Theodore Brameld: *The Use of Explosive Ideas in Education: Culture, Class, and Evolution* (Pittsburgh, 1965).

5 Milton Friedman: "The Role of Government in Education," *Economics and the Public Interest* (Rutgers, 1955). See also Alan T. Peacock and Jack Wiseman: *Education for Democrats* (London, 1964).

6 B. Paul Komisar: "The Paradox of Equality," *Teachers College Record* Vol. LXVIII-3 (December, 1966), p. 251. See also, B. Paul Komisar and Jerrold R. Coombs: "The Concept of Equality in Education," *Studies in Philosophy and Education*, Volume III, Number 3 (Fall, 1964), pp. 223-244; C. J. B. Macmillan's response, "Equality and Sameness," *Studies in Philosophy and Edu-*

cation, Volume III, Number 4 (Winter, 1964-65), pp. 320-332; and B. Paul Komisar and Jerrold R. Coombs' response, "Too Much Equality," *Studies in Philosophy and Education,* Volume IV, Number 2 (Fall, 1965), pp. 263-271.

7 Myron Lieberman is the philosopher of the profession of education. His writings on the nature of the profession of education have been numerous, influential, and persuasive. See Myron Lieberman: *The Future of Public Education* (Chicago, 1960), *Education as a Profession* (New Jersey, 1956), pp. 19-48, and Myron Lieberman and Michael H. Moskow: *Collective Negotiations for Teachers: An Approach to School Administration* (Chicago, 1966).

There is a very delicate argument that needs to be considered when one considers the role of the teaching profession in the determination of educational policy. *Right now,* as teachers succeed in wresting greater power over educational policy from school boards and administrators (as part of their success in achieving better wages, hours, and control of other working conditions), the results *on balance* will probably be positive from the standpoint of education. On one hand, the curriculum (especially in the social studies) should improve as teachers gain freedom to teach what they know and want to teach rather than what is prescribed by outside experts or political propagandists. Teachers will be somewhat less susceptible than businessmen to the lure of new technology (hardware) as a demonstration of their up-to-dateness. Etc. On the other hand it isn't clear that organized teachers will be as responsive to civil rights movements and to the "legitimate aspirations" of poor people as are school boards and administrators who occupy more clearly political offices. On balance the more positive contribution of the teaching profession comes about to this: the teachers are demanding respect for autonomy and individuality, freedom from what they term "bureacratic" control. As they get those values for themselves, they may be a bit more capable of transmitting the same values to children; and *that's* worth more to all children than is the power to *force* teachers to grant mechanical equality to black and white, rich and poor.

That's for right now. Over the long haul it seems clear that administrators will succeed in ingesting "professional" leaders (AFT as well as NEA) into the Establishment where competition will become symbiotic rather than fundamental. Exactly the same point made earlier about the Educationists and Academics applies to the administrators and organized profession of teachers: neither can run the System without the other. Each side will strive for policies which enhance its own power and convenience within the System; neither will look toward a radically different conception of where the educational polity ought to lie.

Index